CW00765673

The Kirkwall Ba'

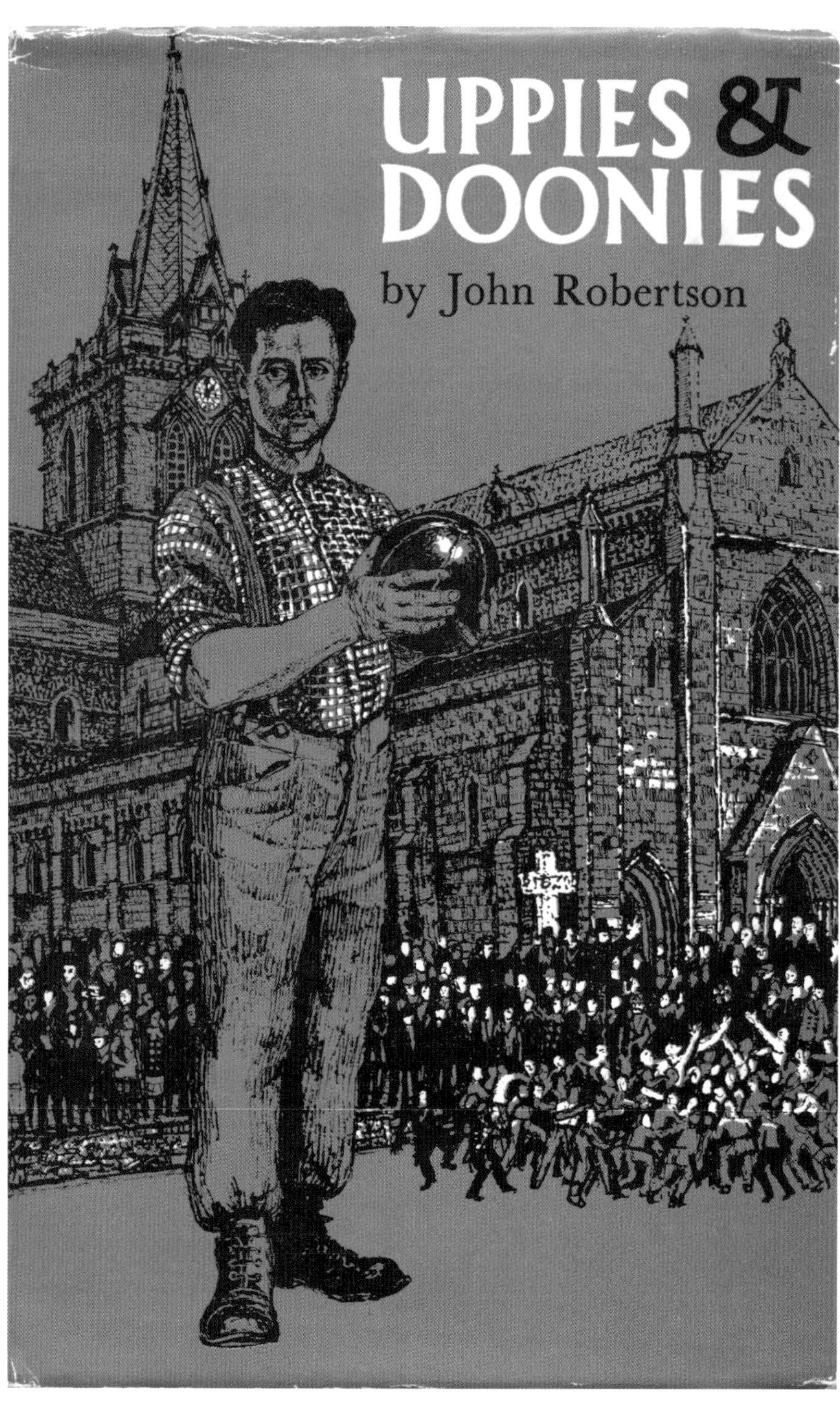

The dustjacket of the orignal book *Uppies & Doonies*,
designed by Gordon Henry.

The Kirkwall Ba'

Between the Water and the Wall

John D. M. Robertson
CBE DL FRSE

Dunedin Academic Press
EDINBURGH

Published by
Dunedin Academic Press Ltd
Hudson House
8 Albany Street
Edinburgh EH1 3QB
Scotland

ISBN 1 903765 42 0

Revised, updated and extended version of
Uppies & Doonies published in 1967

British Library Cataloguing in Publication Data
A catalogue record for this book is available from the British Library

Design, typesetting and pre-press production by Makar Publishing Production
Jacket design by Mark Blackadder
Printed in Great Britain by The Bath Press

for

Susan, John, Fiona, Sinclair

and my grandchildren

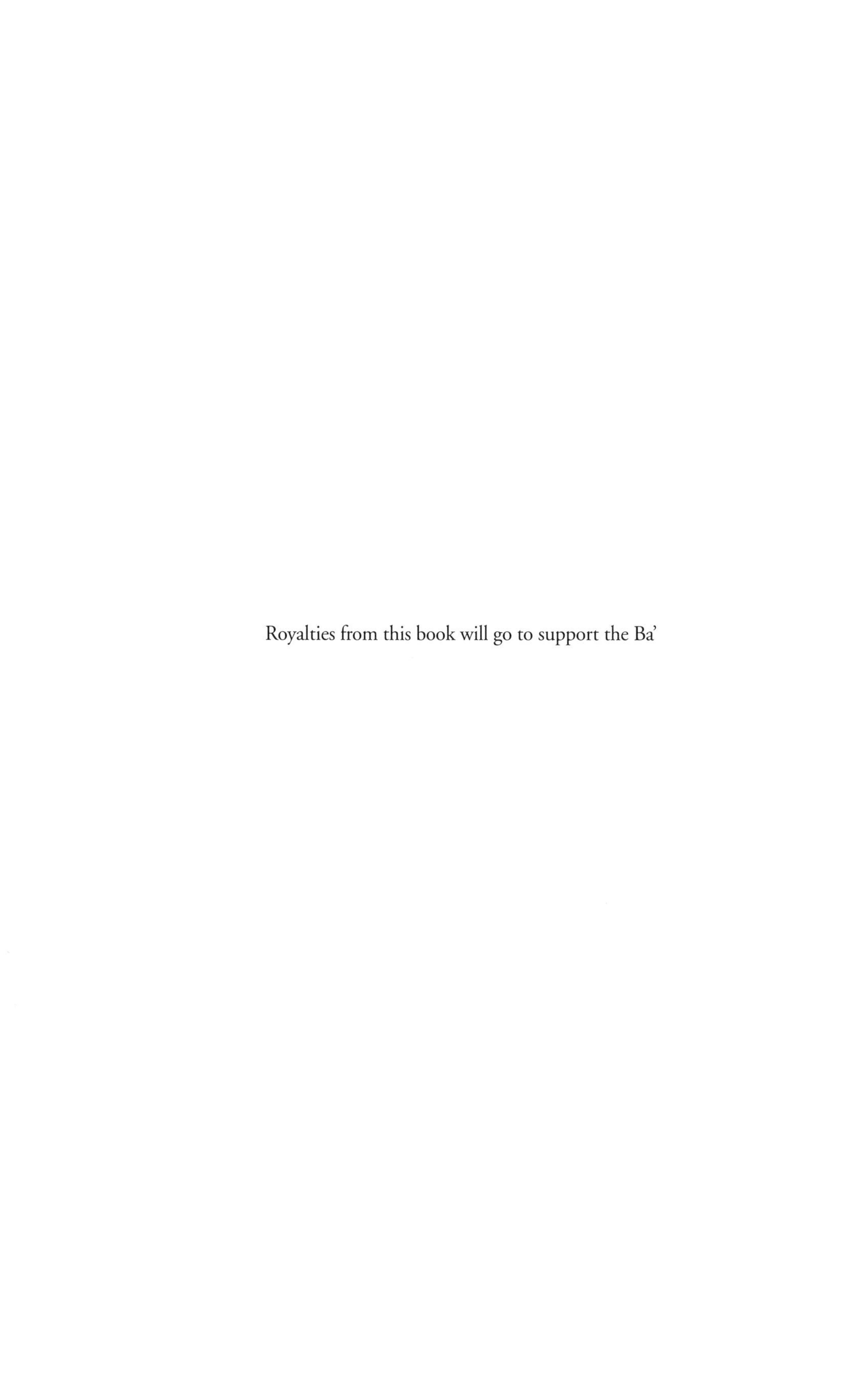

Royalties from this book will go to support the Ba'

Contents

Part III *History of the Ba'*

Part IV *Origin and History of Mass Football*

Introduction

One should make a serious study of a pastime – Alexander the Great

There has been some interest in the issue of an updated version of *Uppies & Doonies*, originally printed in 1967. That volume is now out of print, and I believe that a further book on the Ba', albeit in a restructured and expanded form, will commend itself to Orcadians both in the islands and further afield.

Fresh items in this edition include pieces by Orcadian writers: Ba' song[1] and verse; ba' making; the functions of the Ba' Committee; reports in *The Orcadian* and the *Orkney Herald* (abbreviated in the footnotes as *O* and *OH*, respectively); historical information and anecdotes which have emerged since the 1967 publication; and sketches and cartoons. Further new inclusions are articles and comments from a variety of sources outwith Orkney which depict, sometimes in graphic, even bizarre, form, how others see the game; an updated roll of individual winners; lists of the winning side since records began; a recital of some of those who have donated and thrown up a ba'; recent photographs, not least one depicting a gathering of Ba' winners from the period 1923 to 1999; and illustrations of the Town Hall winner's plaques and the millennium Ba' plaque, funded by public subscription and sited on the Kirk Green.

I very much hope that this volume will prove of interest to all those who esteem the Ba' and that it will encourage present and future generations of Kirkwallians in particular and Orcadians in general to support and enthusiastically to sustain this unique game, played as it is over streets redolent with history. The annual contests hold a special place in the traditions of the Royal Burgh and in its ongoing life.

I have thought it acceptable to append the foreword to the first edition, written by my friend the distinguished author and folklorist Ernest Walker Marwick MA. His comments were typically warm, and are I hope still deserved now.

[1] The subtitle of this book, *Between the Water and the Wall*, is a refrain line in 'Passion and the Glory', a song featuring the Ba' and written by Andy Cant and Stewart Shearer in 1999. A celebration of the game, it is enjoyed by both sides.

Foreword to the first edition

'It's more than a game. It's an institution', wrote Thomas Hughes of cricket. These words seem to me to describe perfectly the Kirkwall Ba' game, even if – while cricket has spread itself over the globe – the Ba' is confined to a brief winter afternoon and a mile of narrow barricaded streets. The spirit, the traditions, the enthusiasm which make cricket more than a game are no less present in the Kirkwall Ba'.

Only enthusiasm of a high order (one would have called it fanaticism if that word had retained its original meaning of 'inspired devotion') could have produced a book like this one.

Has any game so simple, so rigorously confined to a single day, or a couple of days, each year, ever engendered the amount of lore collected in these pages?

And yet, even if the Kirkwall Ba' game is the heart and kernel of Mr Robertson's book, the enthusiasm I mentioned has spilled over until the book has become much more than the history of a local game. It has become, in terms of Orkney, a most valuable social document, illustrating aspects of life never before investigated. And it has also become, through Mr Robertson's determination to trace the game to its ultimate source, a history of football as a popular pastime from its beginnings in ancient fertility rites to its crystallization in present-day soccer and rugby. The way in which Mr Robertson has been able to charge his book with such serious sociological and historical significance fills me with admiration; all this in a context so lively and so full of exuberant humanity that *Uppies & Doonies* will be read with pleasure by people who have never seen a Ba' game.

One important thing ought to be said, for an author cannot say it for himself. Behind every statement, as I can vouch, lies the most meticulous research; not surprising I suppose when one remembers that Mr Robertson studied law at Edinburgh University and took a law degree there.

Even to the most casual reader it will be clear that Mr Robertson writes of the game as a participant. He is in fact a player of many years standing. His Blues in two separate sports, gained as an undergraduate, argue a fitness and skill which have served him well in this most gruelling of contests. It is pleasant to be able to record that he was adjudged the winner of the Men's Ba' of New Year's Day 1966, and that one of his personal treasures is that year's ba'.

Ernest W. Marwick

Acknowledgements

I offer thanks to the many people who have helped in diverse ways in the preparation of the manuscript and in particular: Marie Sutherland for endless hours of research, typing, arranging and re-arranging of material, for sound advice in multifarious ways and for checking proofs. Without her constant support the compilation and completion of this book would have been an impossibility; Dr Alison Parkes for extensive sifting and arranging of material and many valuable recommendations – her help has been very important and of an unusually high order; Ronald Johnston for careful and assiduous proof reading; Ernest W. Marwick and Dr Douglas Grant for much encouragement and advice.

The following, alas some now deceased, have provided information over the years for which I am greatly indebted: Andrew Anthony, Weekend Guardian; Fernand Auberjonois, USA; Nick Baker, Eton College; George Mackay Brown; Margaret Budge; Alan Bullen OBE; Nigel Burton, *Northern Echo*, Darlington; Andrew Cant; Alastair and Anne Cormack; Dr Stanley Cursiter CBE; Derby Local Studies Library; Alec Doloughan BEM; Henry Douglas, Hawick; Mark Entwistle, Selkirk; Mabel Eunson; Ron Ferguson; Alison Fraser; Lucy Gibbon; Gary Gibson MBE; Billy Gillies, Jedburgh; Jeremy Godwin; John Gowans; Mike Grenier, Eton College; Dan Grieve; Guildhall Library, London; Peter Hamilton, Sedgefield; John and Barbara Hanson, Ashbourne; Roddie Hibbert; Yvonne Hithersay, Ashbourne; William Irvine; Ian Landles; Bobby Leslie; Gladys Leslie; Andrew Louttit; Christopher McDougall, USA; Evan MacGillivray; Mitchell Library, Glasgow; Billy Peace; Christine Omand; Public Record Office, London; William Renton, Duns; Arthur Scott Robertson, Shetland; Joe Sandwith, Workington; John Ross Scott; John Shearer; Alan Skene MBE; John Slorance; Clive Thomson; Harry Wright; Keith Wallace, Workington; Sheila Whitehead, Duns; Mathew Whittles; Bryce Wilson; Jim Wilson.

Photographs, illustrations and cartoons have generously come from, and permission to reproduce granted when possible by: Ken Amer; William Hourston;

Tom Kent; Elsie Lennox; David J. Lowe; Thomas MacGregor; the Musée des Arts et Traditions Populaires, Paris; Orkney Library Photographic Archive; Phoenix Photos; Harald Nicolson; Lindsey Porter; J. P. Robertson; James Sinclair; Charles Tait; E. Torricelli; George Washington Wilson collection; Tim Wright; Eton College Library; Ian Bruce on behalf of the Johnston family; and Professor Norihisa Yoshida.

Finally, I have obtained very considrable, indeed essential, material from the files of Orkney's newspapers and its use has been permitted by Mr James Miller of *The Orcadian* and Mrs Kim Foden of the *Orkney Herald*. These two papers provided a mine of rich information into which I have delved and which has been of the greatest possible help. All references from these publications and from other sources have been acknowledged in footnotes.

Part I

The Kirkwall Ba'

FIG. 1: Nearing the Clay Loan, Men's Ba', New Year's Day 1906.

1

Up-the-Gates and Down-the-Gates

The Kirkwall Ba' is a remarkable survival from an earlier age when mass football was played all over Scotland – particularly on holidays, at weddings and in the festive season, and sometimes on Sundays, to the huge displeasure of the Church. Indeed the Ba' is something of a sporting dinosaur: Kirkwall's unique traditional pastime, in which men from disparate backgrounds, and of various ages, roughly and inelegantly garbed, ecumenically annually commingle and provide vicarious pleasure for a host of onlookers. Even in more socially stratified times, the *Orkney Herald* of 1880 reported 'it is no uncommon thing to see Baillies, Town Councillors, doctors, sailors, auctioneers, architects, merchants, navvies, scavengers and nondescripts mixed in one heterogeneous mass, brawling and fighting over the cork and leather trophy.'

Normally the contests take place on Christmas Day and New Year's Day – excepting Sundays. The Boys' game commences at 10.30 a.m. and the Men's ba' is thrown up at 1 p.m. There is no time limit.

For many spectators the Ba' can resemble one of those paintings in which the detail is more stimulating that the picture as a whole. Throughout both days there will be a host of dazzling little cameos, each game thick and rich with humour, character and incident. Every Ba' writes its own story with a wealth of episode.

The contestants in the game comprise two sides, 'Uppies' and 'Doonies', or more properly 'Up-the-Gates' and 'Down-the-Gates'. The object of the Up-the-Gates is to take the ba' Up-street to their goal, while the Down-the-Gates endeavour to force it Down-street to the harbour – the word 'gate' is derived from the Old Norse, Old Swedish *gata*, a road.[1] Just when the designations were first used is not known, but in his book *Orkney*, Dr Hugh Marwick gives some interesting information regarding the two parts of the town:

[1] See also Wright's *English Dialect Dictionary* (London, 1900), which gives: 'Gate: A street in a town; a thoroughfare.'

FIG. 2: Men's Ba' at Burgar's Bay, New Year's Day 1906.

On the east side of the present Broad Street, and separated from it now by a gravelled area, formerly known as the Kirk Green, stands the Cathedral which at the time it was built was probably outside the old town or burgh proper, for the portion of the town higher up in Victoria Street was regarded as Bishop's territory and known as The Laverock. That puzzling name has never been satisfactorily explained, but it has been suggested that it represents the Gaelic word *laimhrig*, a landing stage (derived from O.N. *hlao-hamarr*, loading-rock), and it may have had reference to some special jetty built for the Bishop's use on his way to or from the Bishop's Palace nearby.

That bishopric domain as well as the older town were both included in James III's charter of 1486, which erected 'all and haill our said Burgh and City of Kirkwall, and that part thereof called the Laverock, in ane ffull Burgh Royal.' Though no records survive of any definite clash between the two portions of the town in ancient times there was no doubt considerable rivalry, and the New Year's Day Ba' game, which still survives, probably perpetuates the memory of less friendly intercourse long ago. One recalls the brief entry in the Icelandic Annals under the

FIG. 3: Men's Ba', Christmas Day 1959.

year 1382: 'Then was heard the mournful tidings that Bishop William was slain in the Orkneys.' But to what extent the inhabitants of the burgh may have been involved in that affair we are entirely ignorant.

The ball game just mentioned is a game *per se*, with conventions and rules (or absence of rules) all its own. Such is its popularity that it is now played on Christmas Day as well, and on each day there is a Boys' Ba' in the forenoon, and a Men's Ba' in the afternoon. The opposing sides are known as Doon the Gates and Up the Gates (gate here meaning, of course, the Street), or, more briefly, Doonies and Uppies, and the side on which you play is predetermined at birth. The present Post Office Lane which runs west off Broad Street is regarded as the dividing line between the Old Burgh and The Laverock, and if you chance to be born between that line and the shore you are a lifelong Doonie, while should you enter the world between that and the head of the town you cannot help being an Uppie. Similarly if as an outsider you chance to have entered the town for the first time by the Bridge Street end, you qualify as a Doonie, while if you have entered by the Laverock end you take your place with the Uppies.[2]

[2] H. Marwick, *Orkney* (London: Robert Hale, 1951), p. 123.

FIG. 4: Youths' Ba', Harbour Street, New Year's Day 1908.

In *Kirkwall in the Orkneys* there is the following information:

> After the building of the Cathedral, the double town was ruled by the Earl and the Bishop. Every man residing between the Castle and the Shore was the Earl's man, and all above were vassals of the Church. Thus the division of the townspeople into 'Up-the-Gates' and 'Doon-the-Gates' dates from the twelfth century.[3]

Of course the above extracts do not suggest that these designations were used in the time of earls and bishops, nor that the game itself dates from then. Doubtless, however, long before the Ba' became established there was a certain amount of continuing rivalry, and possibly strife, between the two parts of the town. Differing loyalties and consequent divisions and antagonisms were involved, and the proximity of the two communities produced a natural local enmity that inevitably expressed itself in some sort of contest. In later times mass street football, and then the Ba' game itself provided an ideal medium for the exhibition of this inherent hostility.

As far as ferryloupers – that is non-Orcadians – are concerned the general rule is that the point of entry into town determines on which side one plays. On this basis those who in days gone by came to Scapa pier by the *St Ola* and

[3] B. H. Hossack, *Kirkwall in the Orkneys*, Kirkwall, 1900, chapter 8, p. 95.

FIG. 5: Christmas Day 2000. Uppie men arriving.

FIG. 6: Christmas Day 2000. Doonie men set out for the start.

FIG. 7: Youth's Ba', Christmas Day 1909.

from there straight into Kirkwall by one of the Scapa roads are Uppies; so are passengers landing at Kirkwall airport who enter by Palace Road, and those who arrive in town by the old Finstown Road. On the other hand disembarking at Kirkwall pier makes one a Doonie, as does initial entry to the Burgh by the Ayre Road. Nevertheless, it is true to say that incomers are allowed a certain licence in connection with the side to which they adhere, and this is dependent on friends, relatives, abode, and on occasion personal preference.

Some births take place in Foresterhill Hospital, Aberdeen, and it is not uncommon for proud parents to ensure that their offspring enter Kirkwall by a route that will ensure the desired Ba' allegiance. My own grandson and namesake, on his way home from the maternity ward in Aberdeen, had his week-old hand placed gently on the wall at the Up-the-Gate goal. Doonie infants arriving at Kirkwall airport are often taken by a somewhat circuitous route into Kirkwall to ensure that family territory is reached first, presumably thereafter eschewing digital immersion in the cold waters of the basin.

For the man born in Kirkwall in days gone by, qualification was by place of birth, and thus it was not unusual for members of the same family to support different sides. An amusing story is told of a diehard Uppie father-to-be who, when the end of his wife's pregnancy approached would on no account allow

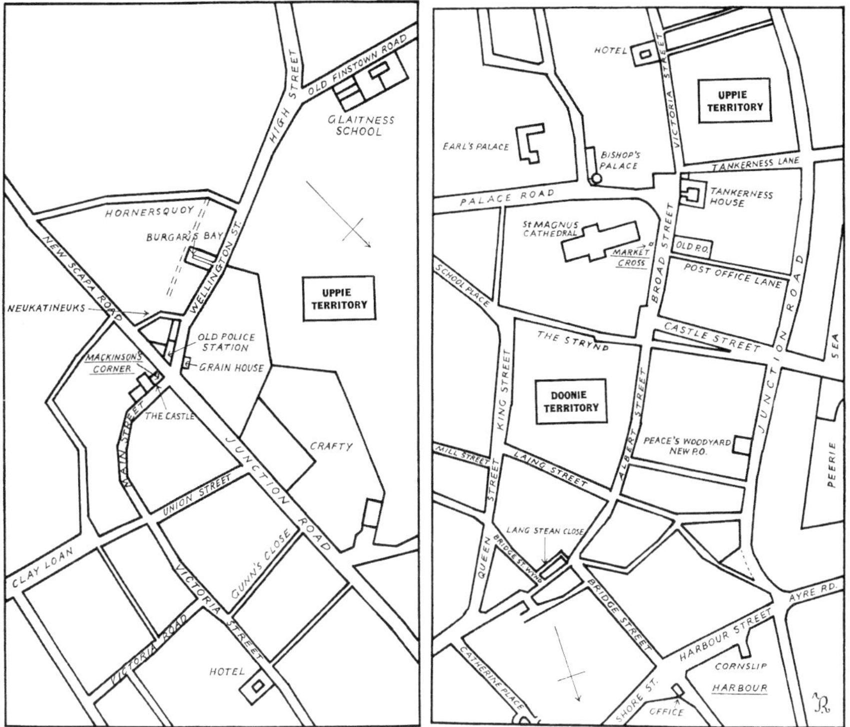

FIG. 8: Street plan of Kirkwall showing Uppie and Doonie territories.

her to stray below the Mercat Cross. One day, to his consternation, he came upon her in Albert Street and shepherding her well above the Cross he chided: 'Noo, noo, lass, we kinno tak the risk o' hivan a blinkan Doonie in wir hoose.'

There was concern regarding the equitable distribution of support following the post war building of several housing schemes in Uppie territory. This anxiety was heightened by the establishment of a modern maternity unit in the Balfour Hospital, which resulted in the virtual disappearance of home confinements. It seemed as if the death knell had been sounded for future Doonie hopes, but this has so far proved to be ill-founded. Families now appear to retain allegiance to the side for which their family has played for years, and to discount where individual members were born. This loyalty seems to be transmitted to the young at an early age: Sandy Budge, a fervent Up-the-Gate and winner of the Men's Ba' on New Year's Day 1970, told me that his nine-year-old grandson had assured him the difference between Uppies and Doonies was that 'the Uppies go up tae Heaven and the Doonies go doon tae Hell'.

The rivalry between Up-the-Gates and Down-the-Gates has also been expressed in other sports. On Christmas Day 1875, as an alternative to the Ba', a game of rugby was held at one o'clock in a field at Soulisquoy. This the Doonies won by a goal to their opponents' try.[4] In May 1886 the St Magnus Cricket Club divided itself into Up-the-Gates and Down-the-Gates. After putting together eighty runs, the Uppies bowled out their opponents for forty-seven.[5]

For many years, and certainly until the 1930s, there was a recognized and well-established feud between Uppie and Doonie boys, and this smouldering antipathy was apparent from time to time throughout the year. The appearance of Up-town lads at the harbour would more often than not result in the cry of 'There's Uppies', and, in the resultant exchanges, insults and sometimes missiles would fly between the opposing groups! Similarly, Doonie boys had to tread warily when setting foot in Victoria Street, and to venture as far Up as Burgar's Bay was regarded as an act of folly, to be undertaken only by the bravest! The rehousing of families from the old lanes at Shore Street, Bridge Street and Victoria Street put an end to this simmering dissension, and now young Up-the-Gates and Down-the-Gates mix freely without any thought of past bickering.

Council Humour

Ba' damage was discussed at the Orkney Islands Council Policy and Resources Committee meeting in January 1985. Convener Edwin Eunson, with tongue in cheek and clearly wishing to play down the matter, suggested that one of the merits of the Ba' was that it removed the aggression from participants who then lived quietly for the rest of the year! At that same meeting, while admitting his Up-street bias, he commented that the Doonies 'had all the advantages' of a far wider goal. When another councillor, Scott Harcus, opined that most of the recent problems about damage seemed to have arisen since country folk joined in the contest, Mr Eunson entreated him, 'Please don't say that, they're mostly Up.'

On 3 April 1986 *The Orcadian* reported:

> The intelligence of Doonies has been called into question by OIC Convener, Mr Edwin Eunson. At an OIC meeting last week, Mr Eunson referred to a request from the Ba' Committee for a 'Past Winners of the Ba'' display in Kirkwall Town Hall. This had been considered by the Education Committee which had thought that a vast amount of space might be required. However, Mr Eunson disagreed and, on the Education

[4] *Northman*, 1 January 1876.
[5] *O*, 29 May 1886.

> Committee's discussion of the matter, added: 'Most of the Kirkwall members present were Doonies anyway and so not very intelligent.' It is believed that Mr Eunson is not a Doonie. A meeting is to be held with the Ba' Committee over their request.

This humorous comment was made in good part, and did not prevent Up-the-Gate Eunson from successfully defending his seat at local elections that year, his ward fortunately being deep in Uppie territory! A lifelong supporter of the Ba', he went on to complete a third term as Convener.

A Tradition to Maintain

Is there still a place today for our fine old game? This is an era of mechanization and indifference, of dazzling opportunities and easy money, of expansion and insecurity, of centralization and neglect; a time of shifting population, anonymity and the drab flood of mass living; a period which cares little for historic local survivals. It is thus all the more important that at this time of the apathetic majority, when people prefer watching to playing, the passive to the active, and tradition tends to be disregarded, the considerable heritage we have in the Kirkwall Ba' should be recognized and preserved with determination.

Wherein lies the appeal of the tussle? Is the attraction in its long history; in the physical challenge; in the joy and abandon of the mass effort? Is it a revolt against convention and mediocrity; a mild form of exhibitionism; a chance to repay old scores; an excellent opportunity of addressing Christmas and New Year over-indulgence? Whatever the motivation, it is nonsense to say that this survival from a bygone age is unwanted and out of place in the twentieth century, that it is irrational to take part, and that those who play are misguided.

Not even its most ardent supporters can say that the Ba' is a sophisticated contest requiring much expertise, but no one can deny that it is quite different from other sports – in its own way it is unique. Played properly and at length it requires fitness, strength, comradeship, restraint, determination, courage and a certain skill. Bodily compression, hard knocks, mutilation of clothing, torn nails, bruised arms and shoulders, skinned knees and stiff backs are equally the marks of victory and defeat, and the property of all whatever their station in life. Whether the benefits arising from the exercise are sufficient to outweigh these hurts depends entirely on the individual.

For a period after the 1939–45 war the annual events proved as popular as ever, and the contests were very well-supported, hard fought and keenly contended. In the 1950s and 1960s fewer men took part, but in the last two decades, and

FIG. 9: The throw-up, Men's Ba', New Year's Day 2004.

FIG. 10: Men's Ba', Christmas Day 2000.

FIG. 11: Men's Ba', New Year's Day 1983.

FIG. 12: Boys' Ba', New Year's Day 1979.

fig. 13: Men's Ba' in Spence's Square, Christmas Day 1973.

particularly in recent years, support has grown considerably and nowadays it would be unusual if fewer than 200 men participated. Others are involved throughout the afternoon and on New Year's Day 1993 it was estimated that around 400 played. That encounter made passage to the Uppie goal via the rear of the Phoenix Cinema, across difficult marshy ground into the field at the rear of Wellington Street and as far as the gate at the top of High Street. Thence it found its way down Wellington Street to the goal. This unusual route had only once before been traversed by the Up-the-Gates, on New Year's Day 1960.

The Boys' Ba' too has grown in popularity and in recent years 100 lads have been seen taking an enthusiastic part in the contest.

A view of the Ba' – past and present – was encapsulated in my address to all participants before the commencement on New Year's Day 2000:

> I speak on behalf of the Ba' Committee at this, the first Men's Ba' of the third millennium. Every Ba' is special but today's game is particularly auspicious.
>
> The traditional annual contest is of much significance in the history and ongoing life of Kirkwall. It is unique, widely supported, knows no social barriers and has been played in one form or another for at least two centuries under the magnificence of St Magnus Cathedral, here on the Kirk Green and through the streets of Kirkwall. The Ba' belongs to you and to generations yet unborn. You are its present custodians and your continuing responsibility, not least to your successors, is to keep the game strong and thriving, to respect its traditions, to play it sensibly and to protect and sustain it with pride. Behaviour that would damage its well-being must be avoided.
>
> The Ba' is an important part of Kirkwall's heritage and its celebration makes a real difference between life here in Orkney and elsewhere. On this rare day Uppies and Doonies alike look forward to another 100 years of the Ba' played and enjoyed responsibly on and over the streets of the town, without let or hindrance from any temporal power.
>
> This is indeed a memorable occasion.

FIG. 14: Men's Ba', New Year's Day 1958.

2

Play and Players

The Ba' has its own conventions and rules – or absence of them, for it is true to say that there are no set rules, and certainly none that affect the simple overriding purpose, namely to reach the goal. However, some general understandings have been fairly well established by custom and usage over the years, one of the few being that play is not permitted on Sunday. If Christmas and New Year's Day fall on Sunday, then the games are held on Boxing Day and January 2.

The Mercat Cross

In all respects this is the logical place for the start. The Cross determines precisely the division between Uppie and Doonie territory, and moreover is well positioned above street level in an open space suitable for both spectators and players.

It seems probable that a ceremonial throw-up was introduced in the early part of the nineteenth century, and certainly since 1854 when newspaper records were first kept, every Ba', without exception, has been started from the Market Cross in front of the cathedral. A report on the New Year's Day game 1870 says that play commenced 'at the place where the Market Cross used to be'.[1] This seems to refer to the fact that the Cross was broken on 28 August 1868, and probably had still not been repaired and replaced.

The Throw-Up

Throughout the nineteenth century, and indeed into the early part of the twentieth century, throwing up the ba' was a privilege not widely shared or sought after. Almost invariably the contest was started by the man chiefly concerned with collecting money to pay for fashioning the trophy – such as the blacksmith Bill Somerville or the Nicholsons, Andrew and James.

[1] *OH*, 4 January 1870.

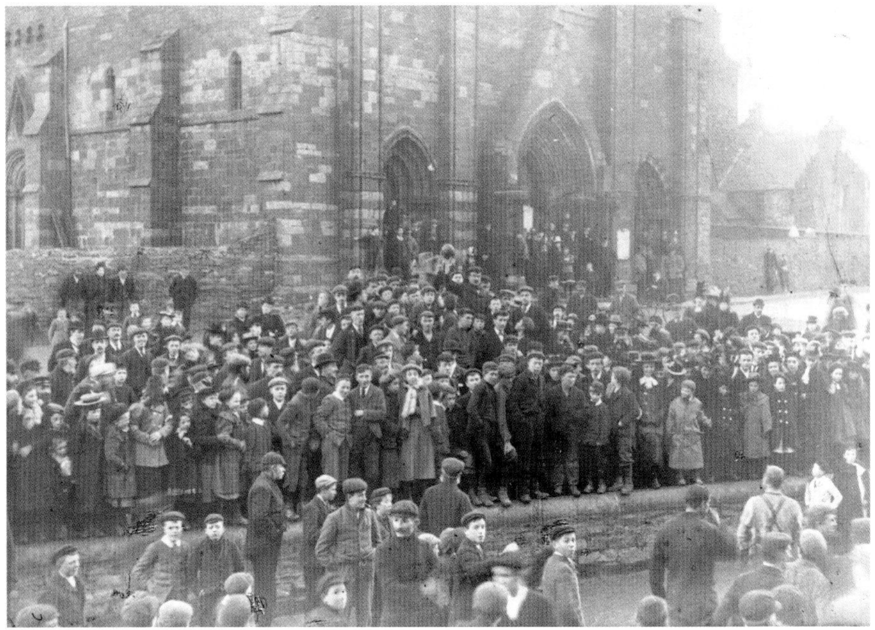

FIG. 15: Waiting for the hour, Christmas Day Men's Ba' 1898.

Gradually the significance of the throw-up was appreciated, a prominent person was accorded the honour and, not unnaturally, the donor was often favoured. The distinction of starting a game is now widely recognized and valued, and lifelong supporters and past winners (usually on a particular anniversary of their triumph) feature prominently. In practice the Ba' Committee makes the selection and those invited normally pay for the ba', although that is not mandatory. At the present time a Boys' ba' costs £45 and a Men's ba' £80. The charge covers material such as leather, thread, packing and an honorarium for the ba' makers. Nationally known figures and various dignitaries have signified approbation by throwing up the ba'. These include two members of parliament, the chairman of the Scottish Land Court, and prominent local people such as the cathedral minister, the convenor of the Islands Council, and in earlier times provosts, baillies and town councillors. All have added distinction to a remarkable event already rich in tradition. Ladies are frequently accorded the honour of throwing up the Boys' ba' and on one occasion only, Christmas Day 1955, the honour of throwing up the Men's ba' was given to Mrs Tom Firth.

The time of the throw-up has altered over the years. When there were only two games each day the Boys' Ba' usually commenced at 11 a.m., although occasionally the start was at 10 a.m. and once at 10.30. The introduction of

FIG. 16: Dan Grieve, family and supporters set out from home to throw up the Millennium ba'.

a Youths' Ba' on New Year's Day 1892 meant that the Boys' game had to start earlier, and several actually began at 8 a.m., others at 8.30 or 9 a.m. The Youths' Ba' was normally thrown up two hours later at either 10 or 11 a.m. Even so the gap was sometimes not long enough, and on New Year's Day 1903 and New Year's Day 1907 the Boys' game was unfinished when the Youths' game started. The Youths' and Men's games also sometimes overlapped, and indeed at one o'clock on New Year's Day 1902 the Youths' Ba' was just leaving Broad Street three hours after the start. Notwithstanding, after a delay of about ten minutes the Men's ba' was thrown up. With the abolition of the Youths' Ba' in 1910 the start of the Boys' game reverted to its original time of 10 a.m., and was delayed to 10.30 on Christmas Day 1968.

It is properly regarded as a considerable honour to be invited to throw up a ba' and some people, particularly those associated with the Boys' game, can spend a sleepless night worrying about being late. In the 1940s a well-known, popular player who lived in Laing Street was asked to throw up a Boys' ba'. Light had hardly broken on the morning of the great day as he awoke with a start and in guilty panic. Tumbling out of bed, he quite ignored his wife, pulled on trousers and a ganzie, rushed out and in his haste dropped the ba' which bumped and rolled its way to John Sclaters, drapers, Albert Street.

FIG. 17: The throw-up, New Year's Day 1986.

FIG. 18: One o'clock, Christmas Day 1988.

Gathering his wits and the trophy, he hurried over fresh snow that showed clearly to his unsteady gaze the marks of recent scuffles. Concerned, he cursed his late carousal, his dilatoriness and folly, and thought he could never come to terms with the opprobrium of the Ba' fraternity. Hastening past J. and J. Smith, drapers, and the blackened shell of the recently burned Albert Kinema he found Broad Street entirely deserted. Sweating and with the sour saliva of the night's roistering troubling his lips he squinted through the mirk at the cathedral clock, to perceive that the hands stood serenely at 8 a.m.

Until the mid-1860s men played in the evening of Christmas Day as it was not a holiday. Thereafter for a number of years, with the exception of Christmas Day 1870 when there was another evening contest, the Christmas Ba' started at 2 p.m. at which time most of the shops closed. It was not until Christmas Day 1910 that the start was at 1 p.m., and this is probably connected with the fact that the Youths' Ba' had just been stopped. This brought the Christmas Day Ba' into line with New Year's Day, which has always started at one o'clock. The only exceptions to the foregoing were the Men's New Year's Day game 1881 when the Doonies delayed the throw-up for one hour to enable them to marshal reinforcements, and on New Year's Day 1891 when for some unknown reason the ba' was thrown up at 1.30 p.m.

Many people help the Ba' to run smoothly, and assistance is often given with no publicity or fuss. One instance is that for almost fifty years, custodians Albert Thomson BEM and John Windwick came to the cathedral every Christmas and New Year's Day to adjust the clock which daily gains half a minute. Thanks to the efforts of these men the Ba' always started on time.

An interesting custom observed until the mid-1860s was to start the game with a pistol shot, but now the striking of the hour by the cathedral clock is the signal for the game to begin.

Play

After the ba' is thrown up it can be kicked, picked up or carried, and indeed a player can do just as he likes with it providing the opposition do not stop him. What usually happens is that the ba' disappears into the maw of a grappling mass of players and does not reappear until the game is over. Open play is rare, and the ba' is held tight somewhere deep in the midst of the perspiring interlocked body of men, each side determined not to yield ground.

A 'smuggle' is a popular ploy – when the ba' is spirited away without players on either side knowing that it is no longer in their midst, and baffling many. With most of the players immobile in the scrum the ba' can sometimes find its

FIG. 19: Men's Ba' in Great Western Road, New Year's Day 1999.

FIG. 20: Men's Ba' in Junction Road, New Year's Day 2001.

way into a backwater such as a window ledge, while the main stream of players unsuspectingly surges past. This is a good opportunity for a smuggle, and the tactic is always undertaken with as much secrecy as possible so that a good start may be obtained. However, the side in danger of being beaten is the side likely to resort to smuggling. It would be unwise for a side making steady progress to its goal to chance losing control by attempting anything risky.

Another manoeuvre is to create a diversion to enable other members of the same side who are holding the ba' to make headway against reduced opposition.

When the throw-up takes place there is almost inevitably a wild scuffle and maul before the game settles down and the players form a compact mass. Thereafter the pack can and often does remain static for considerable periods. There are times when it seems that there is something narcoleptic about the scrum – periods of deep sleep when through sheer exhaustion and by mutual agreement hardly a body stirs. Any movement thereafter is normally a steady heave and slither with the interlocked players lurching from side to side of the street, grinding past creaking barricades, squeezed against pitiless railings and the corners of houses, and steaming in closes and doorways. But the regular pattern is liable to alter and erupt, scattering spectators and sometimes enclosing them. From comparative immobility can come detachment, swirling disorder, confusion and ragged fragmented movement, followed by swift polarization. A collapse in the centre, a sudden rally or violent surge are all features of the game, while a smuggle or a moment of legerdemain can change the tide of fortune with dramatic suddenness.

Although numbers constitute an important part in deciding which way the ba' will go, the better coordinated side has a definite advantage, particularly if its players are holding the ba' and are adept at turning pressure to their advantage.

At one time, when the game had come to an impasse, for example when lodged in a narrow close and unable to progress, agreement was reached and there would be another throw-up. This took place at a point in the street opposite where the scrum had stuck. During the New Year's Day game 1933, the ba' was pushed through the gateway at Tankerness House and into the courtyard beyond, where it remained for half an hour. As matters had reached a deadlock the adversaries returned to Broad Street, and the ba' was thrown up again outside the gate. Similarly during the course of the Boys' Christmas Day game 1936 the ba' was thrown up a further four times. During the Women's game on Christmas Day 1945 the ba' was lost for a period, and on being located was thrown up again. Later in the same game there was stalemate on Junction Road and yet another throw-up took place.

FIG. 21: Men's Ba', Christmas Day 1970.

FIG. 22: Men's Ba' in St Magnus Lane, New Year's Day 1987.

FIG. 23: Men's Ba' in Queen Street, New Year's Day 1995.

FIG. 24: Men's Ba', Christmas Day 1988.

FIG. 25: Men's Ba', Christmas Day 1988.

FIG. 26: Men's Ba', New Year's Day 1985.

FIG. 27: Men's Ba', New Year's Day 1980.

FIG. 28: The narrow entry to Victoria Street taken at the beginning of the twentieth century. The houses and shops on the left were demolished in the 1930s.

FIG. 29: Men's Ba' at the Big Tree, New Year's Day 1994.

This arrangement was sometimes used when a Boys' game was being spoiled by the participation of over-age players. On New Year's Day 1925, as excitement mounted, adults of both sexes joined in and the ba' was forced into Victoria Street. There Bill Somerville, a blacksmith, who was deemed the official collector of monies for the ba's, stepped in, and though there is no record of this happening before (or indeed since), the ba' was taken back to the Market Cross and thrown up again. On New Year's Day 1929 the participation of youths caused the game to be stopped at the Crafty, and after the youths had desisted, another throw-up took place there.

It could be said that one throw-up is sufficient and anything further interferes with tactics, and therefore with the course of the game. Certainly a reduction in the periods of immobility tended to shorten the length of the contest. Nowadays the game is allowed to take its normal course and stalemates resolve themselves.

The game is not exclusive to men, women having quite a say in matters. Indeed any number of people, irrespective of physique, age or sex may take part. Games vary in length, there is no time limit and play of more than four hours is not unusual.

Distances Travelled

The traditional route for the Uppies is via Victoria Street and Main Street, and for the Doonies along Albert Street and Bridge Street. This puts the Uppies at a disadvantage of 50 yards. The distance from the Market Cross to the steps at the Harbour Office (via Albert Street and Bridge Street) is 484 yards, while the distance from the Market Cross to the Old Castle (via Victoria Street and Main Street) is 534 yards. However, there is no stipulated passage to the goals. On more than one occasion the course has been through the Peerie Sea, and when this happened on New Year's Day 1951 the players had to contend with a treacherous layer of ice. During another game on New Year's Day 1960 the scrum passed through the slime and mud of a duck pond at Pickaquoy. The ba' has been taken over roof tops and through gardens, closes, insufficiently barricaded houses, the Albert Hotel and into the doorway of the Congregational manse – the game is catholic in its path. Unusual routes are described in more detail in Chapter 11, 'Interesting Games and Unusual Incidents'.

A Natural Disadvantage

The old saying that if a Ba' remains for any length of time on Broad Street it will go Down holds more than a little truth. There is a slight incline from the Market Cross to the top of Broad Street, and this is a handicap to the Uppies, particularly if there is ice or snow on the ground. Additionally, before the houses opposite the Royal Bank of Scotland were removed in 1930, the Uppies had considerable difficulty in navigating the narrow opening into Victoria Street.

In the New Year's Day game 1895 a thaw had set in and the streets were slippery. Despite this the Up-the-Gates thrice took play during the first hour to within a dozen yards of Victoria Street, at two o'clock actually reaching the top of Broad Street, but were unable to storm their way through. Denied entry into Victoria Street and virtual success, the Uppies wavered and the Ba' eventually went Down.[2] On New Year's Day 1896 'for the first hour play was wholly confined to the upper part of Broad Street, and on four occasions it looked as if the Up-the-Gates were to succeed in forcing the ball into Victoria Street – twice indeed the very top of the street was reached, but they were driven back each time'.[3] Eventually this game, too, was won by the Doonies. In the New Year's Day game 1909, after half an hour's play the Ba' was still in the vicinity of the

[2] *O*, 5 January 1895 and *OH*, 9 January 1895.
[3] *OH*, 8 January 1896.

Market Cross, and Doonie hopes were high 'for it has been often proved that if the Ba' remained any length of time in the Broad Street it invariably went down'. This, however, was to be the exception. 'Several times the Up-the-Gates tried to rush the brae at the top of Broad Street but they were as often repulsed', but then by a clever manoeuvre the scrum was split into two, and the ba' was driven through into Victoria Street.[4]

The Players

It is a feature of the game that young and old alike take part, and although over the years a player learns how to pace himself and avoid the worst of the knocks, because of the strenuous nature of the game, nowadays the tendency is for many men to cease prolonged involvement on reaching their forties. This is perhaps a reflection on the move away from manual work to more sedentary occupations.

Some participants are active for many years. A few stalwarts, having started in the Boys' Ba', graduate to the Men's game at the age of fifteen or sixteen, and even in their late forties still contribute usefully for periods. A small band continue even longer, but the role of middle-aged players is not significant, and is decidedly risky. Indeed their participation is often almost involuntary, as they become so carried away as to allow themselves to be drawn into the struggle.

One remarkable Up-the-Gate, defying the assaults of time, continued until his sixties, and performed well too. His daily work was physical and kept him in good shape. Andrew Thomson had started when he was ten years old and for more than half a century he never missed involvement in a Ba'.

In a game of so much physical contact some arguments are inevitable, but generally the game is conducted in a spirit of keen but reasonably friendly rivalry. Accidents are likely to occur when play is loose and the scrum swings wildly. Now that numbers are so significant the pressures are great, particularly for those on the outside when squeezed against buildings. When the crush is severe, it is possible to lift one's feet and be carried for a few yards. When a man goes down, is injured, or is in a painful position, perhaps against a barricade or the corner of a wall, the pack can usually be persuaded to ease back. This enables those underneath to regain their feet and those in pain or difficulty to withdraw or to wriggle free to a safe position. The police are tolerant, and drunks are unwelcome and expelled. From time to time tempers become inflamed and fists fly, but disputes tend to be extinguished fairly quickly, often by the contestants themselves, and in the main good humour and forbearance prevail. There was an interesting example of

[4] *OH*, 6 January 1909.

FIG. 30: Men's Ba', Christmas Day 1966.

FIG. 31: Men's Ba', New Year's Day 2001.

this on New Year's Day 1887, when the good temper at that particular period of the game was such that 'when the players were passing the foot of Laing Street they struck up "Auld Lang Syne" in which all joined so long as they could find breath to sing'.[5] During the Christmas Day game 1938, when play had reached a standstill in Victoria Street, the stalemate was enlivened by a spirited rendition of

[5] *OH*, 5 January 1887.

FIG. 32: Men's Ba', Christmas Day 1985.

FIG. 33: Men's Ba', Christmas Day 1993.

'The Lambeth Walk'. Others joined in with gusto, and warming to their work the songsters then swung into several other popular tunes. 'Ole Faithful', 'Pack Up Your Troubles' and 'Daisy Bell' swirled upwards from the sweat-streaked choir, whose performance lacked nothing in volume. Next came 'Two Lovely Black Eyes', which was perhaps quite appropriate, and 'The More We Are Together' which, if not entirely accurate, added a touch of humour to the proceedings. An encore of 'The Lambeth Walk' completed the repertoire and brought to an end that part of the day's entertainment.

FIG. 34: Men's Ba', Christmas Day 1993.

Ba' Clothes

Old clothes are normally worn, and boots and shin guards are considered to be de rigueur. An old Kirkwall character is alleged to have declared on seeing the Down-the-Gates appear at the approach of one o'clock: 'Here come the Shories in their seaboots and ganzies.' Caps used to be worn but these are now not favoured. However, it is not unknown for men dressed in their best clothes to be seen in the middle of the unkempt mass of contestants. In such cases excitement and the urge to join in have proved too much even for those who have vowed only to watch.

So difficult is it for retired players to watch passively that various stratagems have been used in the past to overcome the magnetism: one man stayed in bed all day, another veteran sailed to Shapinsay, only to discover on his return late in the afternoon that the game was still in progress at the Uppie goal. The attraction was too much for the erstwhile seafarer and he became involved – and the lifelong enthusiast continued along that path for another twenty years. A fairly widespread ploy is to wear one's best suit and attend, preferably accompanied by spouse, but that too has been known to fail miserably. On Christmas Day 1938, as the scrum reached Tankerness House gateway several well-known Doonie businessmen playing with much spirit added a touch of sartorial elegance with soft hats, lounge suits and tweed coats. Their efforts gave only temporary respite and did little for the condition of their apparel.

Some men discard their clothes if they have been on the losing side. Conversely, those on the winning side may choose to have their garments washed, carefully put away and worn the following year to encourage a similar result!

On New Year's Day 1988 a young perfervid Up-the-Gate confided that she intended to gather parts of jackets, shirts, jerseys and stockings torn and discarded during a game – the detritus of a Ba'. She planned (to my knowledge yet unfulfilled) to wash the items and fashion them into an object such as a quilt or rug. Although not elegant, the resulting confection would certainly be unusual, providing a patchwork of various hues and differing thicknesses, and perhaps exuding strange aromas. Each fragment could tell quite a tale.

Tom Sclater, a strong man who won a Men's ba' on Christmas Day 1953, wore a leather glove on his left hand as a ploy. Tom was usually in the thick of things, either holding or close to the ba', and various hands attempting to locate it were misled by the feel of this decoy leather.

Clothes are not the only possessions to be lost: Dave Johnston, shortly afterwards a Doonie winner, played with a glass eye which was partly dislodged in the course of a rough passage of play. He did not realize that it had been swivelled in its socket after he had received a heavy knock when the scrum stuck in an Albert Street close. Jack Rendall and Dave's brother Robert alerted him to his strabismus (with the aid of a few expletives), the matter was rectified and the stalwart Doonie continued playing unperturbed, with eyes that were now looking in the same direction!

Style of Play

Hossack's *Kirkwall in the Orkneys*, printed in 1900, says (p. 465), referring to the early 1840s: 'In those days to have lifted the ball would have been very risky for the lifter; the ball was kicked or dribbled but never held, so it went all over the street and green . . . When the ball was *played*, skill, agility, and fleetness of foot came to the front while the animal strength and courage of the opposing factions was proved by another test.' By 'another test' Hossack meant the Queen's Birthday Bonfire on the Kirk Green; this celebration gradually faded out on being removed to Warrenfield about 1845 and the last Bonfire was held there in 1858.[6]

Thus we know that in the 1830s and earlier the ba' was seldom if ever picked up and carried. By 1840 the game had become less mobile and the ba' was normally held tight in a scrum on the streets – in other words the Ba' had

[6] See Chapter 14, 'Early Records of the Kirkwall Ba''.

assumed its present form. What happened was that the contest was attracting more popular interest, although considered by the press a sport for ruffians. As more people watched, and more players took part, the practical consideration of space encouraged and indeed necessitated this important change of style.

It is interesting to note that for a number of years there was still a tendency to include a certain amount of foot play. In the New Year's Day game 1875, after the Uppies had succeeded in breaking the Doonie domination by means of a smuggle, there was some cavilling at the manner in which the victory had been secured. However, the general feeling was that the Doonies could not really sustain their complaint 'as they are generally the first to lift the ball from the ground'.[7] In the Christmas Day game 1876 we find that a hard fought struggle lasted for about three hours and 'finally the ba' was kicked down the street'.[8] Again, in the New Year's Day game 1888 an attempt was made to revert to the old style of play. At that time there were still a number of men in the town who could recall when the ba' was played on the ground from first to last, and others who had taken part in contests when play was as much on as off the ground. It was hoped that by making the ba' considerably larger than usual it would be impossible to carry. The plan failed, although those players holding the outsize ba' must have been in some discomfort.[9]

The following descriptive account of the game is contained in Hugh Marwick's *Orkney*:

> Before the game is due to begin the Kirk Green is usually thronged with spectators, but the waiting players on the street may at first be comparatively few. On the stroke of the hour the ball is thrown up where the two 'towns' meet and immediately a locked struggle begins. There is no rule against handling, and only on the rarest occasions is there any chance of a player having a kick at the ball. It duly disappears from sight somewhere in the midst of a sort of vast scrum, a closely packed mass of madly heaving, pushing, perspiring humanity . . . Doonies struggling to force their way with the ball down the street, and the Uppies as resolutely pushing up the street, which, for the most part, is so level that gravitational assistance is almost negligible.
>
> Even on the coldest day a cloud of steam soon rises from the swaying pack, and excitement among the spectators mounts equally fast. Should the pack be forced a few yards down the street one after another of the

[7] *Northman*, 9 January 1875.
[8] *O*, 30 December 1876.
[9] *OH*, 4 January 1888.

FIG. 35: Men's Ba', Christmas Day 2000.

> Uppie spectators rush to the aid of their side to help to stem the Doonie pressure, and so *vice versa* until the original number of players may be doubled or trebled. Such is the magnetic lure of the game that quite staid elderly men, who have donned their best Sunday clothes with the express intention of not being tempted to join in, have been known to cast discretion to the winds and dash to the help of their side, regardless alike of clothes or age.[10]

Unexpected Players

An old player, in relating tales of bygone days, informed me that in 1921 he took part in the Christmas Day game with the late Sheriff A. Martin Laing, who felt that it was only right and proper to take part in the customs and activities of local people. The Sheriff, who had been a rugby player, was to have turned out on New Year's Day as well, but thought better of it, later remarking that the Ba' was a much tougher and rougher game than rugby!

When the Sheriff was playing, Robbie Newlands, a well known character who lived in a loan near the Sheriff's house, would (perhaps with an eye to the

[10] H. Marwick, *Orkney*, pp. 123, 124.

future) enjoin the players 'Take care of the b—r, but don't hurt the b—r, that's the Sheriff.' Subsequently Robbie was summoned to the court for a minor offence, probably not for the first time. There the Sheriff started the proceedings by declaring that he was indeed sorry to see such a respectable man and a neighbour of his own in court. This gave Robbie much gratification.

Doctor George R. C. Russell had a practice in Kirkwall for some years, and he was an enthusiastic player, winning a ba' around 1895. Apparently one Christmas Day, Mrs Russell, who was not a devotee of the game, thought that the time had come to put an end to her husband's annual foolishness, and marched him off to the Episcopal church. This in no way damped the good doctor's zest for the contest, and after the service he went straight to the game. There, handing his tile hat and gold-topped malacca cane to a spectator, and still clad in frock coat, he plunged into the fray. In the course of play one of the contestants broke a leg and was removed to the side while help was summoned. A perspiring and dishevelled doctor emerged from the scrum, set the man's leg on the barrow where he was lying and, duty done, re-joined the struggle.

The Russell story was related to me by the distinguished artist Dr Stanley Cursiter, the Queen's Limner in Scotland, proud possessor of a miniature ba', perfectly made and given to him seventy-five years earlier by John Costie, shoemaker, Main Street, Kirkwall. Dr Cursiter told me that in 1895 Mr Costie was paid 30*s*. for making a ba'. This was quite a sum of money, and gives a good idea of the amount of work required for each Costie ba'.

In the 1930s Dr Ali Sinclair had his surgery in Queen Street. He would go to the Ba' scrupulously dressed in a dark suit and bowler hat, but soon after he arrived the call of the contest would become too much and Dr Ali, in his sartorial elegance and complete with bowler, could be seen in the thick of play.

Surgeon Ian McClure lost a leg with the Royal Flying Corps in the First World War but this disability did not stop him, complete with wooden leg, playing in the Ba.'

Fights and Injuries

In former times good humour did not always prevail, there was more acrimony and fights were frequent. The game then was played by men who set great store by physical strength.

When the game was really football, with the ba' on the ground, the tendency was to settle arguments after the contest. In the mid-1840s the Doonies scored their first success for a number of years. They were jubilant, and after the cheering had died down and the ringing of ships' bells had stopped, they mustered pipes and drums and in the evening marched into Uppie territory. The Uppies, smarting after their defeat, did not take this provocation meekly and a free fight developed. The upshot was that the invaders were utterly routed and, minus pipes and drums, swept in disorder as far Down as the Bridge.[11] With the change in style of play around 1840 there was more physical contact between the players, tempers tended to be easily inflamed, and the opportunity was often taken to air grievances and settle old scores. There is an amusing story told of how, during a tough game at the end of the nineteenth century, a battered and dishevelled player struggled from the heaving, jostling scrum. Lurching up to an innocent bystander he smote him a resounding blow on the ear and growled 'Tak' that Davit my boy, for there's damn little fair play in there!' In the Youths' Christmas Day Ba' 1908 several free fights took place, in which over a score of players were involved.

Notwithstanding the element of friendly rivalry that is always evident, there can be no doubt that the game is rough and tough. A teacher was discussing blood sports with her class, who readily identified fox hunting and bull baiting as possessing the proper credentials. There was a reflective pause, then a ten-year-old girl's face lit up and she exclaimed 'The Ba'!' Cuts, scratches, bumps and bruises are the general rule, and hardly anyone escapes without some damage. But cracked ribs and fractured arms and legs are not unknown, and in the Christmas Day game 1911 one man sustained a broken collar bone while another fell, was trampled on by the crowd and had two ribs broken.[12] In the New Year's Day game 1938 two men were taken to hospital, one suffering from a fractured ankle. German prisoners, awaiting repatriation and watching the first game played after the war, were amazed at what they saw. They are alleged to have said, 'If you do this for pleasure no wonder you won the war!'

An alarming accident which could have had serious consequences occurred during the Men's New Year's Day Ba' 1933. The scrum had stuck for half an hour in the courtyard of Tankerness House, the players voluntarily broke up and play was restarted with a throw-up from the top of Tankerness House gateway. The crowd numbered almost 1000 and the road was congested. The driver of a car travelling down Palace Road lost control and knocked down four people including a woman whose two-year-old daughter was thrown out of her arms. Fortunately no one was killed but one man was concussed and had to have his face and legs stitched at the nearby surgery of Dr Peterkin, 7 Victoria Street. Surprisingly, though the accident occurred less than twenty yards away, most of the players were unaware of what had happened.

[11] *O*, 7 January 1899.

[12] *O*, 30 December 1911.

Forty-three-year-old Theo Rorie won a Men's ba' on Christmas Day 1969 and had been ever present since the game started after the Second World War. On one occasion in the 1950s, it was a close call. He broke a bone in his foot on Christmas Day but proceeded to play a week later with the injured limb encased in a plaster cast that became progressively more soggy as the game unfolded. To put it mildly, a real enthusiast.

On New Year's Day 1983 several players were injured at the top of Broad Street and had to be taken to Balfour Hospital. One of them, a Down-the-Gate, Mike Anderson, had aggravated an injury received in the Christmas Day Ba'. He returned from the hospital with a surgical collar and, somewhat incredibly, continued playing.

Inevitably in the course of play there are injuries and players readily accept the scratches, strains and bruises that are incident to such a rumbustious game. Abrasions and contusions are often ignored at the time and it may be two or three days later that the outpatients department at Balfour Hospital is attended! Occasionally some injuries are serious. On Boxing Day 1988 there was a large turnout and such was the weight of players that when the scrum collapsed a number of contestants had to be rescued. Three trapped Up-the-Gates passed out, two of whom had to be given mouth to mouth resuscitation, and five distressed men were taken to hospital where one was detained overnight. Fortunately nurses were present on the Kirk Green and provided first aid. This was an alarming incident but it should be said that however large and committed the scrum, when players fall almost invariably restraint is shown and both sides readily back off. The trauma of 1988 was not easily forgotten.

On New Year's Day 1990 three casualties were taken to hospital. Two were discharged the following day but the third, Court Officer Billy Peace (ex-Sergeant), was detained; he had stumbled, fallen and broken a leg near the scrum while guiding children to safety at the foot of the Clay Loan. At the request of a member of the Ba' Committee play ceased until Billy was taken to an ambulance, by no means the Ba's first act of collective responsibility when a player or spectator is injured.

On Christmas Day 2003 former Boys' and Men's winner – and ba' maker – Edgar Gibson fractured his skull on Broad Street when he fell heavily. He was taken to hospital, had fourteen stitches inserted, and was detained overnight.

One player told me (somewhat late one night) that his ambition was to die in the middle of the Ba'. Fortunately there has been only one fatality as a result of involvement. This occurred during the New Year's Day Ba' 1903 when Captain William Cooper of the smack *Caleb*, who had been playing for the Down-the-Gates and was having a rest, suffered a heart attack and died, aged about

FIG. 36: Men's Ba', Christmas Day 1971.

FIG. 37: Men's Ba', Christmas Day 1975.

forty-five, leaving a widow and ten of a family. An attempt was made to stop the game, which by this stage was about to enter Victoria Street, and apparently a considerable number of players did desist. Others continued playing, and the game finished shortly afterwards at the Old Police Station at the foot of Wellington Street.

Safety

Safety considerations are of paramount import. Notices and articles in local newspapers remind participants not to trespass on private property, and spectators are asked not to climb on walls and roofs. Onlookers, especially spectators with children, are exhorted to keep well away from the action. Shop owners and householders are expected to erect safe, stout barricades and car owners are requested not to park in areas where play may occur. Although the Ba' has no explicit rules there are certain conventions that have been put to the test and generally accepted: certainly the most important is that when there is a collapse players should stand back and allow those who have fallen to regain their feet. This is vital, as in recent years the pack has become very large, often swelling to over 200 participants.

FIG. 38: Ba' Committee member Jim Cromarty giving pre-Ba' talk to Kirkwall Grammar School pupils, December 2003. Other committee members involved are Bobby Leslie, Gary Gibson, Graeme King and Mike Anderson.

FIG. 39: Young players at Kirkwall Grammar School listening to advice on safety from the Ba' Committee, December 2003.

The danger of standing too close to the Ba' is real and was all too apparent on Boxing Day 1983 when an eleven-year-old boy was injured in a breakaway and had to be taken to hospital. Fortunately he was able to be discharged the same day.

On Boxing Day 1988 women, children and some elderly folk were standing on Broad Street a few yards from play. The scrum erupted and two women were trapped. Although one got clear quickly it was a full ten minutes before her companion broke free, badly shaken.

At all times the Ba' Committee and its adherents conjure players and spectators of all ages to abide in their conduct by every precept of common sense and fair play.

Orkney Islands Council annually issues the undernoted disclaimer accepting 'no liability whatsoever in respect of any claim for damage or injury to person or property' from the Ba', reminding players and spectators that participation is entirely at their own risk. That said, many councillors and officials hold the Ba' in high regard. It is very doubtful if any authority would attempt to stop this old established custom, and certainly any such move would meet a great deal of resistance from players and public alike.

"ORKNEY ISLANDS COUNCIL WISH IT TO BE KNOWN THAT IT ACCEPTS NO LIABILITY WHATSOEVER IN RESPECT OF ANY CLAIM FOR DAMAGE OR LOSS OR INJURY TO PERSON OR PROPERTY, HOWSOEVER ARISING, FROM ANY PERSON IN RESPECT OF THE EVENT KNOWN AS "THE BA", HELD ANNUALLY IN KIRKWALL AT CHRISTMAS AND NEW YEAR.

FOR THE AVOIDANCE OF DOUBT, PERSONS PARTICIPATE IN THE BA', WHETHER AS PLAYERS OR SPECTATORS, ENTIRELY AT THEIR OWN RISK."

FIG. 40: Orkney Islands Council notice which appears annually in the local newspapers.

Volunteers from the local branch of the Red Cross are unfailingly present at Men's games providing first aid for minor injuries. The Department of Harbours makes safety arrangements timeously in case of a Doonie win, by removing hazards at the Basin and the surrounding area, and by ensuring that lifebelts are available against the possibility of players and spectators getting into difficulties in the dark, cold waters.

Damage to Property

Although doors and windows are well barricaded, inevitably there is a certain amount of damage to property. Broken windows are not uncommon, gates and doors are sometimes smashed, walls dislodged and iron railings bent by the impact of the solid mass of players. In the New Year's Day game 1892 the crush was so great in Main Street that the railings in front of the Balfour Hospital (now the West End Hotel) were torn away.[13] On New Year's Day 1967 Gunn's Close between Victoria Street and Junction Road was tight packed with a mass of men, and such was the pressure in the narrow lane that a considerable length of a five-foot high stone wall collapsed. Players were knocked to the ground, and one or two were pinned by falling stones, but fortunately apart from bruises no one was seriously injured.

FIG. 41: Barricaded property, New Year's Day 2001.

[13] *O*, 9 January 1892.

FIG. 42: Men's Ba', New Year's Day 1996.

Boys Break with Tradition

The longest Boys' Ba' intruded into commercial property and a private home. This was on New Year's Day 1998. In early passages of play the trophy had been forced down a drain in front of the Town Hall and the metal cover dropped over it – a somewhat pointless move on neutral territory. It took ten minutes to recover the orb. Then, quite unnecessarily, the ba' was taken to Jewson's wood yard and hidden behind a water tank in an attic. There it stayed for almost an hour, its whereabouts undisclosed. During this time a number of boys ran over the roofs and considerable damage was occasioned to the asbestos sheeting of a store holding decorative lining boards. Open to the elements, these were subsequently damaged by rain. Sections of slate roof too were affected and it was fortuitous that no one fell through (repairs were to cost hundreds of pounds but fortunately the proprietors took a benevolent attitude). While police were clearing the building, members of the Ba' Committee persuaded the lads to produce the ba' for further play. On the street the game proceeded to the Crafty and thence over a field to Glaitness Road and Wellington Street where alas the ba' was taken into a house. This house had also received an irregular visit on Christmas Day. With some difficulty the intruders were persuaded by Ba' Committee member Bobby Leslie to leave, whereupon they made another run through the field. Emerging at the former Scapa Knitwear site the contest was continued in more traditional style and was concluded by the Uppies at 3.20 p.m. This was a very long game, but of poor quality, and by extensively damaging property and invading the privacy of a home the participants set aside the best traditions of what is essentially a street game.

Police Involvement

Edwin Eunson recalled, in a radio broadcast of Ba' memories on Christmas Eve 1986, that in his youth, 'There used to be fights on the outskirts of the Ba' . . . but the police didn't pay very much attention because there were men there who were quite able and willing to stop any outbreaks of violence with a very firm hand and they had no hesitation in doing so. They kind of policed themselves.'

Billy Peace, a former police sergeant, reminisced of his time on duty in the 1950s that he 'always ended up being a walking coat hanger and safety deposit box. I have been on duty at a Ba' and ended up carrying two cloth caps, two civy raincoats, possibly three or four wrist watches, plus the occasional half bottle and other items.' He also recalled having to push into the scrum from time to time to assist anyone who had fallen, particularly elderly men on the fringe, and attempting to hold back these men from entering the fray.

FIG. 43: Men's Ba', Christmas Day 1966.

In those days, the passive, even benign, attitude of the constabulary (mindful of inbuilt Ba' loyalties) sometimes developed into one of active participation. Billy further recalled that when Constables John Corse and David Sutherland reported for duty at 3 p.m. on New Year's Day 1958, they were told to relieve Sergeant (later Inspector) Charlie Craigie and Constable Harry Garrioch at the Ba'. On arrival at Bain's Creamery, Junction Road, Craigie and Garrioch (both Uppies) exhorted the two other officers to join them in the scrum and push Up. Sutherland accepted this invitation with alacrity, but Down-the-Gate John Corse promptly joined the fray on the other side. There was then the interesting spectacle of three constables and a sergeant in the Ba' – all in uniform. The ba' was duly forced Up and awarded to Vinnie Linklater.

This was not the only occasion of participation by policemen who had intended only to watch and enjoy the afternoon's play. Billy's popularity and addiction to the Ba' was known to the Chief Constable who called him aside one New Year's Eve on hearing that he intended to participate the following day. The Chief's advice was that it would not be in his best interests or that of the Force if he played in the game. It would not set a good example to the public. Reluctantly Billy agreed to stay at home and the following lunchtime, house-bound and morose, he was consoling himself with a stiff dram of Highland Park when an agitated brother-in-law arrived and exclaimed, partly in Gaelic, 'Good grief, why in the name of the Lord are you sitting here and four of your fine pals in full uniform, hats and all, in the thick of things on flaming Broad Street?' (This is a somewhat expurgated version.) These colleagues were Harry Garrioch, Davie Sutherland, Jimmy Archibald and Alex Cowie (the last two both subsequently chief inspectors). Billy's gloom vanished, as did the contents of his glass, and he hastened to join four somewhat relaxed members of the constabulary. What the Chief Constable subsequently said or did is not known.

Billy remembered another Ba' when the Uppie side that he supported was in some disarray. On finding his fellow duty officer, Sergeant Sammy Bews, in the middle of the scrum and shoving Down, Billy recalled:

> That was enough for me and I was straight in urging the Uppies to make a late rally. The next I knew somebody had hold of the tails of my police overcoat and was pulling me backwards. This was Maggie Yule and her daughter Ruby Youngson who gave me a ticking off as I might lose my hat. I remember taking the hat off and giving it to Maggie to look after and went back in again only to be pulled out once more by the women who thought the game was too rough and I might get my uniform ruined. I explained that the public paid for my uniform and on hearing this they pushed me back into the game. I eventually caught up with Sammy in Ayre Road after the ba' had gone over the wall into the sea and his explanation was that he 'was only helping out so that we could finish duty'.

The police force in Orkney has always taken a sensible, even pragmatic, view of the Ba', recognizing that in large measure the game is self-regulating and that police involvement in resolving disputes would be deprecated. This approach is greatly appreciated by players and the public.

It is alleged that in recent times when there were rumours of some sort of restriction being imposed on playing the Ba', a member of the local constabulary (fearing with justification that this would provoke a very firm reaction from players) declared that if there was any prospect of this eventuating he would take extended leave at the festive season, continuing in jocular vein that he might even apply for a transfer! He further averred that colleagues were known to organize shifts so that they were off duty at the time of the Men's game and able to participate.

3

The Goals

The Uppie goal has varied from time to time. Reporting the New Year's Day game 1880, the *Orkney Herald* of 6 January 1880 commented on the fact that it was something like thirty years since the Ba' had gone Up. This refers to the New Year's Day game, as between 1846 and 1880 five Ba's were won by the Uppies, four of them Christmas Day games, namely the Christmas Day games 1867 and 1868; the Christmas Day game 1870 which was played in the evening and went Up-street after a long struggle; the New Year's Day Ba' 1875 which was smuggled Up-street; and the Christmas Day game 1879. The *Herald* report then went on: 'The goal in olden times was said to be where the Junction Road joins Wellington Street' – i.e. where the present goal is, although there was no New Scapa Road at that time. On New Year's Day 1880 the Uppies did manage to win, aided by a number of Caithness men who were working on Scapa pier and who, if successful, were to be rewarded with a barrel of whisky! Delighted with their long awaited win, the Up-the-Gates carried the ba' past the old goal, up Wellington Street and High Street and some 300 yards along Old Scapa Road.

A Horse is Used

Prior to this the 'Fork of the Roads' – the junction of the Old Stromness Road and Old Scapa Road – was for a time the recognized goal.[1] On Christmas Day 1879, after the ba' had reached the head of Junction Road an Up-the-Gate, as probably prearranged, threw it from the centre of the players into the arms of one Bill Sutherland, an employee at the Castle Hotel, as he galloped past on a piebald pony called Missie towards the Up-street goal, which at that period was at the head of High Street. The *Herald* report[2] further states that the rider

[1] *OH*, 3 January 1894.
[2] *OH*, 30 December 1879.

galloped off to Scapa 'amidst the howlings of the infuriated mob' (it was alleged, probably with some exaggeration, that there were about 500 players in the game). It was at this time that there was a vague suggestion that the ba' should be taken to water at either end of the town. This never really merited serious consideration if the Uppie goal was to be Scapa. The Christmas Day game 1882 finished at Glaitness School – a few yards along the old Stromness Road, 'where the champion winner climbed up into one of the few trees in Orkney and led the vociferous cheering and rejoicings of his Up-street compatriots'.[3]

The Ba' taken to Foreland

A Mr MacGregor, brother of the author of the poem on the Ba' of 1882, given in Chapter 12, 'Prose and Rhyme', has left an interesting account of the New Year's Day game 1880. He entitled this *The Year of the Biggest Struggle on Record:*

> This was supposed to have been the most severe ba' fight New Year's Day ever underwent . . . Lawyers, Teachers, Town Councillors, Merchants, and representatives from all kinds of people took part in it . . . the Up-street men, principally through superior weight of body bulk, mastered their opponents by pushing them from Broad Street to Junction Road, and thence out the Old Scapa Road to as far as Foreland. It was a great victory and ended by my dear, now deceased brother Henry, being carried shoulder-high back to the town as one of the champions of the day, and in consideration thereof he was awarded the trophy.

Nearing the end of the game, when the Uppies had pushed along Old Scapa Road, some Doonie players in the middle of the scrum, realizing that they could not now win, used their knives to cut the ba', so that the Uppies would not have anything to show for their victory. All the cork stuffing came out, and in the end only the leather casing was left. Presumably Mr MacGregor had the ba' repacked!

Something similar had happened in May 1869 when a game was played as part of the Queen's Birthday festivities. On this occasion too the ba' was cut up and the contest came to an abrupt end.

3 *OH*, 27 December 1882.

The Ba' at Soulisquoy

At the conclusion of two successive games, Christmas Day 1881 and New Year's Day 1882, the ba' was taken to Soulisquoy where it was hoisted on the mail gig which was stationed there. After the Christmas Day game, George Nicolson who had carried the ba' most of the way, mounted the gig and made the following short speech: 'The Doon-the-Gates hoist the ball on an old schooner, when they take it down the street, but we do it more honour, for we have hoisted it on Her Majesty's mail gig.' He was then accorded three cheers, this bringing the game to a close.[4]

After the New Year's Day game 1882 when the Uppies had reached Burgar's Bay the ba' was taken into a house. It was reported that a well-known mail driver (possibly Mr Nicolson) secured the prize, and going out through a back window proceeded to Soulisquoy followed by a considerable number of people. 'The mail gig was taken out and the hero of the hour made a speech, closing by asking three cheers for the Queen and three cheers for the Master for allowing him to take the ball up and congratulating his compatriots for winning both the Christmas and the New Year ball.'[5]

Burgar's Bay

On New Year's Day 1883 'the crowd moved steadily Up-street with scarcely a halt until Burgar's Bay was reached. This interesting locality seems now to be considered the "goal" of the upper end of the town.'[6] After the game had ended, the ba' and attendant cohort issued forth, and one of the leaders addressed the crowd thus: 'The ba' was carried the whole road by the smallest of the Up-the-Gates – Sandy Sutherland – and not ane o' the Doon-the-Gates was able tae tak' it frae him.' Surprisingly this provocative statement went unanswered, and after some desultory cheering the crowd quietly dispersed.[7] The Christmas Day 1883 ba' found a resting place in a hay loft in Burgar's Bay,[8] and on Christmas Day 1887 it was taken by the Uppies into Grain House, at the foot of Wellington Street.[9] On 1 January 1894 after the scrum had reached half-way between the head of Junction Road and Burgar's Bay the ba' was forced back to the then police

[4] *O*, 31 December 1881.
[5] *OH*, 4 January 1882.
[6] *OH*, 3 January 1883.
[7] *O*, 6 January 1883.
[8] *O*, 29 December 1883.
[9] *O*, 31 December 1887. Grain House is the first house up on the right-hand side of Wellington Street.

station[10] 'into which it was taken, some of the players entering and continuing the struggle for a few minutes in the lobby and kitchen. At length the Up-the-Gates obtained possession and displayed it spick and span as at the beginning of the game from a window in the first storey amid cheers and hisses. The finish caused a little bad feeling, Burgar's Bay having been regarded as the Up-street goal for many years, and for a moment it seemed as if the proceedings were to end in a general fight. Good sense however prevailed, and the crowd gradually dispersed.'[11] Subsequently, the Uppie goal for a few years was considered to be the foot of Wellington Street, although on New Year's Day 1905 the game again finished at Burgar's Bay.

By 1906 the permanent goal was recognized as being where New Scapa Road, Main Street and Junction Road meet, known locally as the Long Corner, Mackinson's Corner or Sandison's Corner. The reason for the final change was that after an exhausting contest the players found it onerous to push the scrum up the slope of Wellington Street.

Goaling the Ba'

In connection with goaling the ba' it is impossible in practice to equate what each side must do, and indeed over the years understandings, requirements and unwritten rules have grown up and in turn been modified.

The Uppies have to take the ba' to a specific location, which as we have seen has varied from time to time. After the present goal was established 100 years ago it was widely held that the game could not be considered over until the ba' was exhibited from the top of the wall there. This has not always been the case in recent years, and claimants for the ba' holding or close to it in the dense mass below the wall are most reluctant to pass the trophy outwith their control. There is also the conviction that to complete an Uppie victory the ba' must touch the wall, and even with the solid press of men this is normally achieved although the process can take time. The Uppies do not have the effective Doonie remedy of concluding matters by pushing ba', supporters and contenders for the trophy into the sea!

In practice what happens at the Uppie goal is that when the scrum reaches the corner, normally after other claims have been defeated, the winner is lifted on the shoulders of his supporters with the ba' safely under his jersey. At other times the ba' is passed to the top of the wall and a fierce squabble continues on a small platform before the winner emerges from the mêlée.

[10] On the left-hand side of Wellington Street, second house up.

[11] *OH*, 3 January 1894.

FIG. 44: Men's Ba', Christmas Day 2000 at the Uppie goal.

Traditionally, to complete their triumph, the Doonies immerse the ba' in water, and a water goal is very much a part of mass football played throughout this country and in France. Once the ba' is in the sea, the game is over, and commenting on this fact the *Orkney Herald* (5 January 1876) said that after the ba' had been kicked into the harbour at the end of the New Year's Day game 1876 an Up-the-Gate was inclined to dispute that the contest had been concluded. However, he 'was made aware of his mistake by two or three fists being simultaneously planted on his face – a somewhat staggering form of argument.' On New Year's Day 1889 the struggle continued half-way down the pier before the ba' could be thrown into the water and the game brought to an end.[12] In the Youths' Ba' played on New Year's Day 1893 the game could not be concluded because of the Doonies' inability to get the ba' into the sea. They then 'pushed their opponents along the Ayre to the first slap, and rushed them down upon the beach.'[13]

The established location of the Doonies' goal was for many years the inner harbour or 'Basin' (usually the corner directly opposite the harbour master's office), where to complete a triumph the ba' was 'trucked'.

[12] *O*, 5 January 1889.
[13] *O*, 7 January 1893.

FIG. 45: Men's Ba', mid-1950s.

'Trucking' the Ba'

In days gone by a Doonie win always resulted in the ba' being 'trucked'. This consisted of hoisting it by means of the flag halyards, or on occasion climbing with it, to the truck at the top of the mast of a sailing ship – if possible the highest mast in the harbour. Sometimes the ba' was secured in a handkerchief and pulled to the truck, or a bold young man with the ends of a handkerchief firmly gripped in his teeth would swarm up to the mast head. By this stage the contest was over, the ba' having made its time-honoured visit to the waters of the harbour. It was considered something of a distinction to climb the mast with the ba', and after cheering from the mass of people gathered below the prize might be thrown down and the winner chosen, although occasionally it was the champion himself who climbed to the truck with his trophy. At one time the ba' was run up and down three times before being fixed to the truck and left there to swing.

The first written record of a ba' being trucked is after the New Year's Day game 1856 when the ba' was 'exhibited at the mast head of a vessel in harbour as a dearly won trophy'.[14] On 1 January 1858 the ba' was 'carried down, kicked into the harbour, and finally fixed upon the fore-top-mast of the clipper *Paragon*

[14] *O*, 5 January 1856.

amid great cheering'.[15] Ten years later the ba' was hoisted on the flagstaff at the 'new' pier.[16] On Christmas Day 1878 there was another variation when the ba' was hoisted to the topmast of the Shapinsay packet *Klydon,* and carried off to Shapinsay![17] The Boys' Ba' commenced at eleven o'clock on New Year's Day 1888, the sides were evenly matched and struggled hard for victory urged on by their elders. Gradually the Doonies progressed and soon had passed Dr Logie's house at the foot of the Strynd and facing Broad Street. With only an occasional rally the Union Bank and Adamson's Temperance Hotel, both in Albert Street, were reached and after an hour and a half's play the ba' was hoisted on one of the masts of the schooner *Luna*. A printer's devil was awarded the trophy and *The Orcadian* recorded: 'Our PD now has the leather trophy hanging above his rollers and ink, thus showing he bore his share in the battle. What chance, therefore, could the Up-the-Gates have of victory, when they had to contend with a little black fellow so closely allied to his Satanic Majesty?'[18]

I have included a unique photograph of trucking the Boys' ba' on New Year's Day 1906 (FIG. 46). Taken by the late Tom Kent, it shows twenty Doonie boys on the masts and rigging of a sailing ship, the *Mary Ann* while the ba' is being hoisted to the truck. This particular Ba' started at 8.30 a.m. and was won by J. Lennie. The photograph comes from a postcard sent by eleven-year-old John Sinclair (who was awarded a Doonie Men's ba' on Christmas Day 1933) in March 1906 to his brother Tommy who was working as a herd boy on the farm of Nisthouse, Woodwick, Evie. Tommy Sinclair joined up, served with the Royal Scots in the First World War and was killed in action in France in August 1918. His wallet was sent to his mother in Kirkwall and it contained this undamaged postcard, then twelve years old and over sixty years old when it came to me. An unusual story, tinged with sadness even after all these years, and involving the remarkable journey of a Ba' postcard from Kirkwall to Evie to France and back to Kirkwall before being produced from a dead soldier's wallet in St Rognvald Street many years later.

The custom of trucking disappeared with the old sailing ships. The first Ba' after the First World War was the Boys' Christmas Day game 1919, and it went Down. But the war had brought about a radical change in local shipping and there were no suitable masts that day in Kirkwall harbour, not even a smack! On this occasion the difficulty was overcome by using the flagstaff at the Harbour Office. A week later the Men's ba' was hoisted to the top of the same flagstaff.

[15] *O*, 4 January 1858.
[16] *O*, 7 January 1868.
[17] *O*, 28 Dec 1878.
[18] *O*, 7 January 1888.

FIG. 46: Trucking the Boys' Ba', New Year's Day 1906.

One of the last instances of trucking a ba' was after the Boys' Christmas Day game 1923 when the prize was hoisted on the mast of the *Tresness.*

The *Elizabeth, Margrethe, No-Joke, Klydon, Pomona, Galatea, Paragon, Adele, Luna, Howard, Thomas Henry, Caber Feidh, Tresness, Alexandra, Express, Pandora, Pioneer* – the list of trucked sailing ships reads like a long-forgotten page from an old Kirkwall register of vessels. Sloops, schooners, brigantines, ketches, cutters and smacks – hard-working proud queens, they plied their trade, came and went, now a roll call of wraiths.

For some years, starting in the 1890s, the Uppies had a custom of exhibiting the ba' from the window of a house at their goal. The last recorded instance of this happening was on New Year's Day 1905, when, after half an hour's argument to decide to whom the ba' was to be awarded, it was displayed in a window of a house in Burgar's Bay.[19] This appears to have been the Uppies' equivalent of trucking, but at best it can have been only a poor imitation.

Recently, and particularly since the end of the Second World War, it has become established that as long as the ba' is immersed in water somewhere along the sea-front, including the Ayre Road and Shore Street, this is sufficient to seal the victory. The scrum sometimes fetches up at a part of the harbour where there is nothing to arrest the impetus of players, and then a number of men – some unwillingly – plunge headlong into the sea. The cold dark winter waters can be dangerous for exhausted players, who with heavy boots are not able to swim far or keep afloat for long. Among those who inadvertently tumbled in on one occasion was a non-swimmer, complete with sea boots. After what must have seemed an eternity he surfaced, one water-filled boot still attached and sorely troubling him. Thrashing wildly, spluttering and gasping, but with real feeling, he exclaimed to those who had managed to stay on the pier above: 'For God's sake boys save me first, I've the most bairns.' On 1 January 1937 a player who leapt into the sea on the east side of the pier got into considerable difficulties. Only a prompt rescue operation by two players averted a possible tragedy.

New Year's Day 1951 saw the ba' thrown in the sea well along the Ayre Road. On another occasion, Christmas Day 1964, players and ba' went over the wall and into a rough sea mid-way along Shore Street, opposite the oil depot.

The Ba' is played irrespective of weather conditions. New Year's Day 1967 was bitterly cold, with the additional discomfort of a strong north-west gale. After a protracted contest in which play surged as far up as Gunn's Close, the scrum was eventually forced down Great Western Road and Burnmouth Road, and shortly before six o'clock the interlocked mass of men spilled over the sea wall

[19] *OH*, 4 January 1905.

fig. 47: Men's Ba', New Year's Day 1969.

and onto the open shore in front of the Ayre Houses. The scene was memorable, with a knot of claimants and their attendant supporters grappling in the wintry sea while the gale drove blinding flurries of snow and hail straight off the bay. In these Arctic conditions dozens of hardy players struggled, sometimes waist deep in the breakers, at other times ploughing through banks of rotting seaweed, and it took twenty minutes of animated argument on the wild darkened shore before the winner was chosen. Only then did soaked, battered players and frozen spectators take refuge from the storm.

The game has finished a number of times at the West Pier, and the Corn Slip has also been favoured.

FIG. 48: Boys' Ba', New Year's Day 1975.

Doonies Row to Victory

The New Year's Day game 1936 was unusual in that most of the play was either in or on water. It was also noteworthy for the novel use of sea transport employed by the Doonies to reach their goal. The ba' was thrown up at one o'clock by its donor, Major Basil H. H. Neven-Spence, MP for Orkney and Shetland. Twenty minutes later the Uppies had swept play into Victoria Street and seemed well on the way to victory. There now occurred a particularly clever move by the Doonies, one of whom wrenched the ba' out of the scrum and flung it well Up-street, where by arrangement another Doonie was waiting. A relay of sprinters carried the ba' down a close and along Junction Road to West Tankerness Lane where two Doonies entered the Peerie Sea and waded across to near the

Pickaquoy shore. Instead of landing on the rubbish dump the Doonies, now augmented in numbers, struck out boldly across the Oyce to a point midway along its north shore. Close to the road and still knee-deep in water the resolute band, with the ba' in their midst, moved eastwards, looking for an opportunity to crash over the Aire and throw the ba' into Kirkwall Bay. Eventually, in the face of determined Uppie opposition, this was achieved, and the ba' was hurled into the open sea. A player swam out and pushing the ba' ahead of him, was pulled aboard a rowing boat which by good organization the Doonies had waiting in readiness. Boat and jubilant crew made off for the Basin. No enormously successful Venetian trading galley making its way up the Grand Canal ever received greater acclamation than this tubby two-oared rowing boat, as with sodden trophy and dishevelled crew it bumped against the teeming Corn Slip shortly after two o'clock. The winner was duly chosen, and thus came to an end a momentous game that had been very much a tactical Doonie triumph, not least of seamanship.

4

Acquiring and Making the Ba'

The Cathedral Session Book contains the following entry for Sunday 7 December 1684: 'It was intimated that ther is non in toun and paroch that marries but shall pay a foot-ball to the scholers of the grammour school.' The boys did not get all the ba's which could have been purchased by the monies so levied, but ba' money was included with proclamation fees down to the passing of the Registration Act 1855. Mr Craig was the last Registrar to raise the charge.[1]

We have confirmation that prior to the 1830s the Session Clerk collected ba' money in addition to the usual fees. This was presumably the payment referred to above: it amounted to 1*s.* 6*d.*, and was collected from each couple when they gave in their marriage banns. Out of the proceeds the clerk presented every New Year's Day a ba' for the grammar school and one for the trades.[2] With the discontinuance of this old practice, inevitably public collection became the accepted method of obtaining the necessary funds. This was quite natural, and in 1858 it is recorded that some of the enthusiastic young people of the town had 'just completed a subscription for the purpose of furnishing the annual foot-ball to our tradesmen on New Year's Day'.[3]

For many years there was a certain amount of dissatisfaction concerning the collection of money for ba's. Prior to Christmas 1898 funds had been collected for the ba's and a correspondent of *The Orcadian* had no doubt but that 'the collectors will have enjoyed their spree over the overplus, as the subscriptions are generally quite sufficient, to put it mildly, to pay for all the ba's'.[4] It was felt that there were too many collectors – boys and men – and there was a widely held suspicion that all the money collected did not find its way to the intended destination.

[1] Orkney Archives, OCR 14/75.
[2] *O*, 24 December 1898.
[3] *O*, 13 December 1858.
[4] *O*, 24 December 1898.

So strong was this feeling that a public meeting was held in the Town Hall, Kirkwall, on 20 November 1910 to consider both the future of the Youths' Ba' (see Ch. 8) and regularizing the collection of money. Provost James Slater was in the chair and he explained that for some years there had been a considerable number of complaints by townspeople who were called upon frequently by both boys and men requesting money. Peter Brass intimated that from enquiries he had made a maximum of £2 10*s.* would defray the cost of the four ba's. To satisfy the complaints William Somerville, blacksmith, and Alex Flett, fisherman, were appointed collectors with Peter Brass as treasurer. The maximum subscription was fixed at 6*d.* for each subscriber. Even after this measure was struck, collection proved difficult to control, but as ba's were always available for play, the arrangements, although somewhat imprecise, were left to take their own course. In 1924 there was a proposal that the ba's be purchased from the Common Good Fund, but this came to nothing.

For some years after November 1910 Bill Somerville, who had his smithy in Somerville Square, Junction Road, where the Royal British Legion now stands, remained a senior figure among the collectors. He is shown on the page opposite holding up the Men's Christmas Day ba' 1912 in the gateway of Tankerness House. Bill approached anyone who might be willing to donate and he gave priority to making the round of public houses. The names of contributors and the sums involved were pencilled into a tattered notebook and despite the rumour that accounting was of a somewhat rudimentary nature a residue was always retained to pay the ba' maker.

Throughout the 1930s and 1940s, James Nicolson of 4 Slater Street annually raised money and ensured that the ba' makers were paid. The game owes him a considerable debt, but the Council disapproved when he commenced a house-to-house collection and instructed him to desist, declaring that he was not properly accredited. Nonetheless he continued, incensing the Council with his obduracy. After throwing up the ba' at a Boys' game in the mid-1930s he was escorted by Constable Tom Mainland to the police station, then in Junction Road. Superintendent of Police John R. Tulloch threatened him with imprisonment. His twelve-year-old daughter Jenny accompanied him and tearfully pled for her father's release, saying that she would not leave the station without him. There was an impasse and in the end father and daughter were allowed to leave. The unrepentant Mr Nicholson started the Men's game that afternoon, and continued his fund-raising activity, probably in a discreet manner, and daughter Jenny went on to marry a policeman!

In 1949 a Ba' Committee was formed. It comprised Dan Grieve, Edgar Gibson, Dave Keldie, Gordon Linklater, Alan Findlay and Jim Harrison. Fund-raising

FIG. 49: Christmas Day 1912, Tankerness House gateway. Those present include: 1) Cumming (cycle repairer), 2) Charles Flett, 3) Billy Somerville, 4) D. Linklater, 5) John Mackay, 6) John T. Flett, 7) Edwin Work, 8) Sandy Grant, 9) Bill Somerville, 10) ? Peace, 11) Jim Rendall, 12) Alfie Mowat, 13) Jim Somerville, 14) John Mainland.

dances were held in the Drill Hall, Junction Road, and the proceeds went to buy leather from which casings were made. Dan Grieve was given a dozen small trawl aluminium mooring buoys from his relatives in Sanday. He fashioned them into ingenious collecting boxes with slots, and painted them in the style of a ba'. Stands were made for these buoys, which were dispersed among the public houses of Kirkwall for two or three years. Additionally animated young mendicants armed with these constructions positioned themselves at the entrance to the Drill Hall. There they fared surprisingly well – particularly after the public houses closed. To supplement their efforts an intrepid colleague ventured inside where he tested successfully the generosity of the dancers.

By 1967 the Ba' Committee consisted of two Up-the-Gates and two Down-the-Gates. For some years thereafter, as *The Orcadian* did not have a representative in attendance throughout the games, the committee, duly expanded to four

FIG. 50: The Ba' Committee 2002. Back row: Graeme King, Mike Anderson, Duncan Currie, Jim Cromarty, Sandy Keldie. Front row: George Donaldson, Dan Grieve, John Robertson, Gary Gibson, Bobby Leslie.

representatives from each side, met a reporter on the morning following the tussles to recount what individual members believed had transpired. General agreement normally prevailed but occasionally diverse opinion produced animated discussion, which invariably was resolved amicably. Unfailingly the proceedings were attended by a degree of conviviality. At the present time the committee comprises five Uppies and five Doonies and its functions are simple: to select those who will throw up (and normally donate) the ba's; to ensure that the ba' makers are put in touch with suppliers of cork and leather; and to nominate places of prominence for display of the ba's. Undoubtedly the annual Ba' happening would take place without a committee, as indeed it did throughout many decades. Nevertheless the Ba' Committee does bring some order to the proceedings, for example by providing notices in *The Orcadian* to exhort sensible safe play and the protection of property and ensuring that Orkney Islands Council notices to that effect are displayed in shop windows. The committee has no responsibility for damage, and in that regard a helpful and proper arrangement continues to be honoured by Orkney Islands Council, as it was by Kirkwall Town Council.

FIG. 51: Boys' Ba' Winners at the Millennium. *Back row:* George Keldie D c99; Davy Leonard D ny99; Nikki Monkman U c98; Keith Harcus U ny98; Balfour Baillie U c97; Stephen Kemp U ny97; Roy Keldie U c95; Keith Leonard D c94; Gary Dowell U ny95; Steven Spence U c93; James Baillie U ny94; Robbie Thomson U c92; David Johnstone D ny92; Chris Burgess U c91; Colin Paterson D c90. *Third Row:* Alastair Watson D ny90; Drew Leslie D ny89; Greig Rorie U c88; Derek Sutherland U ny88; Ian Stout U c87; Ian Gorn U c86; Sigurd Gibson U c85; Ronald Paterson U ny85; Gordon Wilson U c84; Gordon Mulraine U ny84; Bruce Moar U c83; Angus Findlater D ny83; Ian Croy D c82; David Flett U ny82; Alec Findlater D c81; Colin Kirkpatrick D c77; Andy Kemp U ny77. *Second Row:* Edgar Gibson U c97; Graeme Smith U ny76; Laurence Leonard U c75; John Stephen D ny74; Kenneth McConnachie D c73; David Miller D c72; Sandy Keldie D ny68; Leslie Tait D c65; Roy Linklater U c61; David Sinclair D ny61; Dennis Muir D ny60; Eric Kemp U c55; Jim Leonard U ny54; Alan Monkman U c53; Ronnie Muir U c52; Freddie Rorie U ny52. *Front Row:* Eddie Craigie U c51; Gary Gibson U ny49; Alastair Smith U ny48; Pat Baikie U ny47; Jack Donaldson D ny46; Dan Grieve D c36; Gordon MacGillivray D ny31; Mackie Thomson D c23.

FIG. 52: Men's Ba' Winners at the Millennium. *Back Row*: Edgar Gibson U c99; Andy Kemp U ny99; Kenny Garriock U c98; Graeme King D ny98; Stuart Gray U c97; George Rendall D ny97; David Miller D c96; Jack Leslie D ny96; Paul Miller D c95; Stewart Leslie D c94; Benny Thomson U ny94; John Stephen D c93; Jim Linklater U ny93; Alan Craigie U c92; Alan Rorie U ny92. *Third Row*: Leslie Manson U c91; George Currie U ny91; Evan Monkman U c90; Jim Baillie U ny90; John Copland D c89; Sandy McConnachie D ny89; Ian Hutcheon D c88; Fred Corsie D c87; Eddie Barnett D ny87; Erlend Tait D c86; Keith Corsie D ny86; Michael Stevenson D c85; David Johnston D ny85; Brian Anderson D c84; Fraser Byers D ny84; Kenny Eunson U c83; Jim Cromarty U ny83. *Second Row*: Sandy Keldie D c82; Mike Anderson D ny82; Alan Hutchison D c81; Leslie Tait D ny81; Lyall Flett D c80; Ian Smith D ny80; David Johnstone D c79; Billy Jolly D ny79; Mike Drever D c78; Dennis Muir D c77; Bobby Leslie D ny77; Duncan Currie U c76; Calvin Slater U ny76; David Sinclair D c75; Eric Kemp U c74; Brian Kemp U ny74; Brian Smith D ny73; Jim Leonard U c72; Freddie Rorie U ny72. *Front Row*: Ronnie Muir U c71; Alan Monkman U ny71; Jim Dick U c70; Sandy Budge U ny70; Brian Barnett U c68; Gary Gibson U c67; Mattie Stephen D ny67; John Robertson U ny66; Billy Johnston D c65; Jack Donaldson D c64; Bill Sim D c63; Jackie Miller D ny63; George Donaldson D ny62; Billy Stephen D c60; Vinnie Linklater U ny58; Jock Harcus D ny56; Tom Shearer D c55; Dan Grieve D c52.

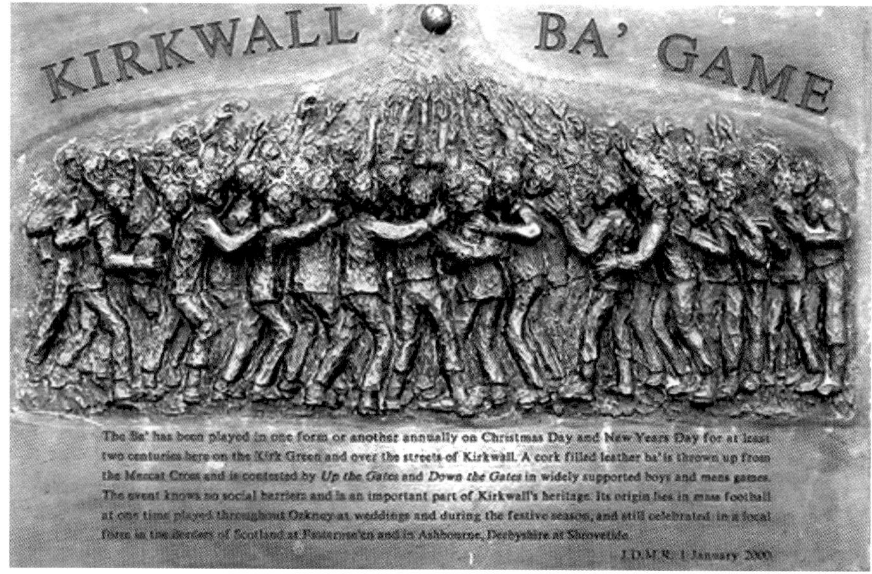

FIG. 53: Ba' plaque at the Mercat Cross, commissioned to mark the Millennium. Money was raised by public subscription.

There has been official recognition of the Ba' with patronage to mark special occasions: on New Year's Day 1975 both ba's were presented by the Kirkwall Town Council to mark its demise; while the Anniversaries Committee and Kirkwall and St Ola Community Council donated ba's in 1987 to celebrate the 850th anniversary of the founding of St Magnus Cathedral and the 500th anniversary of the Royal Charter granted to the Burgh of Kirkwall.

At the approach of the new Millennium, the Ba' Committee agreed to commission a bronze relief panel depicting the Ba'. This cost £4000 and was placed at the Mercat Cross where the annual contests are started. Designed by Gary Gibson, a prominent artist, and with wording by this writer, it was constructed and positioned by Alan Stout, Colin Watson and John and Stuart Dowell, all at no cost. A commemorative book of the signatures of some 350 players and adherents raised the bulk of the necessary funds.

Making the Ba'

It seems likely that a hard, cork-stuffed ba' was first adopted in the 1830s when the game ceased to be street football. Until then what had been used was the inflated bladder of an animal, strengthened with a leather cover. There is no doubt that this change to a solid ba' was made necessary by the greater pressure of the altered game.

FIG. 54: Ba's of different styles, from the late nineteenth-century to the present day. *Top*, clockwise from top left: 1881 New Year's Day Men's ba'; 1893 Christmas Day Boys' ba'; 1888 Men's ba'; 1927 New Year's Day Men's ba'; 1907 Christmas Day Youths' ba'; 1910 Christmas Day Boys' ba'. *Below*, clockwise from top left: 1999 Men's Christmas Day ba' made by George Drever; 1936 Boys' Christmas Day ba' made at an earlier date by Jock Garrioch; 1985 Christmas Day Boys' ba' made by George Drever; 1967 Christmas Day Men's ba' made by Dan Grieve; 1952 Christmas Day Men's ba' made by Sydney Garrioch; 1976 Christmas Day Boys' ba' made by Gary Gibson.

FIG. 55: A collage of the ba' by George Drever showing different styles by makers.

The oldest men's ba' that I have seen (pictured on the cover) was given to me in 1994 by Hamish Crisp, Edinburgh: this was won on New Year's Day 1881 by his great-great-grandfather James Shearer, a Down-the-Gate – as confirmed by faded lettering on the ba'. The trophy is large, weighs 5 lb and is made of four panels of stout leather. I have examined another very old Boys' ba' made in the nineteenth century. Well preserved, it is about half the size of the Men's ba' and was first won by an Uppie, R. Cumming, around 1872. It was played for again on

Christmas Day 1950 when the Doonies won, David Campbell being awarded the valuable old trophy. Mr Campbell told me that he was disappointed at the time as he would much rather have had a new ba'! Another old Men's ba' in my possession is misshapen, and the leather has deteriorated. It was won about 1888 by an Uppie, Andrew Walls, at one time manager of the National Bank, Kirkwall. Both the Cumming ba' and the Walls ba' are identical in design and were obviously constructed by the same unknown maker. Only four panels of leather have been used, and these have been sewn together to form a rough, strong, though imperfect sphere, with the Men's ba' weighing about 2 lb. The result is rugged with little attempt at real craftsmanship as evinced by the fact that the mouth through which the cork stuffing was fed is clumsily finished and measures five inches.

A beautifully fashioned Boys' ba', given to me by the late Willie Oag, Dounby, was won on Christmas Day 1893 by his relative Kenneth Oag (a fifteen-year-old Uppie). Kenneth subsequently fought at the Battle of Omdurman in the Sudan in 1898, when Kitchener commanded an Anglo-Egyptian force which destroyed the power of the Mahdists. Kenneth, later a postman, reminisced: 'Weel, hid wis gey hard wark, I suppose we killed aboot ten thoosand afore breakfast.' Certainly he had faced more dervishes than he would normally expect to meet in the Ba', and it was more bloodthirsty work.

Making the ba' takes considerable time – it is estimated that four days work is required to produce a finished article. This includes cutting, stitching, turning, packing and staining. The stitching alone can take two days. After the ba's are completed they are displayed in shop windows for the public to see and admire.

The ba' itself is a fine piece of craftsmanship and looks like a small football, but this superficial similarity is the only resemblance. It is stuffed with cork dust (which incidentally enables it to float should it be thrown into the harbour). The dust used to come from grape barrels and so could readily be obtained from local fruiterers, but when EEC regulations proscribed this form of packing, suitable cork had to be bought from Portugal. There are eight panels. Half of each alternate panel is painted brown or black; the remainder of the leather is stained a natural colour. At one time it was the custom to paint the panels with a variety of bright colours. As one would expect, the ba' is tough, for something that is to be squeezed, stood on, pushed, pulled, thrown, kicked, and generally ill-treated for four or five hours cannot be of ordinary manufacture. The hand-stitching is undertaken with a strong thread (traditionally eight cord flax). The tannery in Edinburgh where the hides used to be obtained went out of business, so they are now obtained from a wholesaler in London. The weight of the Men's ba' is roughly 3 lb with a circumference of twenty-eight inches, while the Boys' ba' is slightly smaller.

FIG. 56: Linay Linklater packs a Men's ba' in the 1980s.

FIG. 57: The finished product.

It is rumoured, doubtless with little or no justification, that some ba' makers invoke superstition and a touch of magic in attempting to influence the eventual destination of the ba' they have crafted for the following day. The allegation is that in the stillness of the night some trophies have made their clandestine way over flagstoned streets in order to establish acquaintance with the preferred goal:

a dip in the Basin and a drink of salt water, or a reverent touch against the wall at the Long Corner. There is even a canard that one maker secretes with the cork packing a tiny fragment from the wall, and another artisan incorporates a strand of seaweed in the contents, thus encouraging the leather hosts to be vectored home by these talismen. The truth of such mischievous whispers I cannot readily confirm.

When the winner has brought his ba' home it is customary to have it renovated and preserved, although occasionally he may prefer to have the ba' as it was at the end of the game. Usually it is painted, sometimes varnished and put on display in the house or hung in a window facing the street. This latter custom is now not so common.

Of the old ba' makers John Costie, shoemaker, Main Street, is generally recognized as having made the best article, with seven or eight panels. Occasionally Costie ba's turn up unexpectedly. In 1962 the Boys' ba' thrown up by Jock Sinclair had been found by him while clearing a room in the premises of W. T. Sinclair, drapers, Albert Street. This had been won on Christmas Day 1912 by a Doonie, William John Sinclair, known as John, son of W. T. Sinclair. He served in France as a corporal in the Seaforth Highlanders, and like many of his generation, was killed in action in 1918. Another Costie ba', now in the Lerwick Museum, was found in a chest of drawers bought in the early 1920s at a Kirkwall sale. The chest of drawers belonged to Bill Fea, a recluse and a resolute collector of bric-a-brac, who lived beside Bill Muir's creamery at the Gutter Hole,[5] but we will never know how it came into his possession.

In *The Orcadian*, Thursday 12 December 1963, the following letter described how ba's were made before the First World War:

> Sir, it may be of interest to know how the ba's were made by the late Jock Garrioch, the saddler at the shore. Three ba's were made each for Christmas and New Year's days – one for the peedie boys, one for the youth and one for the men. Three different sizes of football cases were brought home from the south. The ends were altered in order to make the ba's round. The Leitch's, the fruiterers was visited to get an empty grape barrel with the cork dust in it to stuff the ba's hard with. When sewn up, the panels alternately were painted black to make them look more attractive. Then each ball was hung up in a shop window either in Broad Street or Albert Street until being thrown up from the Market Cross by a prominent citizen on the festive day. These ba's were always

[5] This was an opening located a few yards on the north side of the Old Castle, Main Street, whence in days gone by an open burn ran to the Peedie Sea.

> made after shop hours, 7 p.m. Jock often worked into the early hours of the next morning. He then used to make the empty barrel into a nice chair for the kiddies. I am, of course, going back sixty years. Yours, etc.,
> H. C. ORGAN.

Mr Garrioch purchased his cases whereas shoemakers like Jim Harrison and John Costie before him hand-stitched the pieces. This technique is continued by present ba' makers to ensure that the ba' stands up to the rigours of the game.

After the Second World War there was for a time no one in Kirkwall skilled in the making of ba's, and as funds were low an appeal brought forth a number of old ba's whose owners generously donated their prized trophies to be played for again. For example, the Men's ba' first played for on New Year's Day 1909 was re-used on New Year's Day 1947, and an 1894 Men's ba' was thrown up again fifty-four years later, in the Men's Ba' on New Year's Day 1948. This ba' was handed back once more and played for in the Boys' New Year's Day game 1949.

In the early 1950s Sydney Garrioch, saddler, Shore Street, and his wife made ba's, following in the pre-war tradition of his father, Jock Garrioch. At the same time Jim Harrison, a shoemaker who had his business in the Strynd, made ba' covers.

After Sydney Garrioch's death his wife, Mary, continued to make some Boys' ba's but most new ba's were made by Jim Harrison. He hand-stitched the cases using a pattern provided by Edgar Gibson Sen. Help with packing was given by players either at his premises or by taking the ba's away and undertaking the somewhat onerous work as time permitted. A variety of people painted these ba's, such as Gary Gibson and Jim Harcus, although on one occasion an unpainted ba' was thrown up, won by Jack Donaldson on Christmas Day 1964 and painted subsequently by Dan Grieve.

Following these uncertain times a fresh impetus to ba' making was given by the making, packing and painting of casings by Dan Grieve (Christmas Day 1965) and Gary Gibson (New Year's Day 1966). Present day ba' makers are George Drever, Edgar Gibson and Sigurd Gibson, with George fashioning a Boys' and a Men's ba' every year. He learned the craft in 1981 from Linay Linklater, and as a boy of six he had watched Jim Harrison making ba's in his Strynd workshop. George produced his first ba' in 1983. Edgar and Sigurd Gibson became skilled under the tuition of their father Gary, with Edgar making ba's since 1984 and Sigurd since 1992. Annually they make one ba' each. All three ba' makers are ba' winners.

Orcadians in other parts of the world maintain a keen interest in the game, and several ba's have been taken by emigrants to Canada and the United States,

Dan Grieve, 1965–1977 *Gary Gibson, 1966–1995*

Linay Linklater, 1977–1989 *George Drever, 1983–present*

Edgar Gibson, 1984–present *Sigurd Gibson, 1992–present*

FIG. 58: The ba' makers.

as treasured mementos of life in Kirkwall. In the 1960s a lady living in Canada donated her father's 1895 Boys' ba' and his 1902 Youths' ba'. These were used in the Boys' game on Christmas Day 1964 and by the men on New Year's Day 1967. Robert Sinclair, Uppie winner of the Youths' ba' on New Year's Day 1902, took his trophy to Racine, Wisconsin, USA. Alexander Milne won an Up-the-Gate Men's ba' on New Year's Day 1906 and emigrated that year to Canada. His grandson Sandy Milne wrote on 22 April 2004 to *The Orcadian* from North Vancouver, British Columbia, confirming that he was the proud possessor of the trophy. George Shearer's Doonie ba' of New Year's Day 1920 was taken to the USA shortly afterwards and is now in the keeping there of his grandson Eric.

From time to time donations of money for the Ba' fund are sent by exiled Orcadians who remember with pleasure and nostalgia the games of their youth.

The following lists ba' makers, past and present:

John Costie	1895–1920
Jock Garrioch	1900–1925
J. Bertram	1926–1930
Willie Voy	1929–1935
Jim Harrison	1951–1964
Sydney Garrioch	1952–1960
Mary Garrioch	1955–1960
Dan Grieve	1965–1977
Gary Gibson	1966–1995
Linay Linklater	1977–1989
George Drever	1983–present
Edgar Gibson	1984–present
Sigurd Gibson	1992–present

At July 2003 the number of ba's made by present day and recent ba' makers was:

Gary Gibson	45
George Drever	33
Dan Grieve	23
Edgar Gibson	20
Linay Linklater	18
Sigurd Gibson	11

5

Popular Support

In the mid-nineteenth century the game seemed to be in decline. On New Year's Day 1861 'only a small number took part in the scuffle'.[1] A year later 'the playing was confined to some two dozen of the lower and rougher sort',[2] but on New Year's Day 1863 'there was a considerable influx of country people, some of whom had probably visited the town for the purpose of witnessing the Annual Foot-Ball Fight'.[3] Again, on 1 January 1868 there was 'a large attendance of actors and spectators'.[4] Between then and 1879 support fluctuated, reaching a particularly low ebb on Christmas Day 1872 when there was no game, and a week later on New Year's Day 1873 when very little interest was aroused.[5] We are told that on New Year's Day 1879 more than 100 players took part although 'of late this game has been a mere ghost of its former self'. It was then suggested that either the intense cold had encouraged some to play or 'the increase in numbers may be a sort of revival before the custom dies'.[6]

Judging from the number of players and severity of the encounters the game reached its apogee in the late 1870s and early 1880s, and we find various references to the considerable support from players and spectators at that time. For example, on Christmas Day 1879 when 'a crowd of young men rushed into an indiscriminate scrummage – the mêlée at one time consisting of something like five hundred old and young combatants'.[7] In the New Year's Day game 1880, 'for two hours and a half the hundreds of players fought through the narrow streets . . . and we believe the spectators anxiously watching the game at various points could be counted by thousands while in the crowd round the ball several

[1] *OH*, 8 January 1861.
[2] *OH*, 7 January 1862.
[3] *OH*, 6 January 1863.
[4] *OH*, 7 January 1868.
[5] *O*, 4 January 1873.
[6] *OH*, 8 January 1879.
[7] *OH*, 30 December 1879.

hundreds would be packed in a condensed and surging mass of humanity'.[8] The following year there was 'a huge mass of combatants – at least five hundred had been or were engaged in the struggle up to this time.'[9] The number of players on 1 January 1884 was estimated at about 400.[10] On New Year's Day 1885 'fully two thousand people gathered in Broad Street at one o'clock either to watch or take part in the annual struggle over the ball.'[11]

At this time the population of Kirkwall and St Ola totalled 4786 (Burgh 3925 and Rural Area 861), compared to a figure of 5672 in 1961 (Burgh 4293 and St Ola 1379).[12] The population of Kirkwall alone in 2001 was 6206, a comparable figure for St Ola being no longer available because of boundary changes.

Writing in *The Orcadian,* 12 January 1889, a correspondent had this to say: 'But the men's ba' is the exciting affair of the day. Half the town turns out to see it from the Cathedral esplanade – if I may call the gravelled space by such a fine sounding name – and the other half lie out through their windows and cheer either side on to victory, just as their sympathies may lie.'

In this period numbers were considerably swelled by recruits from country districts, and in 1881, to make sure of repeating their victory of the previous year, it is said that meetings had been held by the Up-the-Gates and 'the "fiery cross" sent round to Orphir and other districts to ensure a full muster of the clan.'[13] On New Year's Day 1883 'Up-street representatives from both town and country districts were there in force.'[14] A year later 'a considerable number of countrymen from Deerness, Tankerness and Holm proved strong allies of the Up-the-Gates.'[15] John Sinclair, who won a Men's ba' on Christmas Day 1933, told me that in 1911 he was in service at Fea in Birsay. He spent his 1912 New Year's Day holiday in Kirkwall and played in the Men's Ba' that day, cycling the twenty-one miles to Kirkwall the previous evening, and pedalling back to Birsay after the game.

Recruitment of country players was sometimes undertaken in style. Geordie Wick, a tower of strength for the Up-the-Gates in the 1920s, set out one mid-morning from Gaitnip in a four-wheel brake pulled by two spirited ponies and, making his way through the parish of St Ola, collected a dozen or so stalwarts. However, the men were expected to find their way home from Kirkwall.

[8] *OH*, 6 January 1880.
[9] *OH*, 5 January 1881.
[10] *OH*, 2 January 1884.
[11] *O*, 3 January 1885.
[12] These figures were taken from *The Population of Orkney, 1755-1961* by Robert S. Barclay BSc PhD FRSE.
[13] *OH*, 5 January 1881.
[14] *OH*, 3 January 1883.
[15] *OH*, 3 January 1894.

FIG. 59: New Year's Day Men's Ba', 1939. Players featured include: Bill Costie, Jim Cooper, David Findlay, Herbert Borwick, Mac Rosie, Jim Keldie, George Cook, Jim Leonard, Angus Harcus, Stevie Twatt, W. H. B. Sutherland, Tom Drever, Fred Cooper, Jim Pottinger, Jim Sinclair, George Leslie, Gordon Linklater, John Cutt, Ian Smith, Bobby Sinclair, Alfie Walls, Jackie Shearer.

FIG. 60: New Year's Day, Men's Ba' mid-1930s. Players featured include: A. G. Webster, D. Bews, D. Kemp, C. Leslie, A. Shearer, Jack Brass, W. Langskaill, G. Cook, M. Rosie, J. Hourston, J. Monkman, R. Park, W. Schollay, S. Wick, R. Heddle, E. Gibson, D. Walls, John Donaldson, W. H. B. Sutherland, Norman Linklater, Will Johnson, M. Rosie, C. Muir, S. P. Robertson. Also Messrs Kelday, Bews, Flett, Hay and Sinclair.

FIG. 61: Men's Ba', mid-1930s.

FIG. 62: Men's Ba', Christmas Day 1947.

A number of players also came in from the country districts to play Down, but for a long time the Down-the-Gates drew their main support from the resident population at the Shore – the 'Shories'. They also numbered among their best players the sailors from the many sailing vessels that crowded Kirkwall harbour, including the crews of the Leith clippers.

The Ba' comprehends all classes and many walks of life. This was affirmed by *The Orcadian* of 5 January 1901:

> Police, education, weather – nothing seems to make any impression in doing away with enthusiasm over this old pastime. Our municipal fathers and rulers, our teachers and other professionals, for the nonce, hob nob with the labourer, farm servant, and the trades man, and all are determined to win, no matter by what means. In the boys' ba' bearded men may occasionally be seen, and as often as not fathers, for the time being, bitterly opposed their sons, and *vice versa.*

We know from old reports and photographs that in the early part of the twentieth century games were still very well supported, although numbers were down somewhat. After the First World War, when the game was restarted on Christmas Day 1919, there was a resurgence of interest, and on Christmas Day

FIG. 63: Men's Ba', late 1940s.

FIG. 64: Men's Ba', late 1940s.

1920 several hundreds were engaged in the struggle.[16] There was an unusual occurrence a week later on New Year's Day 1921 when only a dozen or so Doonies turned up at the start of the game. As a result the Uppies had the easiest of wins, the ba' being rushed into Victoria Street two or three minutes from the start. Apparently there had been wholesale dissatisfaction among the Doonies regarding the awarding of the trophy after their win on Christmas Day, and large numbers stayed away as a protest. In subsequent years participants varied between 100 and 150. Spectators continued to be numerous, and on New Year's Day 1938 a crowd of nearly 1000 saw the Men's ba' thrown up.[17]

With the cessation of the Second World War the number of contestants and spectators increased once more. Writing in the *Orkney Herald* in 1947 the well known sports columnist David Horne, contributing under the pseudonym 'Cubbie Roo', wrote: 'one hundred and seventy-five men were counted – by observation and from photographs – in the Men's Ba' on New Year's Day.

[16] *OH*, 29 January 1920.
[17] *OH*, 5 January 1938.

FIG. 65: Men's Ba', New Year's Day 1955.

FIG. 66: Men's Ba', New Year's Day 1960.

FIG. 67: Men's Ba', Christmas Day 1971.

There were many more present, some of them with "kent" faces but with names slipping the memory, besides sailors, soldiers, and airmen and a few strangers – so that my estimate last week of 200 would not be far out'.[18] Again on Christmas Day 1948 there were close on 200 players.

In the 1950s and 1960s interest in the Men's game declined somewhat; but gradually, and particularly in the last two decades, there has been a revival and now a well-supported game can boast upwards of 200 players. Men and boys from country districts regularly participate and over the years players from Birsay, Burray, Deerness, Evie, Firth, Sandwick, South Ronaldsay, Stenness, Stromness, Stronsay, Scapa and other parts of St Ola have taken part. Exiles

[18] *OH*, 14 January 1947.

FIG. 68: Men's Ba', Christmas Day 1978.

too are keen to play and they contribute to numbers by travelling home from Shetland, Aberdeen, Edinburgh, Glasgow and London at the festive season.

It is pleasant to record that numbers in the Boys' game have increased appreciably in recent years and at the present time upwards of 100 lads take part.

The minister of St Magnus Cathedral invoked the Ba' during a watchnight carol service in 1990. He did so to improve the volume of singing and at the same time to obtain a view as to the likely outcome of the forthcoming Christmas Day tussles. The Reverend Ron Ferguson reserved one verse of a hymn exclusively for the voices of the Doonies in the congregation. The following verse was allocated to Uppie vocalists. He judged that the decibels fell in favour of the Uppies and opined that they would be victorious the following day. Alas for the Uppies the popular support that evening proved a false dawn.

Players and adherents confide that most Kirkwallians will continue to support this remarkable survival with only a few killjoys being antipathetic. Large numbers attend the throw-up, particularly if the weather is fine, and after watching the opening passages of play on Broad Street some folk retire for lunch, returning in mid-afternoon to follow the game to its completion. At the Millennium Ba' on New Year's Day 2000 crowds thronged the length of Broad Street and the Kirk Green and it is estimated that 1500 spectators were present at 1 p.m.

With such dense crowds of participants and onlookers the opportunity for a smuggle is much reduced. This is particularly so in the confines of Victoria Street and Albert Street.

So this old custom, which accepts no social barriers, has waxed and waned in popularity over the years. Kirkwall men, nevertheless, do still fervently support their Ba', played over flagstoned streets imbued with history, and the tradition of street football has prevailed against the counter-attractions now offered by a more affluent society.

FIG. 69 (OVERLEAF): Cathedral minister the Reverend Bill Cant throws-up the Men's ba', New Year's Day 1987.

6

Attempts to Stop or Transfer the Ba'

At various times since mass football was first played on the streets of Kirkwall the Ba' has incurred the displeasure of the press, the Justiciary and the Town Council.

The first organized attempt at interference occurred in 1825 and details are given in the Town Council minutes. Between the minutes of 20 November 1825 and those of 11 February 1826 there is the following proclamation:

> Whereas sundry Idle and disorderly persons have occasionally disturbed the public peace of the Burgh of Kirkwall by playing at football through the Streets and liberties thereof whereby the Inhabitants and Community have been much annoyed and molested, and their persons and property hurt and endangered, Notice is hereby given that all and every person and persons are strictly prohibited and discharged from such conduct and practice in time coming, Certifying all those who shall presume after the publication hereof to play football through the Streets or within the precincts of the Burgh, that they will be apprehended and brought before the Magistrates to be dealt with according to Law; And all the Burgh officers, Constables, and other Conservators of the Peace within the Burgh are required to apprehend and bring before the Magistrates all transgressors against this order. By order of the Magistrates (Signed) John Mitchell Town Clerk.

The proclamation is not dated but as it was only subsequently placed before the Town Council for ratification, presumably it had been published as a matter of urgency, and probably with the New Year's Day game 1826 in mind. Mr Mitchell must have signed the proclamation with a certain amount of misgiving or perhaps mental reservation since, as will be seen shortly, in the 1840s he is mentioned as being a staunch supporter of the game!

The cause of the proclamation is revealed in a minute of the meeting held on 11 February 1826, which reads:

> The Clerk laid before the Council a Petition from a number of Burgesses and other Inhabitants praying the Council to pass an Act discharging and prohibiting the practice of playing FootBall through the public streets, a practice which had given much annoyance and disturbance to the Community, and that after consulting with the magistrates he had caused publish a Proclamation through the Burgh prohibiting the continuance of such a practice in future, of which the Council approve.

In 1841 play continued despite magistrates' orders, as a letter from a Kirkwall correspondent in that year's 22 January edition of the *John O'Groats Journal*, Wick, states: '. . . the male population turned out to the foot-ball as usual. This was done notwithstanding strict orders from three of our magistrates . . . Robbie Miller (who gave their orders) was, however, disregarded, and indeed the boys kicked up such a bobbery on his endeavouring to give publicity to the manifesto, that not a word of it could be heard . . . The game has been played in Kirkwall on such occasions for time immemorial, and some folks will have it that there was no good reason for attempting to put it down.'

An attempt to substitute another locality came in 1845. On 4 January of that year a letter from Sheriff Substitute C. Gordon Robertson was laid before the Town Council, and this requested permission to carry out 'certain ornamental improvements' on the Kirk Green, which apparently were to include the planting of trees and flowers. On 15 January the magistrates granted permission. As the success of his scheme would be endangered by street football the Sheriff issued an edict abolishing the Ba'. The result was that an even greater crowd turned up at the next game, on New Year's Day 1846, when 'the Chamberlain of the Earldom was guarding the narrow pass at the head of Broad Street, and to him went the irate judge, actually threatening imprisonment. The Town Clerk, Mr John Mitchell, overhearing the words, shouted out "You'll need to put us all in jail", and plunged into the scrimmage from which he by-and-by emerged with only one tail to his coat.'[1] I have examined the records of the Kirkwall Sheriff Court and there is no mention of this matter. It appears likely that the Sheriff made a personal pronouncement that had no force in law. However, he was not easily put off, and two days later on 3 January 1846, the Council discussed 'a letter from Mr Robertson, Sheriff Substitute, respecting the practice of playing football within the Burgh'. The relevant minute continues ' . . . the

[1] B. H. Hossack, *Kirkwall in the Orkneys*, p. 465.

Council concur in the views expressed by Mr Robertson, and the Magistrates are authorised to confer with him as to the best means of substituting some more suitable locality'. The Sheriff left Orkney later that year and nothing more was heard of the proposal.[2]

In 1858 there seems to have been a proclamation issued forbidding the game, but notwithstanding this on Christmas Day that year, boys attempted to start a contest. The arrival of the police put an end to their plans. The lads had to make a swift exit down the closes, which then led directly to the Peerie Sea. Through the icy waters the boys struggled to escape from the law, getting thoroughly soaked for their pains.[3]

A hundred and fifty years ago the local press was unremittingly censorious. On 9 January 1855 *The Orcadian* reported: 'We have always regarded this uproar on the streets as most indecorous and absurd, and we would recommend that a piece of ground be given for this holiday sport, and players absolutely prevented from disturbing the town.'

The *Orkney Herald* of 8 January 1861 said that on New Year's Day a crowd 'had clustered round the Cross waiting for the great annual foolery of ba'-playing to begin. The ruffian sport was over in an hour.'

A year later the *Herald's* view was that play was confined to 'the lower and rougher sort. And indeed we wonder how any respectable man could take part in that absurd looking medley of pushing and kicking and knocking one another's heads, with an occasional bloody nose, and frequent falls in the gutter, which goes by the name of playing at football. A few did take part in it of whom better things might have been expected, but the number is rapidly diminishing.'[4]

Reporting the New Year's Day Ba' 1863 *The Orcadian* of 3 January was unequivocal in its disapproval. Seemingly the attendance on Broad Street was less than in previous years, 'a sign we think, of an improved and healthy feeling in regard

[2] One hundred and fifty years later another Sheriff, Colin Scott Mackenzie, who presided over the courts in Kirkwall and Lerwick, held the Ba' in higher regard, describing it as 'the mark of a vibrant and robust community and a tradition that must be protected'. He presented to the Ba' Committee an engraved rock crystal tablet to commemorate his time as Sheriff and commented at the ceremony 'some people, like Sheriff Substitute C. Gordon Robertson, think of it [the Ba] as an ongoing breach of the peace, but I think it takes us away from the wool basket of our present civilisation'. Explaining that analogy he recounted how the wife of a Viking who did not seem too willing to go raiding exclaimed 'If I'd known you wanted to live forever I would have kept you in my wool basket'. The Sheriff continued 'There are too many wool baskets around today'. The tablet is inscribed 'Presented to the Ba' Committee by Sheriff Colin Scott Mackenzie DL, BL, FSA Scot., Her Majesty's Sheriff of Orkney, 1992–2003, in support and encouragement of a fine and ancient tradition' and has a Latin inscription, *Palma Non Sine Pulvere* – no prize without struggle.

[3] *O*, 27 December 1858.

[4] *OH*, 7 January 1862.

to this custom'. The game was started with a pistol shot and after an hour's play the ba' was 'conveyed triumphantly to the topmast of a vessel in the harbour'. The paper was scathing in its general comment: 'During the melee, shirts, caps, and other articles of clothing were flying about the streets. The roads, owing to the late rains were exceedingly muddy, and as knock down blows were neither few nor far between, the appearance of many engaged in the struggle may easily be imagined. It was evident that those who went most respectable into the affray came least respectable out of it; while the used up and patched up appearance of some of the "brave boys" gave sad signs of the hard and sanguinary nature of the struggle. It was no small relief when the end came.'

The Orcadian did not seek to discourage healthy and vigorous enjoyment among the young men of Kirkwall, and neither did it wish to interfere with ancient customs but the paper believed that 'the exhibition on New Year's Day, in the game of "football" – where at times, when sparring room could be obtained, the spectators were treated to a "scene" from the prize-ring – was certainly not only productive of no good, but of much positive evil, and we can only hope that the good sense of all parties may see it to be their duty next year to find amusements of a more manly and at the time more genial description.'

The *Orkney Herald* of 6 January that year was equally condemnatory: 'This game, which, as conducted in Kirkwall, should have perished with the era of cock-fighting was evidently, in the estimation of a large portion of the populace, the principal event of the day. The game or the Battle of the Ball as it might more appropriately be called is of very old standing, and this year the civil strife raged with all the fierceness of Federals v Confederates.'[5] The *Herald* report concluded, 'Really it is high time that our citizens, young and middle-aged, should bethink themselves of some more rational amusement. It is as barbarous as the Christmas diversion of the young Shetlanders, who drag a burning tar-barrel through the streets of Lerwick on Christmas Day.' On 29 December that same year the *Orkney Herald* referred to the game as 'a riot', 'a preposterous kind of amusement', 'outrageous' and 'barbarous'.

In 1864 came another suggestion that the event should be banned: 'The spectacle was a most unsightly one and ought to be summarily stopped by the authorities.'[6] On New Year's Day 1867 there were a large number of spectators 'who took as much interest in this barbarous pastime as the Spaniards in their bullfights'.[7]

A further attempt to change the location occurred in 1868 when, according to the local press, it was felt that the police should try to prevent the contest being

[5] The sides in the American Civil War which was raging at that time.
[6] *OH*, 5 January 1864.
[7] *OH*, 8 January 1867.

held on the public streets. Mr T. Traill of Holland offered the players the use of a field and also promised to provide refreshments, but the game was played on the streets as of yore.[8]

Wednesday 28 December 1870 was observed as the Christmas holiday in Kirkwall, and commencing at eleven o'clock that day the Kirkwall games were held under the patronage of the provost and magistrates. The venue was a 'capacious park' belonging to presumably the same Mr Traill, and situated a short distance above the Market stance. This would be on the Tankerness Road not far beyond Warrenfield. The object was doubtless the introduction of a more civilized alternative to street football, but at four o'clock that afternoon, as soon as the contestants and spectators returned to town, a Ba' game was played. This lasted for two hours before the ba' was taken Up-street.

In 1872 it was considered that the game had neither skill nor amusement but was 'a brutal riot in which whichever side can muster the greatest number of roughs – and the Down-the-Gates always manage this – carry the day.'[9]

On Christmas Day 1875 Kirkwall Football Club held a match on a field at Soulisquoy, the idea being to introduce rugby as an agreeable substitute for street football. The numbers involved are unknown; the sides were Up-the-Gates and Down-the-Gates and that it was designed as an alternative to the Ba' was underlined with a one o'clock start. There were a large number of spectators and they indulged in 'a hearty laugh every now and again as some player was collared and got his length on the soft, muddy ground, or worse still when a "scrummage" was engaged in, a dozen or more would be all in a heap . . . The ground being so wet and slippery made it impossible to make a good running or doubling during the game, the result being that when a player attempted to dodge an opponent he generally got doubled himself.' The game went on for two hours before heavy rain put an end to the proceedings, and the result was a win for the Down-the-Gates by a goal to try. The *Northman* report doubted whether this attempt by Kirkwall Football Club to introduce 'a more civilized game in place of the usual street riot' would be of avail unless backed by the authorities. No support was forthcoming, arrangements for a similar game on New Year's Day 1876 came to nothing, and the Ba' took place on the streets as usual.

In 1877 there were 'bloody noses, red scars and tattered garments' and it was recommended that the 'foolish custom' should be brought to an end in the interests of public order and safety.[10]

[8] *OH*, 7 January 1868.
[9] *OH*, 3 January 1872.
[10] *O*, 6 January 1877.

At a special meeting held on 24 December 1877, the Town Council decreed that on Christmas Day 1877 and New Year's Day 1878 there would be no football playing on the streets. Drainage and water works were going ahead at the time and it was feared that not only might damage be done to the clay pipes collected on Broad Street and elsewhere through the town, but also there was the possibility of injury to the players. Mr Gold, the factor of Papdale Estate, was approached and he granted the use of Carters Park on the understanding that any damage done to the dykes or gates would be paid for by the Council. This seemed to the councillors to offer a satisfactory alternative, but to give added weight to their decision they resolved that the constables should attend 'and take the names of all parties engaging in the game of football on the thoroughfares of the Burgh tomorrow and first proximo and at once report them to the Burgh Fiscal for prosecution'. It was also agreed that handbills and tuck of drum should give notice of the resolution.[11]

On Christmas Day there was some ball play on Broad Street notwithstanding the prohibition, but the fun was to come on New Year's Day. Both sides dutifully gathered in the Carters Park to take part in the game there, but after the throw-up the sides joined together, kicked the ba' through the adjoining parks, down Palace Road and into Broad Street. Constables Grant and Costie who were on duty with batons drawn were soon removed, the Superintendent of Police got hold of the ba' but a player neatly knocked it out of his hands, the game commenced, and ended an hour later with the ba' being hoisted to the topmast of one of the vessels in the harbour.[12]

The sequel to the above took place at a meeting of the Kirkwall Town Council on 14 January 1878. When references were made in the minutes to the prohibition of football playing some of the councillors were seen to smile. The Provost did not know what was being done about the matter, indeed all he could tell was that the game had been played! The Council was divided, the traditionalist members not wanting to take further action, feeling that as the matter had passed over very quietly nothing more should be done about it! It was finally decided that if the Fiscal got substantial evidence the Council should back him up, and prosecute the ringleaders. This was the end of the matter.[13] Only a year later a baillie, a town councillor and an ex-councillor were all seen to take a prominent part in the game, as recorded on 11 January 1879 in 'Notes on Local Topics by a Lounger':[14]

[11] Town Council Minutes, 24 December 1877.
[12] *OH*, 2 and 9 January 1878; G. MacGregor, *History of the Kirkwall Ba' Game (Stirring Events)*, 1914.
[13] *OH*, 16 January 1878.
[14] *O*, 11 January 1879.

> On going to the street, I found that the ball had been thrown up during my visit to dreamland, and that the majority of the usually quiet and respectable town's people were engaged in a furious game at football. Here was a veritable bailie pushing on the game, by word and gesture. 'Push her off my shop, boys!' was his rallying cry. When the crowd was pressed to the middle of the street, the bailie then shouted, in a voice of thunder, 'Down street with her, boys, down street with her!' Was I still dreaming? No. Here was an ex-councillor waving his stick on high, and pushing downwards. Yonder was a Town Councillor, a member of the School Board, and a member of the Harbour Trust. And they were all pushing downwards. I was struck with this. I had almost always pulled in a different direction from them in their public capacities, but thought I would go with them on this occasion. So I rushed into the ring, and hoisted my walking stick above the heads of the players, that all and sundry should know where the ball was. This did away with all hope of success for the up-street boys, and their resistance become more feeble, as I, with all these local magnates at my back, pushed everything before me, till I had the satisfaction of throwing the ball into the basin.
>
> After the tussle was over, I could not help thinking of the fickleness of our municipal rulers. So recently as last year, they had denounced this game as savage, and one that should be done away with, and now they not only countenanced it, but took a very prominent and ludicrous part in the fray.

On 2 February 1883, a contributor to *The Orcadian* believed that because of the game's rough and dangerous nature people did more damage to themselves when playing than by their manual labour for the rest of the year. He was certain that the game had been the cause of shortening the lives of many useful and able men. Because numbers were never equal, in his opinion the system of play made it impossible to ascertain which side had the better men. He therefore proposed that twenty of the best players be chosen from each side and the contest be fought in an open, flat park, and further that umpires should note the number of goals scored in a specific time. He also wished the game to be played 'in the good old school way in which we were brought up' – presumably the style of open fluid play in which only feet were used. He also recommended that players should be selected solely from those who lived within the Burgh. If these stipulations were observed he felt that it would be known which end of the town really possessed the best players and also 'the old dangerous and uncivilized street nuisance' would be eliminated. Needless to say these proposals, though well meaning, were quite unacceptable and ignored.

There is an undated document (*c.*1895) in Kirkwall Town Council records addressing representations made to the Council regarding the three Ba's that were then being played on both days: Boys', Youths' and Men's. The document is headed 'Complaints having from time to time been made regarding the annoyance and damage to property caused by the playing of three foot-balls on Xmas Day and the like number on New Year's Day, the magistrates have thought proper to invite as they hereby do an expression of opinion on the part of occupants of property along the route of said Balls whether or not the playing of them on the public street should be henceforth discontinued.' Under the heading 'To Be Continued' there are eighty-three signatures, and only twenty-three others wished the games to be abolished. Several supporters added qualifications such as 'one each day'; 'two each day'; 'one ball on New Year's Day'; and 'Two Balls on New Year's Day only'. One enthusiast wrote 'As long as possible'! I was pleased to find that on the list of those who wanted the game to continue was the signature of my maternal grandfather, D. M. Wright, who owned a chemist's shop in Albert Street.

The most recent genuine attempt to transfer the Ba' to another location occurred when the game was about to be recommenced after the First World War. At a meeting of the Town Council in December 1919 it was suggested that the public might be asked to play the Ba' game in the Bignold Park. After some desultory discussion the Council decided they had no power to do anything, and so the matter was dropped.

It is fortunate that this came to nothing, and that the Ba' continues to be celebrated on the streets of Kirkwall. Playing in a field would strip it of a great deal of character, and there it would certainly not command the same attention from the public. Indeed just this happened when the Queen's Birthday Bonfire was removed to Gallowha' in the 1840s.[15]

In 1931 there was a suggestion that the Ba' games be replaced by football matches in the Bignold Park. This was because of the cost to the town of repairing broken windows, damaged walls, doors, etc, but the idea had practically no support.

On the return of peace in 1945 a request to permit resumption of the Men's and Boys' Ba' did not meet with unanimity in the Town Council chamber. A minute of its meeting held on 15 November states: 'A letter was submitted from Cpl. D. J. Keldie, 10 Thoms Street, dated 30th October 1945, asking the Council to grant permission for resumption of the Christmas and New Year's Day Ba's. Dean of Guild Archibald moved and Councillor Flett seconded that the Ba' be continued as formerly Councillor Spence moved and Bailie Slater seconded that

[15] B. H. Hossack, *Kirkwall in the Orkneys*, p. 466.

the letter be allowed to lie on the table for this year. Three members voted for the amendment and six for the motion which was thereupon declared carried. Three members did not vote.'

Notwithstanding that slightly grudging approval, the Council hardened its collective heart on 20 December: 'In connection with a Women's Ba' advertised for Christmas Day the Council expressed their disapproval of all such as were not approved at last monthly meeting.'

However, as recorded in Chapter 9, 'The Women's Ba' and Women in the Ba'', the fair sex were not to be denied their outing and, disapproval or not by the city fathers, two Women's Ba's took place that festive season.

An attempt to stop the Ba' was made in 1947. The reason was that the return of servicemen made the game for a year or two more boisterous and uninhibited than ever, and the damage to property, particularly shop windows, became excessive. The attempt was in the form of a proposed petition to the Town Council, but no support was forthcoming.

Thus, sustained by the wider public and bolstered by the sensible approach of most councillors and Council staff, the Ba' has survived tenaciously, and indeed flourished, for over 200 years. During that time it has prevailed against a high-handed sheriff, some curmudgeonly councillors, a frequently unsympathetic press, and the disparagement of those bereft of pride in Kirkwall's history.

FIG. 70: Boys' Ba', Christmas Day 1973.

7

The Boys' Ba'

We noted in Chapter 4, 'Acquiring and Making the Ba'', the Cathedral Session Book's entry for Sunday 7 December 1684: 'It was intimated that ther is non in toun and paroch that marries but shall pay a foot-ball to the scholers of the grammour school.' These football games would not have been played on the streets, but rather on the Ba' Lea which stretched at one time from the foot of Dundas Crescent as far out as Warrenfield.[1] Another likely place for Boys' football was the Kirk Green. From there the final translation to the streets was an easy matter, and probably took place along with the Men's Ba' in the late eighteenth or early nineteenth century. Boys had long taken an interest in the Men's game. Andrew Louttit, recollecting his early life in Kirkwall (an account written in 1917 when he was eighty-seven years old) remarked: 'During the play on Broad Street we boys dodged about on the outskirts of the body of men, and if we were fortunate enough to get a kick at the ball felt quite proud.'[2]

There is confirmation that prior to the 1830s a Boys' game was held on New Year's Day, and the ba' was presented to the grammar school by the Session Clerk who paid for it out of the ba' money collected when a couple gave in their marriage banns.[3] This was obviously a continuation of the enactment of 1684 and ba' money was charged in the proclamation fees down to the passing of the Registration Act 1855.[4] The old custom of ba' money died out, but the boys of Kirkwall found other means of obtaining a ba' to continue their annual New Year's Day tussle.

The history of the Boys' Christmas Day game is somewhat different. Prior to 1880 any Ba' play on Christmas Day, with a few exceptions, was a small affair, being confined mostly to boys and young lads.[5] This was not by design but was

[1] B. H. Hossack, *Kirkwall in* the *Orkneys*, p. 401.
[2] *Orkney View*, December 2000/January 2001.
[3] *O*, 24 December 1898.
[4] B. H. Hossack, *Kirkwall in* the *Orkneys*, p. 434.
[5] *OH*, 29 December 1880.

due rather to the fact that the Christmas game, which was fairly well established by 1855, did not have the same standing in the eyes of the community as the New Year's Day game, which was considered an historic institution.

On Christmas Day 1858 some boys attempted to start a contest, but there had been a proclamation forbidding the game, and the arrival of the police on the scene resulted in the lads departing in headlong flight down closes and through the Peerie Sea.[6]

Gradually, however, in the 1870s the Christmas Day game increased in popularity and became a full-scale Men's Ba. Probably as a result of this increase in stature a proper Christmas Day Boys' game was introduced in the late 1870s.

The first reported game for the younger generation was on Christmas Day 1881 when 'the juvenile portion of the community following the example of their elders, had a game, the ball being thrown up at the Market Cross at 10 o'clock'. The contest was played with great spirit on Broad Street, and eventually the ba' was taken to the harbour where it was hoisted to the topmast of the Norwegian schooner *Adèle*. The game must have been fairly rough as a boy called Henderson was thrown on the pavement and had his collarbone broken.[7]

From 1881 to 1892 the earlier game each day was termed the Boys' Ba', and the town crier went his rounds on 1 January 1882, announcing that the Boys' ba' would be thrown up at eleven o'clock and no one above fifteen years of age would be allowed to play.[8] The youngsters met in force at the Mercat Cross and the ba' was thrown up by 'a plucky little fellow dressed in leggins and prepared for a good "stick out"'. The fifteen-year-old rule was ignored and soon young men entered the fray and shortly afterwards the ba' was taken Down-street. One young protagonist remarked that it was no wonder as 'there were aboot a hunder shories at her.'[9] On Christmas Day 1884 'two or three hundred youngsters were soon striving to carry the ball either to the harbour or to High Street'.[10]

A year earlier, on New Year's Day 1884, the Bellman intimated between nine and ten o'clock that the Boys' ba' would be thrown up at ten o'clock. At the appointed hour a ba' was thrown up from the Cross and hustled Down-street with hardly any opposition. However, at eleven o'clock another Boys' ba' was thrown up and this turned out to be a sterner contest. In this second game an attempt was made to restrict play to those of the correct age, and a

[6] *O*, 27 December 1858.
[7] *OH*, 28 December 1881.
[8] *O*, 7 January 1882.
[9] *OH*, 4 January 1882.
[10] *OH*, 31 December 1884.

number of youths kept watch, anyone over age being summarily ejected.[11] But on Christmas Day 1885 we are told that in their game the boys were 'interfered with by old boys with beards'.[12]

Although I know that an Up-the-Gate lad, Bob Cumming, was the recipient of the trophy in 1872, it was not until 1 January 1888 that there is mention of the practice of the ba' being awarded to a boy, who alas was not named in the newspaper report. After a game lasting an hour and a half, the prize was taken to the harbour and hoisted to the top of one of the masts of the schooner *Luna* amid great cheering.

On New Year's Day 1892 for the first time, three Ba's were played on the same day. What appears to have happened is that the boys, realizing that their game had become more or less a young man's contest, determined to start another game strictly for boys. Accordingly they went the rounds collecting money and so initiated the third Ba'. The first Boys' ba' under the new arrangement was made of canvas and shaped like a rugby ball. A week later an old leather Men's ba' was used, but thereafter a proper Boys' ba' was made, half-size and perfectly fashioned.

The introduction of the Youths' Ba' necessitated that the boys started their game at an earlier hour, and on New Year's Day 1896 the game began as early as eight o'clock! Even so, on occasion the Boys' game was quite a protracted struggle, and was still being played when the Youths' Ba' was started.

Age Limit and Interference

The age limit has varied from under fourteen to under sixteen. As we have seen, on 1 January 1882 the town crier announced that no one above the age of fifteen would be allowed to play – presumably a boy of fifteen years and one day was ineligible. With the commencement of the Youths' Ba' on New Year's Day 1892 the rule was that only boys of under fourteen years of age could participate, and this limit was retained when the Youths' Ba' was abolished in December 1910. In the 1920s and 1930s all boys under the age of fifteen were eligible, and this was the arrangement until New Year's Day 1949 when, consequent on the alteration in the school leaving age, the limit was raised by a year to include all boys below the age of sixteen.

The history of the Boys' game is something of a catalogue of interference by girls and older players. As we have seen, the introduction of the third Ba' in 1892 had been caused by participation of youths in the Boys' game. But boys

[11] *O*, 5 January 1884 and *OH*, 2 January 1884.
[12] *OH*, 30 December 1885.

continued to be obstructed in their play, and the abolition of the Youths' Ba' in November 1910 had the effect of turning the attention of still more over-age players to the Boys' contest.

At the abolition meeting the maximum age for boys had been set at fourteen, but in the very next game the rule was broken, initially when older lads took part, and eventually when both men and women joined the contest. When the Uppie goal was reached these over-age players were shamefaced at their unwelcome involvement. Among the legitimate players there was some reluctance to make a claim, and eventually the trophy simply had to be handed to one of them. Even at that it was subsequently believed that the selected winner was over the age limit! It was then suggested, but without effect, that another alteration to the rules for the Boys' game be made, and that only schoolboys should be eligible.[13] There was a great deal of feeling over the matter, and a week later on New Year's Day 1911 any one over the age of fourteen venturing into the game was forcibly ejected.

On Christmas Day 1912 all players were initially of the correct age, although youths who stood in a tight circle round the scrum hampered play considerably. After a time these youths began to play, others followed and spectators became so incensed that they tried to remove the ba'. When this proved impossible everyone joined in. The ba' eventually went Down, and afterwards the bulk of the players slipped shamefacedly away. The *Orkney Herald* was tempted to name the guilty players, but refrained from doing so on condition that their conduct did not recur.[14]

The sequel was a public meeting held in the Town Hall to discuss proposals for the better regulation of play. A suggestion that the Youths' Ba' be restarted as a means of siphoning off the older players was ruled out of order, as was a suggestion to abolish the Boys' Ba'. Eventually it was agreed that the age limit for boys should be fixed at fourteen, and three Up-the-Gates and one Down-the-Gate formed a committee to see that fair play was given to the boys, and to act as 'chuckers-out' when necessary. The committee was also given powers to bring their number up to twelve. During the course of the meeting there was a light-hearted suggestion (which was heartily endorsed by the audience) that apologies should be demanded from the married men who had taken part in the Boys' game.[15] The result was that a few days later, on New Year's Day 1913, the boys had complete freedom and indeed were surrounded by a solid cordon of their elders. So tight was this barrier that anyone coming out for a breather

[13] *O*, 31 December 1910 and *OH*, 28 December 1910.
[14] *OH*, 1 January 1913.
[15] *OH*, 1 January 1913.

had difficulty in getting back into the game.[16] However, only a year later the rule regarding age limit was broken again, and on Christmas Day 1913, bigger and bigger boys joined in until once again the game became one for young men.[17]

On Christmas Day 1919 the game was ruined once more by the participation of older players, and few boys could be seen in the struggling mass. As the *Orkney Herald*, 31 December 1919, said: 'It would take a long stretch of imagination to call a married man – with boys of his own – a boy.'

On New Year's Day 1922 'the game was a great one but was again marred, youths and even men joining in. The rule, however, was broken by the Uppies and Doonies alike.'[18] On Christmas Day 1922, 'the affair resolved itself into practically a Men's Ba'.'[19] On Christmas Day 1926 the Boys' game was being won by the Doonies, but near the Big Tree the girls seemed to think that the game was too slow and entered the struggle. For a while a mass of girls could be seen struggling and pushing before they in turn gave way to youths, and a little later 'the issue was being waged between players who could be classed as of "twenty years and over".'[20]

The Boys' Christmas Day game 1932 was started with the announcement that only boys of fourteen and under could take part, and for a time after the throw-up it did remain a game for boys only. Then women, youths and men entered the struggle and because of interference by these older players play had to be stopped and the ba' thrown up again on four further occasions on Junction Road. Eventually the game was won by the Down-the-Gates after two and three-quarter hours' play.[21] Despite interference, Kirkwall boys retained their fervour for the game. On New Year's Day 1934 there was amused sympathy for one young Uppie, aged seven, who was so determined to join in that he had to be forcibly held back. Frustrated in his efforts, the young enthusiast burst into tears.

On Christmas Day 1934, 'throughout the game there was far too much interference by grown-ups who sometimes, through over-enthusiasm, or so one likes to think, took the game out of the boys' hands altogether. At other times they formed so close a cordon round the players that the youngsters could scarcely hope to move the ba' either up or down.'[22] On occasion, onlookers would take hold of a boy spectator and pitchfork him into the game, naturally the opposition did likewise, and from then on it was an easy step to personal interference.

[16] *OH*, 8 January 1913.
[17] *OH*, 31 December 1913.
[18] *OH*, 4 January 1922.
[19] *OH*, 27 December 1922.
[20] *O*, 30 December 1926.
[21] *O*, 28 December 1932.
[22] *OH*, 2 January 1935.

FIG. 71: Boys' Ba', New Year's Day 2004.

FIG. 72: Boys' Ba', New Year's Day 2004.

So over the years the Boys' game has been bedevilled by the unwanted attention of older players. The *Orkney Herald* of 10 January 1923 reported Kirkwallians as saying, rather aptly, that 'the Ba' is a terrible thing for bringing on age', and 'while on Broad Street the combatants were very young, they gradually grew older till at the final shove several had grown whiskers'.

Even at the present time the boys are not always left to have their game completely unmolested. No lasting solution has ever been found to counteract the interference of those seniors whose only excuse has been that they were carried away by excitement.

Girls

In the 1920s girls were very active in the Boys' game. Indeed they played well, taking a significant part in the proceedings and it was suggested that as they were so keen the girls might have a game of their own.

On Christmas Day 1921 and New Year's Day 1922, girl players were prominent on both sides. Feminine vigour was apparent again on New Year's Day 1923 when 'young girls at times out-numbered the boys, while one or two older women were seen in the fray periodically'.[23] A year later the game had become 'almost a young women's Ba', and chiefly through their efforts the leather was forced into Victoria Street'.[24] On 1 January 1925 'shortly after the commencement, young girls joined their brothers in the struggle and before long even married women had joined in the fray'.[25]

A reminder was issued from the Market Cross on Christmas Day 1925 that the game was only for boys of fourteen and under. In this game also a good many young girls took part, and by the time play had reached the Bridge the struggle had become one between a band of girls, boys being in the minority.[26] A week later 'girls were more than ever conspicuous on their respective sides.'[27]

Shortly after the throw-up on New Year's Day 1929, boy players 'were soon joined by their big sisters . . . the boys were being out-numbered and practically swamped by their sisters and it looked as if the Boys' Ba' was wrongly named.'[28] On Christmas Day 1933 James Nicholson, Slater Street, threw up the Boys' Ba' at 10 a.m. Waiting on Broad Street was a crowd of sixty lads and some girls. Play moved to Junction Road and after halts at the power station, the gas house,

[23] *OH*, 3 January 1923.
[24] *OH*, 9 January 1924.
[25] *OH*, 7 January 1925.
[26] *O*, 31 December 1925.
[27] *OH*, 9 January 1926.
[28] *OH*, 2 January 1929.

Mackay & Wallace's garage, Mellis' garage, the police station and Baikie's wood yard the scrum reached the Basin shortly after noon. The trophy was awarded to Jim Norquoy, Queen Street, the ba' being retrieved from the water by a player described by the *Orkney Herald* of 27 December 1933 as 'a hardy young Amazon, Miss Mary Muir', who had played in the game for two hours. The mettlesome young lady became for many years a kenspeckle, enthusiastic figure at the Ba', knowledgeable about the game and popular with players on both sides.

On 1 January 1936 'by the time the Royal Hotel was reached, many women and young girls carried away by excitement, had flung themselves into the fray, and, whether it was thanks to the efforts of the ladies, or not, the Uppie rate of advance certainly speeded up a lot.'[29]

Enthusiasm

In the early part of this century Kirkwall boys were most enthusiastic about their game, and every effort was made by both sides to muster as many players as possible.

The roll call started about 5 a.m. on Christmas Day 1908, door knockers were rattled and horns and bugles blown to make sure that tardy sleepers were awake.[30] A year later people who lived in houses with boys of ba' playing age got little rest after six o'clock.[31]

There was a recrudescence of the boys' exuberance on Christmas Day 1911 and long before daylight Kirkwall lads were on the move. The *Orkney Herald* of 27 December reported:

> A great unrest seemed to have taken possession of the boys of the burgh. Some unhappy youngster had apparently been bereft of sleep through thought of the coming struggle and having got out of bed carried the infection to his chums; for about 3.30 am the stillness of the morning was broken by ear-piercing shreaks [sic] from paper trumpets, followed by the yells of the youngsters as they hurried from place to place; doors were banged and bells pulled. This was done intermittently all night to the great annoyance of many people. We trust the boys will keep their exuberant spirits under control on New Year's morning; for if they persist in this form of hooliganism there is a probability that the means will defeat the end, and the boys' ba' may be relegated to the things that have been.

[29] *OH*, 8 January 1936.
[30] *OH*, 30 December 1908.
[31] *OH*, 29 December 1909.

FIG. 73: Boys' Ba', Christmas Day 1910.

In days gone by distance was no obstacle to the young, and the winner of the New Year's Day game 1909 was Bob Reid,[32] Shore Street, who at the time was in service on a farm in Evie. On New Year's Eve, after finishing his day's work he walked the fourteen miles to Kirkwall, and the following morning won his trophy, the game starting at 8.30 am. Later that day he returned on foot to Evie, his holiday over. This ba' was presented by Sir Arthur Bignold, then MP for the Northern Burghs. On Christmas Day 1921 the Boys' ba' was won by Thomas Scott, who had walked from Mirkady, Deerness. Also present that day was thirteen-year-old Tom Sclater, who had trudged the nine miles from Netherhouse farm on the Lyde Road, Firth (he won a Men's ba' in 1953).

Dick Mowat, subsequently my neighbour, won a Boys ba' (now in my possession) on Christmas Day 1910 in a game bedevilled by adult players of both sexes, some as old as forty. The contest was for lads not exceeding fourteen years of age. He was serving with the Post Office whose employees at that time worked throughout Christmas Day. As the throw-up time of 10 o'clock approached the pull of the Ba' became irresistible, Dick absented himself, played a prominent part in the game and was awarded the trophy. Hastening back to duty, happy and dishevelled, he faced suspension, or worse. Perhaps work had been light that day or his superiors may have been keen supporters of the game, but good sense prevailed, a stern lecture sufficed and Master Mowat kept his job and the ba'.

[32] He was awarded a DSM in the course of naval service during the First World War.

FIG. 74: Boys' Ba', Christmas Day 1982.

Between the wars the number of players was considerable, and when the Boys' ba' was thrown up from the Market Cross at 10 a.m. on Christmas Day 1933 there were no fewer than sixty lads waiting to play.[33]

Before the Second World War, when the winner had been elected his companions usually showed their uninhibited delight by carrying him away shoulder high. A particularly good example of this occurred in the Boys' New Year's Day game 1936 when the Uppie winner was chaired home from the Castle, up Clay Loan, across Dundas Crescent and along and down George Street – quite a feat of youthful endurance!

The war caused the senior game to be banned from Christmas 1939 until the cessation of hostilities. But the boys of the town did not philosophically accept the cancellation of their favourite festive season sport. On the forenoon of Christmas Day 1939 about thirty young players banded together and a struggle took place against the east wall of the Bignold Park, a Boys' ba' being used. Play went on for half an hour and the result was somewhat inconclusive, both sides claiming victory!

[33] *O*, 28 December 1933.

The School Game

Writing in January 1948 in a letter to *The Orcadian,* Bill Park, the winner of the Men's Christmas Day game 1909, recalled how at school in the early 1890s the Ba' was the main topic of conversation from September to January. He remembered how the boys were all eager for the coming struggles, and anxious as to the health and wellbeing of their favourites.

For many years a Ba' was played in the grammar school playground during break time and lunch hour. This took place in the period November/January, a turnip was provided for each game, and boys of all ages took part. Sometimes two games would be in progress at the same time, one for the seniors and one for the juniors. For a period there were established playground goals for Uppies and Doonies, and the Uppies had to contend with the slope, just as they do on Broad Street. The game continued until the bell rang or the turnip disintegrated. Dave Keldie, Men's ba' winner on Christmas Day 1951, said to me, with a twinkle in his eye, that as far as he knew these were the only ba's which were actually eaten after the game! Latterly, however, the game became more of a rough and tumble scrimmage without a definite aim. This game was certainly in existence in the 1880s, and was popular right up to the outbreak of the Second World War. In recent years the custom has been observed only by the juniors, and is now restricted to boys at the primary school.

FIG. 75: Boy's Ba', New Year's Day 1987.

FIG. 76: Boy's Ba', Christmas Day 1991.

Similarly in the 1920s and 1930s Kirkwall boys of all ages would play the Ba' in the streets of their locality every November and December. The tussle started at The Brig using a turnip thrown from a stone pillar at the side of Stevensons, booksellers. One goal was Cumming & Spence, grocers, 17 Albert Street, and the other was John Slater, wine merchant, 20 Bridge Street.

Pre-war Uppie boys too practised annually in Victoria Street also with a turnip, which was thrown from the railings of the Miss Hourston's ivy clad house at 75 Victoria Street. The goals were the foot of Clay Loan and Croy's shop at No. 46.

Boys' Brigade social evenings were held in Victoria Street Hall (now the Baptist church) when a Men's ba', or a medicine ball, was used, the game being played over the wooden floor.

The Boys' Christmas Day Ba' 1952 formed part of a special Home Service programme, and the start was delayed for forty minutes to fit in with the broadcast. The description of the scene was excellent and was listened to with great interest by Orcadians at home and away.

In the Fifties and Sixties the number of boys taking part seldom exceeded fifty, but gradually there was a resurgence of interest. Numbers have increased from the mid-Eighties, since when up to 100 enthusiastic boys under the age of sixteen participate. With such support smuggles and run-away victories are less common. Indeed in recent times there have been occasions when the boys were still in contest when the senior game started two and a half hours later at 1 p.m. Two such examples were on New Year's Day 1995 and New Year's Day 1998 when the boys finalized their tussles at 1.35 p.m. and 3.17 p.m. respectively.

FIG. 77: Boy's Ba', Christmas Day 1998.

Boys now play on the side with which their family is associated, irrespective of their place of birth. The location of housing schemes and the fact that (apart from mothers flown to the specialist unit in Aberdeen) all births now take place in the Balfour Hospital deep in Uppie territory would create an unacceptable imbalance in numbers.

8

The Youths' Ba'

A third Ba' – for youths – was started on New Year's Day 1892, and this game was intended for those who had not reached the age of twenty-one.

Increasingly in the 1880s and 1890s over-age contestants had taken part in the Boys' game, and as we have seen it was in an attempt to regularize the position that the Youths' game was started.

While the Youths' Ba' was designed for the 'halflins' or 'those who are not quite yet men', in practice what happened was that older players took part and the contest became in reality a second Men's game.

The effect of the introduction of this third Ba' can be gauged from the events on Christmas Day 1898 when the game 'in which several who had something more than a sprouting moustache on their lip took part, was keenly fought . . . The men's game at two o'clock was a very hollow affair.'[1]

On New Year's Day 1902 the Youths' ba' had been thrown up at ten o'clock and did not move out of Broad Street for almost three hours. Thereafter although progress to the Uppies' goal was fairly swift, when one o'clock arrived no one knew whether or not the Men's game would be started on time. After some wrangling, the ba' was thrown up at seven and a half minutes past one. Doonies were in the majority, and with a series of rushes reached the harbour in eight minutes, and the ba' was hoisted to the topmast of the steamer *Express*. When the crowd was returning up the pier with the ba' they were confronted by those folk who had been following the Youths' Ba'. The Uppies in this second throng contended that it had been mutually agreed to postpone the Men's Ba' throw-up till two o'clock, and accordingly proposed that the game should be played again. This the Doonies would not accept, feelings ran high, some Uppies tried to take the ba' from the player to whom it had been awarded, and perforce he took refuge in the Harbour Office until the crowd dispersed.

[1] *OH*, 28 December 1898.

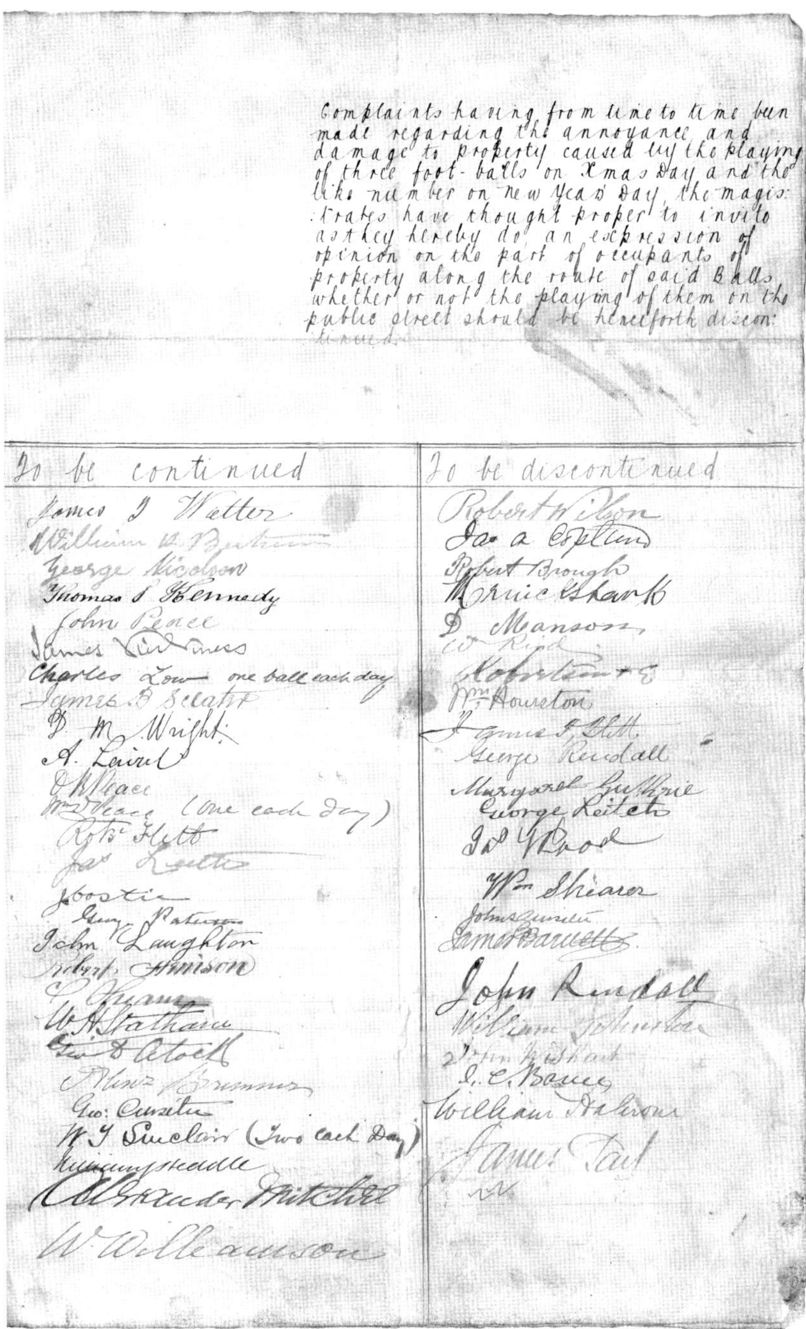

Complaints having from time to time been made regarding the annoyance and damage to property caused by the playing of three foot-balls on Xmas Day and the like number on New Year's Day, the magis:trates have thought proper to invite as they hereby do an expression of opinion on the part of occupants of property along the route of said Balls whether or not the playing of them on the public street should be henceforth discon:tinued.

To be continued	To be discontinued
James J Walter	Robert Wilson
William W. Bertram	Jas A Copland
George Nicolson	Robert Brough
Thomas S Kennedy	M Cruickshank
John Peace	D. Manson
James [illegible]	W Reid
Charles Low one ball each day	Robertson & Co
James B Sclater	Wm Houston
D. M. Wright	James Flett
A. Laird	George Rendall
J K Peace	Margaret Guthrie
Wm Peace (One each Day)	George Leitch
Robt Flett	Jas G Reid
Jas Leitch	Wm Shearer
J Bostie	John [illegible]
Geo Paterson	James Barnett
John Laughton	John Rendall
Robert Harrison	William Johnston
[illegible]	[illegible]
W. H. Statham	J. C. Baxter
Geo D Ratch	William Dalrymple
[illegible]	James Tait
Geo: Carston	
W. J. Sinclair (Two each Day)	
[illegible]	
Alexander Mitchell	
W Williamson	

FIG. 78: Undated document from Town Council records, probably *c.*1895 and certainly before 1910 when the Youths' Ba' was abolished and after New Year's Day 1892 when it was first played.

To be continued	To be discontinued
Robt Spence	James Bews
James Corsie	
T. T. Smith	
Mrs Dongey	
W Wallace	
J. Anderson	
John Cassells	
John Maxwell	
Robert Miller	
Wm Ferguson (2 each day)	
Duncan Stewart	
Wm Geo. Sennory (as long as possible)	
Margaret Peace	
Gibson & Halcrow (2 balls on New years day only)	
Wm Slater. one each day	
Mary Foulis	
William Hay	
W [illegible]	
R. Gowdie	
Thomas Flett	
R. L. Harrold (one ball each day)	
James Farquhar	
James A. Bews	
John Garrioch	
Wm Hourston	
Saml Reid Senr	
Peter Brass Jr	
James Sinclair one ball on New years day	
W. J. Gibson	
John L. Havens (one each day)	
Wm [illegible]	
[illegible]	
Robert McKenzie	
James Lightfoot	
John Hamilton	
David S. Aim (One each day)	
Wm Corsie	
Peter Shearer [illegible]	
Peter Shearer Jun	
Joseph Couris	
W Swanney	
Mrs Geo Leslie	

To be continued	To be dis-continued
David Marwick	
Mrs Smith	
Angus Buchanan	
Thos. W. Slater	
John Smith	
Mrs J Horne	
Mrs John Wilson	
William Fea	
Robert Stove	
Mrs Mc Kay	
George R. C. Russell	
Robert Barron	
Wm D Baikie (2 balls both days)	
Macrae & Robertson (2 balls each day)	
83	

The ba' was kept locked in the office safe that night, and eventually smuggled away the following day under an overcoat. This noteworthy ba' was used again forty-five years later in the Boys' New Year's Day game 1947 and is now on display in the Masonic Lodge, Kirkwall.

The enmity thus engendered was not forgotten, and *The Orcadian,* 4 January 1902, said that the bad feeling that had been aroused would not readily die down, but would probably simmer on until an outlet was found for it in the following year's game. This highlighted the need for a change and it became increasingly apparent that the acceptance of the Youths' game as the Ba' par excellence was seriously affecting the Men's contest.

From 1905 the pattern of events was usually that the Youths' game was a protracted and hard fought struggle while the Men's game was over quickly and resulted in an Up-the-Gate victory. By New Year's Day 1905 the interest had been largely taken out of what was being termed the 'old Men's Ball'.

It was therefore almost inevitable that at a meeting in the Town Hall on 20 November it was decided to discontinue the Youths' Ba'. The proceedings were chaired by Provost Slater and there was a good attendance that Saturday evening. The Provost explained that the intention of the meeting was not to try and do away with the 'ancient custom of Ba' playing,' but many people had expressed the view that with fewer Ba's the interest would be greater. After some debate, when it was agreed that in practice the Youths' Ba' had become another Men's Ba', Peter Brass moved that only two Ba's be played on each of Christmas and New Year's Day. William Costie, postman, seconded the proposal which was passed with a large majority. Collecting for the Ba's was the other matter of importance addressed and this is included in Chapter 4, 'Acquiring and Making the Ba''.

In 1912 there was another public meeting, this time to deal with the problem of interference by men in the Boys' game. During the meeting there was a plea for the reinstatement of the Youths' Ba', and the circumstances are worth repeating. A young man sitting in the front of the largely attended meeting opined that the trouble was being caused by the lack of a Youths' Ba'. He obviously felt keenly about the matter, for:

> As he spoke he gesticulated wildly, waving both hands in the air, now turning towards the audience and anon facing the platform. The audience being simply convulsed with laughter. While he spoke he drew nearer and nearer to the platform. Fixing the chairman with his eye and with his hand pointed direct at his head, he exclaimed wildly, 'Do you see what I mean?' The Chairman involuntarily ducked his head and Councillor Morgan half-rose as if to protect him from a feared attack. But their fears were groundless. The speaker after his deliverance resumed his seat amid the plaudits of his companions.[2]

His eloquence was in vain, the suggestion was ruled out of order and any lingering hopes of reviving the Youths' Ba' vanished.

[2] *OH*, 1 January 1913.

9

The Women's Ba' and Women in the Ba'

Female participation in the game is by no means of recent origin, and the records give many instances of ladies taking an active part in Boys', Youths' and even Men's games.

On Christmas Day 1866 the ba' was being forced Up-street after a good 'spat', when 'an Amazon who ought to have been home with her mamma caught it and threw it down.'[1] In the course of my researches I have come more than once upon vague references to a game played probably in the late 1860s, in which the leading role was taken by a woman. It seems that when the ba' was thrown up it landed right in the lap of this determined young lady, who thereupon made for the harbour without a moment's hesitation. Behind her on Broad Street pandemonium reigned, but the intrepid lass, gathering up her skirts with one hand and clutching the ba' with the other, sped on past the Big Tree and down Bridge Street. At the pier she was caught by the pursuing pack, and in the ensuing struggle swept into the water. But she had won the day for the Doonies, and while the ba' itself was doubtless awarded to some lesser mortal, the heroine of the hour, wet but supremely happy, was carried home shoulder-high in triumph.

On New Year's Day 1888 at a crucial moment in the game Doonie reinforcements rushed into the fray, and these included one or two of the fair sex.[2] On 1 January 1936 a number of women, carried away by excitement, joined the Boys' Ba' and were instrumental in speeding up the rate of progress to the Uppie goal.

David Horne Senior, in writing a poem to commemorate the restarting of the game after the First World War, discusses the position occupied by women in the Ba'. He treats the matter lightly and I suspect that he little thought there would be a Women's Ba' twenty-five years later.

[1] *O*, 1 January 1867.
[2] *O*, 7 January 1888.

New Year's Day Ba' 1920[3]

Awa wi' gloomy thoughts this day;
Let War his blunt teeth gnash!
For once again this New Year's morn
Brings in the auld stramash:
Let kings be hanged, or empires fa' –
Wha cares! This day we play the Ba'.

And Kirkwall folks and soldier lads,
Wedged in a seething mass,
Are cheered on by the watching crowd –
At times some anxious lass
Puts her fair shoulder to the wheel,
As if the contest were a reel.

And then I think o' women's rights,
And women's votes and a',
And wonder dimly if next year
We'll hae a Ladies' Ba';
And certies! if they try the ploy,
They'll stand their ground as weel's a boy!

We menfolks then, frae vantage point
Up on the Market Green
Will view the surging crowd below,
While Alice, Jess and Jean,
Alang wi' Peggy and Betsy Ann,
Push 'Up' or 'Doon' like ony man.

And when some breathless lassie stands
(The raging battle o'er)
Victorious at the Head o' the Toon,
Or maybe at the Shore,
Possessor o' the Ladies' Ba' –
The witch will steal oor hearts awa.'

This may be but a silly dream
That never comes to pass;
Yet Kirkwall's crown shall ne'er grow dim,

[3] David Horne, *Songs of Orkney*, p. 106.

While sturdy lad and lass
Stand side by side, and play the game,
In wars abroad, or ba's at hame.

For Viking blood runs strong and deep
Here as it did langsyne;
And ilka lass inspires her lad –
She sent him to the Rhine –
She'll send him yet far frae the Ba'
To ding a tyrant to the Wa'!

On two occasions games exclusively for women have been played, namely Christmas Day 1945 and New Year's Day 1946. These proved unattractive and did not meet with general approval.

Both struggles were won by the Uppies, the Christmas Day game taking one and a half hours to complete and the ba' being eventually awarded to Miss Barbara Yule. The New Year's Day game was over in five minutes and the winner was Miss Violet Cooper. The contests were dour and uncharitable, and interspersed with hair-raising incidents, with participants on both sides revealing special qualities hitherto quite unsuspected!

The following shortened report comes from the *Orkney Herald* of 1 January 1946:

> An innovation this Christmas, and in the view of many citizens, not entirely a welcome one, was the provision of a ba' contest for women . . . There was considerable opposition to the holding of this game, on the grounds that it would prove to be an undignified exhibition . . . The contest began at 11.30 a.m., and a good number of the town's 'Amazons' had gathered when the ba' was thrown up by Mr. David Flett, town librarian. Soon after play commenced however there was an extraordinary development, the ball being smuggled out of the ruck of players and 'mislaid' by, it is said, some individuals hostile to the women's game. While the New Year's Day ball was being procured, to use as a substitute, the missing article was found in the Cathedral churchyard, and thrown up anew.
>
> . . . the ball was gradually carried up into Victoria Street, but there the Doonies rallied, and . . . regained their lost ground pushing the ball down past the Market Cross to Castle Street, where the scrum swirled down to Junction Road, and an Uppie breakaway there took the ball as far as the Police Station.

There, after a stalemate, there was another throw-up:

> There was nothing gentle about this contest of the members of the gentle sex, but fortunately none of the participants suffered any hurt beyond scratches and bruises. A couple of players were said to have fainted during the excitement of the scrimmages, but the casualties, for the most part, were confined to permanent waves, hats, scarves, shoes, and stockings.

The reaction of the spectators can be gathered from the following short poem by 'Seamew' which appeared in the same paper:

Thoughts on Beholding the Women's Ba'

This is a queenly sport: those lovely maidens
Tenderly tugging one another's hair,
Bashfully biting, chanting in sweet cadence,
'Uppie' and 'Doonie'; earth has not a fair
Where such a show is staged free and for nothing,
And so much female beauty is exposed
Through rents and rips in what began as clothing –
The scene is heavenly, but my eyes are closed,
Shall I again behold so sweet a pastime,
Lighting with loveliness the Kirkwall streets?
Or will the Council say this is the last time
Our maidens shall perform those magic feats.

The proposal that a game for women be introduced to the Ba' season had gathered momentum in late 1945. *The Orcadian* of 6 December announced that at 11.30 a.m. on Christmas Day and New Year's Day there would be a game for women and girls. However, the Town Council decided on 20 December: 'In connection with a Womens Ba' advertised for Christmas Day the Council expressed their disapproval of all such as were not approved at last monthly meeting.' At the November meeting the Council had granted permission for the resumption of the Men's and Boys' games, and no mention was made of a game for women.

But the ladies were not easily deflected and turned out in force on both days. The following account by ex-Provost James Flett, owner of David Spence's bookshop, Broad Street, captures splendidly the atmosphere and many of the cameos that enlivened the Christmas Day game:

> Never was there a truer saying than: 'The hand that rocks the cradle rules the world!'

To have seen the hands that were raised on Broad Street, Kirkwall, on Christmas Day, 1945, when the first 'Ladies' Ba" was thrown up, no man would have dared to dispute that old adage – in fact, no man would have dared to open his mouth at all, women looked at men so threateningly.

Women were there arrayed in every kind of garb: the haram skirt, the kilt, the sailor trousers, riding breeches, slacks, tights and khaki – all the colours of the rainbow gleamed before the Market Cross as the magic hour of battle approached.

Strange to say, a 'mere man' was entrusted to throw up the sacred symbol of contest. (What a nerve that man must have had!! I understand he is still alive!!)

To be truthful, I must admit there were some of, shall I say, 'the tender sex' who were a little backward at first. However, encouraged by an old lady who had resided in Burgar's Bay for the better part of a century and who boasts of a pedigree and offspring enough to stock a city, the timid ones stepped forth when the ba' was thrown to the street.

There congregated wives of sailors, soldiers and airmen; A.T.S., W.R.N.S. and N.A.A.F.I. girls; cooks and table-maids; slavies, land-girls and laundry-maids – a formidable array to uphold the merits of womankind!

The crowd closed in as the ba' landed on the forest of uplifted arms and then a seething and entangled mass of drapery and napery swayed and crashed against barricaded doorways and windows.

Down the street moved the struggling mass until near Castle Street, when something most unusual happened – the ba' disappeared altogether!!! Consternation followed! Threats were thrown at some nearby young lads who slunk away with guilty looks! Women ran hither and thither – all of no avail – the ba' was really lost!!

Slowly the crowd of disappointed players wended its way back to the Cross as if to make a solemn vow of vengeance against all mankind before so sacred an emblem!

All was silence for a few minutes – even the lady with the fiery locks, who had urged on her Doonies by screams and pressure was silent now. In an undertone was heard the repeated remark: 'was it no a dirty trick? – I wish I knew wa' stole the ba!' Nothing on earth would have saved that man from utter destruction had he been discovered then!!

But, lo! a shout of joy was heard on the Market Green and the man who had thrown up the ba' was seen advancing with the lost treasure tucked under his arm.

For the second time he mounted the steps of the Market Cross – that old relic of past ages where strange scenes and tragic incidents had been enacted in the lives of by-gone generations of the people of Kirkwall. After viewing the smiling crowd before him, he made the following announcement: 'The ba' is here – It was found in the kirkyard.' No Royal Proclamation from the Cross was ever more heartily acclaimed!

To the superstitious the knowledge that the ba' had been in the churchyard may have been looked upon as a bad omen for the success of their side! But the question was: 'Did the villain who stole the ba' intend to bury it there?'

However, once again the ba' was hurled through the air and once again the tussle commenced with renewed vigour. Across Broad Street the surging, screaming, sweating batch of females went until they were brought to a sudden halt at 'Makum Green's' house, where they appeared to pause for their 'second breath.' This they soon regained and made a sally past my [Spence's] shop-front – for which they have my most grateful thanks!!!

By now the Doon Street women appeared to be more numerous or perhaps had more stamina in them than the Uppies as the ba' went hastily past the Cross on its way down street.

At Castle Street the side-walk kerb is blamed for knocking the 'tenderfoots' off their feet for, suddenly, nothing was seen but arms and legs beating the air. In the midst of the confused affray a nimble little wench was seen to extricate herself from the entanglement and set off with the ba' down Castle Street for all she was worth, followed by a screaming, mud-bespattered mob of Kirkwall 'beauties!'

Like a streak of lightening she turned the Gas Works corner on her way to Burgar's Bay, but, when opposite the Police Station (a dangerous place for the brawl), she tripped and fell – the ball flying out of her grasp! The second lady in the race nimbly picked it up and with the speed of a deer reached the goal and was at her own home with the prize before her followers realised the game was over.

But, no! the game was by no means over. The lady who fell disputed the second girl's right to the ba'. After mustering her clan from that delightful suburb known as Burgar's Bay she sallied forth at the head of the contingent to the home of the possessor of the ba!

Common courtesy was thrown to the wind – the door was kicked, the handle turned, and in went the uninvited intruders. With the demand: 'The ba's no yours; you have no right to it – you're a Doonie!' The ba' was snatched from the possessor's grasp.

It is only natural that the goodman of the house – the proud parent of so worthy a daughter who first claimed the prize – should resent the Burgar's Bay invasion. He did his best to quell the rabble by argument, following up by attempting to throw them out. But, nothing doing!! He soon discovered he had made a mistake and was glad to be left alive – although he lost in the scuffle a shirt, which had cost him five clothing coupons and hard-earned cash, one of the intruders going off with a sleeve as a souvenir!!

With the ball in their possession, the lawless intruders made a hasty retreat back to the Bay where the aged and infirm generation, who had been left in charge of the cradled population, almost wept with joy at so gratifying a close to so strenuous a day!!

* * * * * * *

The fervent prayers of the City Fathers – of which I have the honour to be one – is that never again may the Ancient City and Royal Burgh of Kirkwall be disturbed by so undignified a section of the community as was seen on the streets on Christmas Day, 1945.

Wifely Assistance

In the 1920s, after the Uppies had triumphed, a group of claimants crashed into the house that stands above the Uppie goal at Mackinson's Corner, making their explosive entry through the rear of an adjacent old building known as the Castle. After a protracted wrangle in which crockery and furniture were broken, one of the men smuggled the ba' to his wife who, unnoticed, carried it to the street. One version of the story is that the prize was hidden in a basket of washing; while another more colourful account is that it was tucked away under her petticoat. With the ba' in her possession she returned to the goal and as a concluding gesture touched the ba' against the wall, and unmolested walked home. This ba' is now in the National Museum of Scotland.

Another clever move that concluded a heated argument over the choice of winner took place in the early 1930s. At Mackinson's Corner an Uppie man briefly wrenched himself free from the knot of struggling players, handed the ba' to his wife and said casually 'Tak that home mother'. Nobody dared to interfere, and the woman walked away with the prize safely under her arm, leaving behind the unsuccessful, somewhat perplexed claimants.

A similar ploy was used in the early 1930s by an Up-the-Gate who, having just won a ba', handed it to his wife to avoid harassment by other persistent claimants. As she walked briskly along Junction Road a prominent Down-the-Gate reproached her, 'My Hell, Bella, whits a Doonie lik you doin carryin an Uppie ba'?' His remonstrance was unavailing; the lady was not at all discomposed, she gave a bright smile and enjoined, 'Chust this wance'.

In days gone by some of the more vociferous, militant and colourful personalities present at both Boys' and Men's games were women. From the ranks of the gentle sex came formidable marshals who exhorted, directed, enlisted and encouraged. Opponents who had infiltrated were perfunctorily dispatched to their own side, innocent bystanders dragooned and battle-weary participants regrouped. Shirkers and slackers were berated, and by energy, choice language and often personal example these Amazons exerted quite an influence on the fortunes of their side. This is less noticeable today, but even at the present time the game is not entirely a male preserve!

10

Winners of the Kirkwall Ba'

Periods of Dominance

There have been several periods in the history of the game when one side has exerted and maintained supremacy for a number of years. During the 1830s and up to 1846 the Uppies were unbeaten, mainly on account of the strong-playing Scapa men. That district was then more densely populated than it is now, and its men were renowned for their Ba' playing prowess. Among their number was a group of athletic brothers, and it is said that the Up-the-Gates never lost a game in which they played.[1]

The longest period of dominance by one side was between 1846 and 1875 when the Doonies had an uninterrupted run of success in the New Year's Day Ba' – which was the Ba' that mattered in those days. At last on New Year's Day 1875 after play had been forced down to the Bridge, an Uppie called Bill 'Crusoe' Robertson executed a successful smuggle. Assisted by John Costie (the man who made the ba's) he moved quietly along the Lang Stean Close (the narrow lane between Leonard's and Stevenson's shops, leading into Bridge Street Wynd) into Queen Street and along Mill Street. At Willow Road, Oliver Laughton and John Sclater (later Provost) took up the running, and together these two hastened through the 'Keelie' park to Palace Road. There Davie Finlay, a ploughman from Orquil, took the ba' via the Clay Loan to the Uppie goal, and thence to the Head of the Town (the Burgar's Bay area) where he secreted himself with his trophy under a bed until the hue and cry had died down.[2]

Although the Christmas Day game at this time was considered of little moment, it is only fair to record that during the foregoing period the Uppies did manage three Christmas Ba' successes. From New Year's Day 1897 to New Year's Day 1914, of the thirty-five Men's games played only two were won by the

[1] *OH*, 4 January 1922.
[2] *Northman*, 9 January 1875.

FIG. 79: Twelve consecutive Doonie winners. *Left to right*: Ian Smith, New Year' Day 1980; Lyall Flett, Christmas Day 1980; Bobby Leslie, New Year's Day 1977; Dennis Muir, Christmas Day 1977; Norn Donaldson, New Year's Day 1978; Leslie Tait, New Year's Day 1981; Mike Drever, Christmas Day 1978; Alan Hutchison, Christmas Day 1981; Bill Jolly, New Year's Day 1979; Mike Anderson, New Year's Day 1982; Sandy Keldie, Christmas Day 1982; David Johnstone, Christmas Day 1979. The Uppies have recently matched this with twelve consecutive wins between Christmas Day 1998 and New Year's Day 2004, although no photograph exists of the group.

Doonies, the Uppies having twenty-one consecutive victories. The seventeen Boys' games played between Christmas Day 1927 and Christmas Day 1935 produced only one Uppie victory. Between New Year's Day 1977 and Christmas Day 1988 the Down-the-Gates triumphed twenty-four times out of twenty-six consecutive Ba's. In more recent times the Up-the-Gate men have marked up twelve successive victories between Christmas Day 1998 and New Year's Day 2004 .

So complete and sure was the Up-the-Gate domination in the Men's Ba' before the First World War that it became customary for men from the two most prominent Uppie Ba' playing families, the Costies, Main Street, and the Gunns, Glaitness Farm, to meet at the farmhouse on the evening before a game to discuss which Uppie player's claim to the ba' should be supported. When the seemingly impossible happened and the Doonies prevailed in the first Men's game after the war, some Uppie women – particularly those who lived at the Head of the Town – were both incredulous and tearful.

When the scrum was at the Brig on New Year's Day 1977 an old man of eighty-three, himself a Men's ba' winner and a Doonie stalwart for many years, could contain himself no longer and gave a determined push. Breathless and reluctant he disengaged himself from the fringe of play and declared that in recent years he had become fearful that never again would he see the ba' forced in time-honoured fashion down Albert Street and into Bridge Street. 'Man' he exclaimed with fervour, 'it's worth £1000'. The Doonies went on to score a decisive victory, a rare success since New Year's Day 1968, and the harbinger of a sustained winning run.

Choosing the Winner

The game must be one of the remaining few played by the true amateur, for no one taking part receives any reward except that after the game is over the winning side elects a player who is given the ba' as his personal property. By tradition the trophy is awarded to a member of the winning side who has played hard and well for a considerable number of years. On New Year's Day 1933 Harry Clouston, a New Zealander of Orcadian extraction who was hiking round the world, played a prominent part in the Men's Ba'. At the end of the game a section of the crowd shouted that it was 'the hiker's ba'', but the old rule held and quite properly the ba' was presented to a veteran of many games.

Once a man has won a ba' he can never claim another. He may have already acquired a Boys' ba', and over the years there have been a number of dual winners. The only known instance of two members of a family being awarded a ba' on the

FIG. 80: Christmas Day 2003. Raymie Stanger gets the prize.

same day occurred on New Year's Day 1949 when Edgar Gibson, aged forty-six, gained the Men's ba' and his son Gary, aged fourteen, won the Boys' ba'.

Nowadays there is no real distinction between winning a Christmas Day ba' and a New Year's Day ba'. This was not always the case, and certainly up to the 1930s the latter was considered the more desirable. This was probably because the game itself was bigger, and having been in existence for many years before the Christmas Day game, it was looked on as the more important.

For some years a stalwart Uppie was a strong claimant for the trophy. His best chance always seemed to arise at Christmas Day games when he would under no circumstances allow his name to go forward, preferring to wait for a New Year's Day ba'. But this never happened – either the ba' went Down or someone else's nomination prevailed. With succeeding generations pressing their claims the opportunity of winning a ba' is usually fleeting, and eventually after years of

FIG. 81: Selecting the winner, Men's Ba', Christmas Day 1996.

FIG. 82: Uppie winner Kenny Eunson, Christmas Day 1983.

endeavour the veteran's chance of winning either ba' disappeared, and he retired empty-handed.

Although there are records of players being awarded the ba' before 1880, it was around this date that choosing a champion to receive the trophy became established as a recognized and important part of the game. Prior to this the vast majority of ba's were won by the Doonies, and the ba' was 'fixed' or 'exhibited' at the truck of a vessel, and left to swing there to underline the Down-the-Gate triumph. At the conclusion of the New Year's Day game 1876 the Doonies tied the ba' in a handkerchief and hoisted it to the masthead of a vessel in the harbour where it swung for the rest of the afternoon.[3] Christmas Day 1878 saw the ba' hoisted to the topmast of the Shapinsay packet *Klydon* and carried off to Shapinsay.[4]

Outstanding play by an individual Doonie was recognized on New Year's Day 1865. That day Captain Biglan, who commanded the *Elizabeth*, was thought to have had 'the principal part in gaining success for the Down-the-Gates party', and accordingly the ba' was hung at the topmast of his vessel.[5]

In 1897 successful claimants began to be named in the press as a regular feature, although on rare occasions between 1880 and that year there is written evidence of the champion, and the part he played. Henry MacGregor was

[3] *OH*, 5 January 1876.
[4] *O*, 28 December 1878.
[5] *O*, 10 January 1865.

FIG. 83: Doonie winner Drew Leslie, New Year's Day 1989.

awarded the trophy in 1880, being carried back from Foreland shoulder-high,[6] and the winner of the New Year's Day ba' 1884 can also be identified. This game was won by the Down-the-Gates largely due to the efforts of a Farayman called Hercus who 'made a splendid run with it down Castle Street and Junction Road . . . it was kicked into the harbour, the winning player remarking he would take it to Pharay yet.'[7]

There are usually several claimants for the prize, and establishing the outcome can be a noisy, time-taking and boisterous business, with contenders and their adherents urging their case often with clamorous immodesty. In days gone by when the Doonies could not agree on their champion the difficulty was overcome by an arbiter – normally the captain of a vessel in the harbour. He made his choice from the players disputing the ba', basing the decision on the volume of applause greeting the name of each player as it was shouted. Nowadays popular acclaim and level of physical support is what settles the issue, and generally the choice is satisfactory, the award being gained primarily on the basis of sterling play over the years. Ages vary from outstanding players in their

[6] G. MacGregor, *History of the Game of the Kirkwall New Year (Stirring Events)*, Kirkwall, 1914. In this publication the year is wrongly given as 1882.

[7] *OH*, 2 January 1884.

FIG. 84: Doonie winner Paul Miller, Christmas Day 1995.

late twenties, to veterans in their forties. After the Second World War, winners of Men's ba's were older than normal because of the six years when no contests were held. The chance to win a ba' does not often present itself, and there have been many outstanding players who have not gained one of the coveted prizes. There is a delightful story from the early 1930s concerning a Down-the-Gate Men's ba' winner. The day after the game, accompanied by the harbour master and two captains of North Isles steamers, the champion is said to have celebrated in a private room at the St Ola Hotel. The ba' was carefully washed, placed in a large crystal bowl, and a considerable quantity of whisky added. The four men then took their leisure, replenishing their glasses and drinking in comfort and contentment.

Several suggestions have been made with a view to eliminating argument at the end of the game: that there should be a free vote; that the oldest claimant should be awarded the trophy; or that the man who has played longest should be successful. Those well meant suggestions would be difficult to put into practice, and the controversy at the end is all part of a game that has never had any rules.

FIG. 85: Uppie winner Nicholas Monkman, Christmas Day 1998.

In 1987, Orkney Islands Council generously provided panels in the Town Hall detailing past winners of Boys', Youths', Women's and Men's ba's. The recording of winners was more casual in earlier times, and alas a number of names have not been preserved for posterity. I was fortunate in ascertaining, through the kind offices of the late D. B. Peace (a keen Down-the-Gate who played for many years, including the Youths' game at the beginning of the twentieth century) and David Oddie (a stalwart Up-the-Gate during the 1960s, '70s and '80s), the name of the Boys' Ba' winner on New Year's Day 1900, which had not been mentioned in the newspaper reports of the game. He was George F. Linklater who subsequently wrote to me in 1968 from Dartford when aged eighty-three. One of a family of thirteen, he left Kirkwall in 1901 and became a publisher's traveller. He recalled that the ba' he won was fiercely contested, with a score of lads wading and swimming through the Peedie Sea which in those days encompassed a much larger area.

The roll of honour is of significant interest to Kirkwallians who recognize the names of brothers, fathers, uncles, grandfathers and great-grandfathers. Similar lists are on display in Ashbourne, Derbyshire, where Royal Shrovetide Football – a remarkable game and first cousin of the Ba' – is played annually on Shrove Tuesday and Ash Wednesday. The Ashbourne panels also feature the names of those privileged to turn-up the ball.

Family Success

Donald and George Bertram were declared joint winners of the Youths' Ba' on Christmas Day 1898 after what the *Orkney Herald* described as 'a battle of words and some fierce gesticulations among the jealous players'. On Christmas Day 1948 Gordon and Nelson Rorie were awarded the ba', and Jack and Rognvald Paterson gained the prize on New Year's Day 1985.

A unique run of family success in the Boys' Ba' was completed on New Year's Day 1999 when Davy Leonard won a Boy's ba'. Davy was the last of three brothers to claim the trophy for the Doonies: eldest brother Ewen triumphed on New Year's Day 1993 and Keith on Boxing Day 1994.

The Men's Ba' too can boast the success of three brothers with George Donaldson winning on New Year's Day 1962, Jack gaining the trophy on Christmas Day 1964 and Norn triumphing on New Year's Day 1978.

When Up-the-Gate Graham Brough won his Men's ba' on Christmas Day 2000 it completed a trio of unusual wins for his family. His grandfather Albert Brough and great-grandfather James Brough both played for the Doonies and won ba's on Christmas Day 1926 (Boys) and Christmas Day 1903 (Men's), respectively.

The Rorie family are the most prolific in terms of Ba' success and eleven trophies have been won between 1939 and 1992 by various members.

There are instances of Ba' success running in families who can boast variously great-grandfather, grandfather, father, son, brother, uncle and nephew being awarded the trophy. Notable in this regard are the Craigie, Currie, Donaldson, Findlay, Gibson, Groundwater, Keldie, Kemp, Leonard (U), Leonard (D), Linklater, Miller, Monkman, Rorie, Stephen and Tait families. Additionally there are numerous instances of two ba's being won by relatives. It should be said that many families have played for generations and never won or sought a ba'. They have taken part solely for the love of the game.

Winners' Comments

To win a ba' is the highlight of many people's lives and a wonderful experience for the victor and his family. The feeling of euphoria has been described in different ways. The following comments, as reported in *The Orcadian*, are typical.

Following his success on Christmas Day 1997 Stuart Gray commented: 'It was terrific, I don't think it has really sunk in yet. It was a team effort and I was delighted to be chosen to win it.'

Graeme King, Men's winner on New Year's Day 1998, when asked how it felt to emerge the victor, responded: 'Tremendous. It was a great experience and one that I will never ever forget. I can't put it in words, but if you could bottle the feeling I've got you could make a fortune.'

After his triumph on Christmas Day 1999, Edgar Gibson explained the personal significance of his win: 'It really was the greatest day of my life and the most significant honour anyone in my family could ever achieve.'

Forty-five-year-old Norman Craigie, Uppie Men's winner on Christmas Day 2001, confided: 'I'm nearly 46 now, so it was a case of now or never, but I'm absolutely delighted to have won, and I'll keep on playing for a wee blink yet.'

Danny Bain won a Down-the-Gate Boy's ba' on New Year's Day 2002 and immediately after his victory said: 'I don't know how I feel, it's just . . . the best!'

After being raised by his team mates on New Year's Day 2004, Doonie Boys' winner Julian Thomson said: 'I'm delighted, absolutely delighted. It means so much and I've not taken it all in yet. I'm delighted, I'm over the moon.'

Many participants and spectators share the champion's joy, as holding his much coveted prize he is escorted home by jubilant supporters. Protagonists from both sides then repair to his home where they receive warm hospitality which can continue for more than one day, visitors and other players calling with congratulations and to admire the ba'. This pleasant custom in its present enlarged form dates from the 1960s and melds erstwhile contestants into a convivial group, discussing and celebrating the outcome and by extension the Ba' itself.

Players' Tributes

In the story of the Ba' nothing is more illustrative of the camaraderie of players and the mutual respect permeating and binding the sides than the actions which transcended traditional Ba' rivalry at Christmas 2003.

Stewart Ritchie, a thirty-four-year-old popular Down-the-Gate, prominent in the game as boy and man, tragically died in a house fire earlier that year. His memory was recalled and long involvement with the Ba' recognized as Doonie players – about 100 strong – en route to the throw-up, stopped at the Brig and observed a minute's silence.

Furthermore, at meetings of Up-the-Gates and Down-the-Gates, substantial sums of money were raised for his family.

Winners of the Kirkwall Ba's

MEN'S BA'

Date	*New Year*	*Christmas*
1897	No record	Peter Campbell (U)
1898	Archibald Bews (U)	James Fox (U)
1899	Harry Cowper (U)	John Costie (U)
1900	No record	No record
1901	R. Gunn (U)	Robert Budge (U)
1902	D. B. Peace (D)	Robert Mowat (U)
1903	T. Wylie (U)	James Brough (D)
1904	J. Linklater (U)	John Cromarty (U)
1905	R. Linklater (U)	William Wick (U)
1906	A. Milne (U)	J. Dennison (U)
1907	William Somerville (U)	William Garrioch (U)
1908	Tom Nicolson (U)	William Costie (U)
1909	William Harrison (U)	Corporal W. Park (U)
1910	James Johnston (U)	Alexander Voy (U)
1911	Jack Schollay (U)	John Mackay (U)
1912	John Mowat (U)	Alexander Flett (U)
1913	Robert Matches (U)	James Kelday (U)
1914	John Herdman (U)	No game – First World War
1919	No game	Peter Hercus (D)
1920	George Shearer (D)	Alex Walls (D)
1921	Alex Groundwater (U)	Thomas Linklater (U)
1922	James Craigie (D)	James T. Herdman (U)
1923	Robert Newlands (U)	James Mackay (U)
1924	Andrew Nicholson (U)	J. Harcus (D)
1925	James Bews (D)	J. Muir (D)
1926	William Mackinson (U)	William Laird (U)
1927	Robert S. Robertson (U)	David Fox (U)
1928	William Mackinson Jr (U)	Gillies B. Hercus (U)
1929	Thomas Sinclair (D)	Robert Gunn (D)
1930	William Bews (D)	James Linklater (U)
1931	D. Johnston (D)	James Linklater (D)
1932	William R. Park (U)	James Sinclair (D)
1933	Bob Johnstone (D)	John Sinclair (D)
1934	David Kemp (D)	Andrew Shearer (U)
1935	David Heddle (U)	David D. Marwick (D)
1936	James Thomson (D)	Charles Kelday (D)
1937	John Miller (D)	Alex G. Webster (D)
1938	W. H. B. Sutherland (D)	William Sinclair (U)

Date	*New Year*	*Christmas*
1939	William Rorie (U)	No game – Second World War
1945	No game	Hector Aitken (D)
1946	John Hourston (U)	Bob Park (U)
1947	Alie Groundwater (U)	W. Schollay (U)
1948	Jim Crisp (U)	Tommy Miller (D)
1949	Edgar Gibson (U)	Walter Scott (D)
1950	Tommy Thomson (D)	Geordie Borwick (D)
1951	Johnnie Walls (D)	David Keldie (D)
1952	Andrew Thomson (U)	Dan Grieve (D)
1953	George Cook (U)	Tom Sclater (U)
1954	Pat Johnston (D)	Jack Crisp (U)
1955	John Flett (D)	Tom Shearer (D)
1956	Jock Harcus (D)	Jim Kelday (U)
1957	Jim Harrison (U)	Bob Muir (D)
1958	Vinnie Linklater (U)	John Sinclair (D)
1959	Douglas Campbell (U)	Gordon Rorie (U)
1960	Davie Fox (U)	Bill Stephen (D)
1961	Bill Wilson (D)	Bobby Sinclair (D)
1962	George Donaldson (D)	lan Linklater (U)
1963	Jack Miller (D)	Bill Sim (D)
1964	Ronnie Drever (D)	Jack Donaldson (D)
1965	Jackie Scott (D)	Billy Johnston (D)
1966	John Robertson (U)	George Craigie (U)
1967	Mattie Stephen (D)	Gary Gibson (U)
1968	Bert Grieve (D)	Brian Barnett (U)
1969	Andy Rendall (D)	Theo Rorie (U)
1970	Sandy Budge (U)	Jim Dick (U)
1971	Alan Monkman (U)	Ronnie Muir (U)
1972	Freddie Rorie (U)	Jim Leonard (U)
1973	Brian Smith (D)	Alan Findlay (U)
1974	Brian Kemp (U)	Eric Kemp (U)
1975	Gordon Rorie (U)	David Sinclair (D)
1976	Calvin Slater (U)	Duncan Currie (U)
1977	Bobby Leslie (D)	Dennis Muir (D)
1978	Norn Donaldson (D)	Michael Drever (D)
1979	Billy Jolly (D)	David Johnstone (D)
1980	Ian Smith (D)	Lyall Flett (D)
1981	Leslie Tait (D)	Alan Hutchison (D)
1982	Mike Anderson (D)	Sandy Keldie (D)
1983	Jim Cromarty (U)	Kenneth Eunson (U)
1984	Fraser Byers (D)	Brian Anderson (D)

Date	*New Year*	*Christmas*
1985	Davie Johnston (D)	Michael Stevenson (D)
1986	Keith Corsie (D)	Erlend Tait (D)
1987	Eddie Barnett (D)	Fred Corsie (D)
1988	John Cromarty (D)	Ian Hutcheon (D)
1989	Sandy McConnachie (D)	John Copland (D)
1990	Jim Baillie (U)	Evan Monkman (U)
1991	George Currie (U)	Leslie Manson (U)
1992	Alan Rorie (U)	S. Alan Craigie (U)
1993	Jim Linklater (U)	John Stephen (D)
1994	Benny Thomson (U)	Stuart Leslie (D)
1995	Barry Reid (D)	Paul Miller (D)
1996	Jack Leslie (D)	David Miller (D)
1997	George Rendall (D)	Stuart Gray (U)
1998	Graeme King (D)	Kenny Garriock (U)
1999	Andrew Kemp (U)	Edgar Gibson (U)
2000	David Flett (U)	Graham Brough (U)
2001	Martin Flett(U)	Norman Craigie (U)
2002	Ian Brough (U)	Garry Cooper (U)
2003	Bruce Moar (U)	Raymond Stanger (U)
2004	Gordon Mulraine (U)	

YOUTHS' BA' (started New Year's Day 1892)

Date	*New Year*	*Christmas*
1897	No record	William Cooper (D)
1898	J. W. Inkster (D)	Donald and George Bertram (U)
1899	James Groundwater (U)	Peter Reid (U)
1900	No record	James Smith (U)
1901	Jim S. Deerness (D)	Robert Fawns (U)
1902	Robert Sinclair (U)	John R. Miller (D)
1903	John Spence (D)	George Durno (D)
1904	W. Scott (D)	Robert Harcus (D)
1905	Charlie R. Smith (D)	William Work (U)
1906	J. Harcus (D)	Stewart Wilson (D)
1907	W. A. Nicolson (U)	Pat Gunn (U)
1908	David Thomson (D)	Jeremiah Wilson (D)
1909	William Groundwater (U)	David Linklater (D)
1910	D. Sinclair (D)	Youths' game abolished

BOYS' BA'

Date	*New Year*	*Christmas*
1897	No record	George Durno (D)
1898	Stewart Wilson (D)	Robert Matches (U)
1899	William Nicolson (U)	Donald Morgan (D)
1900	George F. Linklater (U)	Tom Shearer (D)
1901	Robert M. Mowat (D)	Alexander Smith (D)
1902	David Thomson (D)	James Croy (D)
1903	E. Arthur (D)	John Farquhar (D)
1904	Peter Shearer (D)	Robert Spence (D)
1905	Alexander Mitchell (D)	James Finlayson (D)
1906	J. Lennie (D)	John Croy (D)
1907	B. Rendall (D)	John Muir (D)
1908	T. Learmonth (D)	Alexander Morgan (D)
1909	Bob Reid (D)	Herbert Williamson (D)
1910	Johnnie Kennedy (D)	Dick Mowat (U)
1911	David Nicolson (D)	Frankie Sinclair (D)
1912	Jackie Nicolson (U)	William John Sinclair (D)
1913	William Halcro (U)	James Harvey (D)
1914	Jim Fox (U)	No game – First World War
1919	No game	James Cooper (D)
1920	Alie Groundwater (U)	Edwin Halcro (U)
1921	David Linklater (U)	Thomas Scott (U)
1922	A. Sinclair (D)	Rognvald Keldie (D)
1923	J. Kemp (U)	M. Thomson (D)
1924	James Mackinson (U)	J. Simpson (U)
1925	Philip Brass (D)	Johnnie Taylor (D)
1926	Archie Findlay (U)	Albert Brough (D)
1927	John Bruce (U)	Albert Thomson (D)
1928	Ronald Muir (D)	Calvin Slater (D)
1929	Bertie Rosie (U)	Tom Cooper (D)
1930	R. Gunn (D)	Charlie Smith (D)
1931	Gordon MacGillvray (D)	John Bews (D)
1932	Johnnie Walls (D)	David Hay (D)
1933	Jim Bews (D)	Jim Norquoy (D)
1934	Jim Duncan (D)	James Thomson (D)
1935	John Sinclair (D)	Herbert Flett (D)
1936	George Craigie (U)	Dan Grieve (D)
1937	James Pottinger (D)	Gordon Linklater (D)
1938	David Flett (U)	Stanley Moar (U)
1939	Norman Cooper (D)	No game – Second World War
1945	No game	Evan MacGillivray (D)

Date	*New Year*	*Christmas*
1946	Jack Donaldson (D)	Ian Argo (D)
1947	Pat Baikie (U)	Cecil Sutherland (U)
1948	Alastair Smith (U)	Gordon and Nelson Rorie (U)
1949	Gary Gibson (U)	Tom Heddle (D)
1950	George Stout (D)	David Campbell (D)
1951	John Mooney (D)	Eddie Craigie (U)
1952	Freddie Rorie (U)	Ronald Muir (U)
1953	Leslie Campbell (U)	Alan Monkman (U)
1954	Jim Leonard (U)	Archie Findlay (U)
1955	Gath Cheyne (U)	Eric Kemp (U)
1956	Alan Findlay (U)	Norman Muir (D)
1957	Brian Barnett (D)	Billy Rorie (U)
1958	Stewart Urquhart (U)	Chris Norquoy (D)
1959	Douglas Thomson (U)	Tommy Borwick (U)
1960	Dennis Muir (D)	Raymond Borwick (U)
1961	David Sinclair (D)	Roy Linklater (U)
1962	Attie Leask (U)	Ian Cormack (U)
1963	Tony Monkman (U)	Bobbie Somerville (U)
1964	Archer Kemp (D)	Rognvald Taylor (U)
1965	Raymond Youngson (U)	Leslie Tait (D)
1966	Norman Cooper (D)	Ian Rorie (D)
1967	David Pirie (U)	David Scott (D)
1968	Sandy Keldie (D)	Billy Youngson (U)
1969	Alistair Clunas (U)	George Drever (D)
1970	Stuart Wood (D)	Billy Wylie (D)
1971	Sammy Tulloch (D)	James Donaldson (D)
1972	Maurice Walls (D)	David Miller (D)
1973	George Mowat (U)/Anthony Rees (U)	Kenneth McConnachie (D)
1974	John Stephen (D)	Brian Hutcheon (D)
1975	Stewart Pottinger (D)	Laurence Leonard (U)
1976	Graeme Smith (U)	Edgar Gibson (U)
1977	Andrew Kemp (U)	Colin Kirkpatrick (D)
1978	Leslie Miller (D)	David Moffat (D)
1979	Neils Newlands (D)	Billy Taylor (D)
1980	Jim Stout (D)	Tam Sinclair (D)
1981	Stewart Ryrie (D)	Alec Findlater (D)
1982	David Flett (U)	Ian Croy (D)
1983	Angus Findlater (D)	Bruce Moar (U)
1984	Gordon Mulraine (U)	Gordon Wilson (U)
1985	Jack and Rognvald Paterson (U)	Sigurd Gibson (U)
1986	Paul Watson (U)	Ian Gorn (U)

Date	*New Year*	*Christmas*
1987	Martin Sutherland (U)	Ian Stout (U)
1988	Derek Sutherland (U)	Greg Rorie (U)
1989	Drew Leslie (D)	Cullen Burns (D)
1990	Alastair Watson (D)	Colin Paterson (D)
1991	Bryan Bain (D)	Christopher Burgess (U)
1992	David Johnstone (D)	Robbie J. T. Thomson (U)
1993	Ewan Leonard (D)	Steven Spence (U)
1994	James Baillie (U)	Keith Leonard (D)
1995	Gary Dowell (U)	Roy Keldie (U)
1996	Darren Rendall (U)	Sean Brough (U)
1997	Stephen Kemp (U)	Balfour Baillie (U)
1998	Keith Harcus (U)	Nicholas Monkman (U)
1999	David J. Leonard (D)	George Keldie (D)
2000	Stuart Rosie (D)	James Linklater (U)
2001	Ryan Garriock (U)	Magnus Flett (U)
2002	Danny Bain (D)	Andrew Sutherland (U)
2003	Graham Peace (U)	Robbie Innes (U)
2004	Julian Thomson (D)	

WOMEN'S BA'

Date	*New Year*	*Christmas*
1945		Barbara Yule (U)
1946	Violet Cooper (U)	

* * * * *

The undernoted were winners before accurate records were started in 1897. Wherever possible, I have given what I believe to be the correct date.

BOYS' BA'

Pre-1890	Bob Cumming (U) 1872
1890-1897	J. W. Inkster (D) New Year's Day 1893
	Kenneth Oag (U) Christmas Day 1893
	Bob Swanney (D) 1894
	Fred Buchanan (U) 1894
	John R. Miller (D) 1895

YOUTHS' BA'

1892-1897	Bob Corsie (D) Christmas Day 1892
	David S. Flett (D)

MEN'S BA'

1875-1890	Davie Finlay (U) New Year's Day 1875 H. MacGregor (U) New Year's Day 1880 James Shearer (D) New Year's Day 1881 – Hercus (D) New Year's Day 1884 Andrew Walls (U) 1888 Bob Cumming (U) 1889 Jim Flett (D) – Foulis (D)
1890-1897	Alex Cassells (D) John W. Deerness (D) Christmas 1895 Dr George R. C. Russell (U) Bob Nicolson (U) 1894 Geordie Wick (U) David S. Flett (D) Dan Meil (D) William Park (U)

Those who have Presented and Thrown up the Ba'

For the first 175 years of its evolved existence the game was started at the Mercat Cross by a person closely associated with the contest and in particular with production of the trophy. Availability of the ba' and its appearance on Christmas Day and New Year's Day was the domain of apparently factionless townsfolk who raised funds from the public, although the accounting of some collectors was alleged to be rudimentary! Gradually, the significance of the moment gained import and willing donors (often burghers of substance or other note) gained pleasure, and doubtless publicity, from its uniqueness.

For many years in the first part of the twentieth century two organizers of note were Bill Somerville and James Nicolson, but there were other stalwart supporters in bygone days whose names have not survived.

Since 1945 the principals (sometimes acting on behalf of others) at the start have been:

	MEN'S BA'	BOYS' BA'
1945 New Year	No record	No record
1945 Christmas	W. H. B. Sutherland	James D Nicolson
	[Mr David Flett threw up the Womens ba', Christmas Day 1945]	

	MEN'S BA'	BOYS' BA'
1946 New Year	No record	No record
	[No record of who threw up the Womens ba', New Year's Day 1946]	
1946 Christmas	James Drever	Jim Nicolson
1947 New Year	Willie Harrison	Mrs Maggie Rorie
1947 Christmas	David Flett	Mrs Maggie Rorie
1948 New Year	Herbert Borwick	No record
1948 Christmas	David Kemp	Jock Price
1949 New Year	David Horne	Bill Annal
1949 Christmas	David Peace	William Hay
1950 New Year	James D Nicolson	David Ross
1950 Christmas	Donald Bertram Snr	Jock Price
1951 New Year	A. Cromarty	Col. Fred Buchanan
1951 Christmas	W. D. Reid	John Flett
1952 New Year	John Sclater	S. Sinclair
1952 Christmas	James Linklater	Dr Hugh Marwick
1953 New Year	Councillor James Flett	no record
1953 Christmas	Gordon Robertson	Pat Johnston
1954 New Year	David Kemp	Councillor Alfie Mackay
1954 Christmas	David Fox	Miss Mary Muir
1955 New Year	Robert Nicolson	Mrs MaryGarrioch
1955 Christmas	Mrs Tom Firth	Andrew Manson
1956 New Year	Baillie James Scott	Mrs Peggie Gibson
1956 Christmas	Brig. S. P. Robertson	No record
1957 New Year	David Spence	No record
1957 Christmas	Albert Maxwell	No record
1958 New Year	A. G. Spence	No record
1958 Christmas	John G. Shearer	Mrs Margaret Cardno
1959 New Year	Ralph Miller	Miss Bella Ritchie
1959 Christmas	Scott Watson	Captain James Peace
1960 New Year	Albert Jolly	Gordon MacGillivray
1960 Christmas	Archie Jamieson	No record
1961 New Year	Robert Garden	No record
1961 Christmas	John Shearer	No record
1962 New Year	Baillie Edwin Eunson	No record
1962 Christmas	D. D. Marwick	John Sinclair
1963 New Year	William Jolly	No record
1963 Christmas	John Flett	Mrs J. Spence
1964 New Year	John Sclater	No record
1964 Christmas	Bill Rorie	Mrs Mima Sclater
1965 New Year	Johnny Walls	Mrs Peggie Gibson
1965 Christmas	Jim Miller	Mrs Violet Couper

	MEN'S BA'	BOYS' BA'
1966 New Year	Alie Groundwater	No record
1966 Christmas	John Sinclair	Mrs Catherine Donaldson
1967 New Year	Edgar Gibson	Mrs Margaret Cardno
1967 Christmas	Jim Kelday	Mrs Bella Park
1968 New Year	Jo Grimond	Mrs Rita Robertson
1968 Christmas	John Brown	Mrs Margaret Stephen
1969 New Year	Douglas Cooper	Mrs Jean Gibson
1969 Christmas	Edgar Gibson	Mrs Mamie Linklater
1970 New Year	Tom Sclater	Mrs Ruby Youngson
1970 Christmas	Bill Sim	Mrs Violet Grieve
1971 New Year	Dan Grieve	Josie Robinson
1971 Christmas	George Craigie	Mrs Ruby Craigie
1972 New Year	John Foulis	Mrs Inga Drever
1972 Christmas	Walter Scott	Mrs Minnie Miller
1973 New Year	Jack Donaldson	Mrs Bessie Webster
1973 Christmas	James Foubister	Mrs W Muir
1974 New Year	Jack Watson	Mrs Ann Park
1974 Christmas	Alec Webster	Mac Thomson
1975 New Year	Provost James Scott	Baillie Andy Wylie
1975 Christmas	William Schollay	Mrs P. Linklater
1976 New Year	George Cook	Mrs Kathleen Stephen
1976 Christmas	Andrew Thomson	Mrs Violet Grieve
1977 New Year	Pat Sutherland	Alistair Pottinger
1977 Christmas	Jock Harcus	Albert Thomson
1978 New Year	Vinnie Linklater	Mrs Elizabeth Linklater
1978 Christmas	Ian Linklater	Mrs Peggie Gibson
1979 New Year	Bill Bews	Mrs Gladys Leslie
1979 Christmas	Tommy Shearer	Ronnie Drever
1980 New Year	John Robertson	Gary Gibson
1980 Christmas	Jim Harrison	Mrs Hazel Groundwater
1981 New Year	Convener Edwin Eunson	Mrs Elizabeth Firth
1981 Christmas	Gordon Rorie	Mrs Isabella Watson
1982 New Year	George Donaldson	Mrs Vera Bell
1982 Christmas	Bobby Sinclair	Mrs Grace Currie
1983 New Year	Bill Wilson	Mrs Evelyn Monkman
1983 Christmas	Gerald Eccles	Mrs Rita Cromarty
1984 New Year	Tommy Brough	Mrs Dorothy Thomson
1984 Christmas	Jim Leonard	Mrs Jenny Bews
1985 New Year	Jackie Miller	Pat Baikie
1985 Christmas	Billy Stephen	Mrs Mary Blair
1986 New Year	John Robertson	Mrs Norma Leonard

	MEN'S BA'	BOYS' BA'
1986 Christmas	Jock Sinclair	Dan Grieve
1987 New Year	Rev H. W. M. Cant	Bobby Leslie
	[to mark the 850th anniversary of St Magnus Cathedral]	
1987 Christmas	Clive Thomson	Dennis Walls
1988 New Year	Jack Scott	Mrs Ellen Smith
1988 Christmas	Gary Gibson	Mrs Emily Celli
1989 New Year	Alan Rosie	John Robertson
1989 Christmas	Jim Dick	George Stout
1990 New Year	Stevie Twatt	Mrs Liz Watson
1990 Christmas	Brian Barnett	Leslie Tait
1991 New Year	John Robertson	Charlie Miller
1991 Christmas	Billy Johnston	Roy Linklater
1992 New Year	Sandy Budge	Miss Meg Firth
1992 Christmas	Linay Linklater	Mrs Ann Bell
1993 New Year	Andy Rendall	Sandy Keldie
1993 Christmas	Freddie Rorie	Mrs Norma Craigie
1994 New Year	Alan Monkman	Mrs Christine Fraser
1994 Christmas	Russell Groundwater	George Drever
1995 New Year	Gordon Linklater	Mrs Helen Wylie
1995 Christmas	Jim Leonard	Mrs Iris Clyde
1996 New Year	Brian Smith	Mrs Avril Cromarty
1996 Christmas	Ronald Muir	Mrs Julia Johnston
1997 New Year	Mattie Stephen	Alie Findlater
1997 Christmas	Ian Tulloch	Mrs Vira Burghes
1998 New Year	Bryce Donaldson	Mrs Sandra Tait
1998 Christmas	Alan Findlay	Alan Lobban
1999 New Year	Brian Kemp	Mrs Inga Oddie
1999 Christmas	Eric Kemp	Adrian Watt
2000 New Year	Dan Grieve	Gary Gibson
2000 Christmas	David Johnstone	Mrs Melba Leonard
2001 New Year	Calvin Slater	Mrs Liz Johnson
2001 Christmas	Duncan Currie	Eddie Craigie
2002 New Year	Bobby Leslie	John Leslie
2002 Christmas	Dennis Muir	Ian Cormack
2003 New Year	Kenny Eunson	Norman Rushbrook
2003 Christmas	Jim Cromarty	Alan Monkman
2004 New Year	Billy Jolly	Mrs Michelle Aiken

11

Interesting Games and Unusual Incidents

Longest and Shortest

The Ba' can vary greatly in the length of playing time, but is always concluded. The shortest Men's game took place on Christmas Day 1952, and resulted in a win for the Doonies in four minutes. The longest contest was on New Year's Day 1975 and lasted for seven hours. The scrum arrived at Mackinson's Corner at eight o'clock and four tired contenders and their supporters disputed ownership of the trophy for a further fifteen minutes. This eclipsed the length of the New Year's Day Ba' 1957 when the trophy was taken by smugglers to the Uppie goal at 7 p.m., although playing time had finished three-quarters of an hour earlier. Another long tussle was on Christmas Day 1971. The New Year's Day game 1972 was also extended and finished at about six o'clock. This contest had been prolonged by the introduction of a canvas-covered ball which distracted the attention of many players and enabled a smuggle and an hour's concealment of the real ba' in the Keeliequoy. The Uppies reached their goal at 6.20 p.m., but the wrangling as to who was to be awarded the prize lasted for a further hour and ten minutes. Other long games were on Christmas Day 1993 and New Year's Day 1996, both won by the Doonies and both taking five and three-quarter hours to complete. Nowadays most contests last for at least four hours and it is not uncommon for play to extend over five hours.

The length of Boys' games also can vary and the first tussle after the Second World War, on Christmas Day 1945, is one of the shortest on record. Seconds after the throw-up a relay of Doonie sprinters sped down Albert Street and Bridge Street and the trophy was dipped in the Basin less than five minutes after the start.

Another quick tussle took place on Christmas Day 1985 and was won by the Uppies in four minutes. They outnumbered their opponents by three to one and with minimal opposition had no difficulty in running the ba' to Mackinson's

Corner. On Boxing Day 1988 the Up-the-Gates once again ran the ba' to their goal in four minutes.

Not surprisingly, Kirkwall boys much prefer lengthy, keen tussles, in the rigours of which they are well able to rejoice. On New Year's Day 1991 the Boys' Ba' lasted from 10.30 a.m. to 2 p.m. when it was won by the Doonies. The longest contest on record was the New Year's Day 1998 game when after a 10.30 a.m. start the trophy was taken to the Uppie goal at 3.20 p.m. However, there was period when the ba' was hidden.

The Longest Hold

On New Year's Day 1980 the Down-the-Gates controlled the game from the outset and by half past two it had reached the close on the Up-side of George Rendall, drapers, now Leonard's stationers. There the scrum remained for another three and a half hours. A visiting player, a Welshman, stationed with the RAF in Shetland, had travelled specially to play, got hold of the ba' and stood on it at the close doorway. Try as they might the Down-the-Gates could not move the scrum and the crowd of watchers grew until there were some 500 well muffled spectators. At quarter past five the Doonies were surprised to find that the wooden door was not secured. Players surged through but three men crammed themselves into a small shed in the lane and obstinately stuck there for a further three-quarters of an hour. They were Evan Monkman, Brian Guthrie and Erlend Tait. With difficulty this small group was prised out, the ba' was pitched back into Albert Street and after some robust passages of play, the scrum swung and lurched down the remainder of the traditional route and the ba' was thrown into the Basin at quarter past seven.

Three Scrums

New Year's Day 1984 was remarkable, not only because it was very well supported by players and spectators, but also because of the possibility that the Men's and Boys' scrums would become enmeshed. When the Men's ba' was thrown up the boys were heavily involved at Tankerness House, only leaving Broad Street at ten past one. The Up-street lads eventually reached their goal shortly after 2 p.m., damaging an unguarded petrol pump on the way. For a short time there were three scrums on Broad Street, the Men's Ba' having split into two, with some doubt as to which group actually had the ba'.

Men's Ba' Played Twice

On two occasions the Men's Ba' was played twice on the same afternoon. This first occurred on New Year's Day 1869 when it was generally felt that the game was over too quickly.

> The personage upon whom the honour had devolved of tossing up the ball, evidently considered himself master of the situation, as he sat smoking his pipe and watching the clock with an easy air of nonchalance. The ball was no sooner tossed off, when the clock struck, than it was picked up by a bonnetless, coatless, Fenian-looking fellow, who rushed away down the street with it in his hands, and seemed bent upon spoiling the game. He was at last tripped up and rolled in the mud, but the ball went on its way in the direction of the harbour, and the people who had gathered to see a sight began to disperse with a feeling that they had been swindled. However, as the youth of the town were not to be baulked of their annual amusement, another ball was obtained, and the battle soon began in earnest in Broad Street.[1]

The second occasion was New Year's Day 1881 and occurred in interesting circumstances. The *Orkney Herald* commented that although the ba' was usually thrown up at the Market Cross at one o'clock, at half past twelve the *St Clair* had been sighted at Thieves' Holm, followed almost immediately by the *Paragon.* When the *Paragon* and the *St Clair* entered Kirkwall Bay they were becalmed. This was a blow to the prospects of the Down-the-Gates, as reinforcements from the crews would arrive too late to play. The ba' was held by the Down-the-Gates who put it under lock and key, and announced that it would not be thrown up until two o'clock. This raised the ire of the Up-the-Gates 'and many and noisy were the declamations made against the cheatriness of those in possession'. The Uppies convened a council of war, an 'air ball' was produced and a few minutes' play 'sent the drummy dancing up street'. Presumably had the Uppies abstained from playing subsequently they could have claimed victory. The Doonies produced the proper ba' at two o'clock and a tremendous struggle commenced, 500 players being engaged at one time or another.

The crowd soon turned Broad Street into a mass of mud, and gradually the scrum moved Up-street until it nearly reached the Clay Loan. Here the Doonies rallied and many men who had not played for years were drawn into the fray. A detachment of seamen from the clipper *Paragon* arrived on the scene and threw

[1] *OH*, 5 January 1869.

themselves into the struggle. Feelings were running high and those who would not lend a hand were classed as 'cowards' and 'unpatriotic brutes'. Probably because of the seamen reinforcements the game gradually swung in favour of the Doonies, and after a protracted and turbulent contest the harbour was reached just as darkness fell. The ba' was thrown in, and amidst tumultuous cheering hoisted to the masthead of the *Paragon*.[2] The *Orkney Herald* concluded its report: 'The ball was never seen outside the crowd from the time it was thrown up until the harbour was reached; and spectators who have watched the game for nearly half-a-century state that it was the keenest they ever witnessed. Strangers could only express their surprise at such a brawl – the only excuse that can be offered in mitigation being that it is a "time-honoured" relic of a barbarous age.'

Through the Peedie Sea

A struggle in the waters of the Peedie Sea is always exciting to watch, and the scene is sometimes enlivened by amusing incidents such as a player completely disappearing from view in one of the holes which make crossing the Oyce a doubtful pleasure.

The Ba' has paid several visits to the Peedie Sea – particularly in the days when the water reached the foot of Tankerness Lane. Mr G. MacGregor[3] described a game that went through the Peedie Sea, probably in the 1870s:

> On this occasion a creditable victory took place in favour of the 'Down-the-Gates' under rather odd circumstances. After the play had undergone a severe test on the Broad Street, the ball was cunningly taken from the centre of the combatants by an 'Up-the-Gate' named 'Toakie' Foubister, and who, after he had run through and reached the foot of Tankerness Lane, followed by a howling crowd, jumped with it, waist-deep, into the waters of the Peerie Sea, and where he was at once joined by a fearless and champion 'Down-the-Gate', R. Brough who grappled with him for its possession. Ultimately, however, after the two men had produced much sensation amongst the crowd of onlookers by thus struggling until they had reached the other side of the water, directly opposite where the 'wee cottage by the sea' now stands, Foubister threw the ba' into the hands of a club-footed 'Up-the-Gate' named Tom Corrigal, who, with others, had run round to meet them there, and who after he had made a bold dash

[2] *OH*, 5 January 1881 and 3 January 1894.

[3] G. MacGregor, *History of the Game of the Kirkwall New Year's Day Ba' (Stirring Events)*, Kirkwall, 1914.

FIG. 86: Through the Peedie Sea, Men's Ba', New Year's Day 1954.

> with it towards the Up-street goal was caught, severely throttled by a number of his opponents and relieved of it. In short, within half-an-hour of this incident, the ba' was goaled by the good old 'Down-the-Gates'.

The most spectacular occasion last century was the New Year's Day game 1951 when, according to *The Orcadian,* 4 January 1951:

> the ba' was heaved into the Peerie Sea and in went quite a number of players. A most remarkable scene followed as player after player got possession and heaved the ba' either one way or another. The Peerie Sea was ice-bound, and at parts bearing the weight of the players, while the ba' itself skimmed over the frozen surface. A water polo game ensued with many amusing incidents, players crawling and skimming on their stomachs all over the place, while some went through the ice. After much passing and re-passing the Ayre Road was finally reached.

A prominent Doonie cut his legs on the ice and had them stitched in the surgery at 7 Victoria Street by Dr Ronald Welsh. So cold were the player's limbs that no anaesthetic was required.

Doonies Swim to Victory

In January 1987 after a tough game the Doonies chose to take the ba' over the dyke adjacent to the West Pier, not realizing how far the tide had receded. The contest proceeded over the beach and onto the foreshore where players were faced with an expanse of unpleasant clinging mud over which fifty of them struggled ankle deep, watched by a throng of spectators on the pier. Encountering extended puddles there was dispute as to whether the ba's contact with this salt water was enough to seal victory. Eventually, far out on the foreshore Bobby Leslie, who had thrown up the Boys' ba' earlier in the day, heaved the trophy into the sea. Then a group of men, including Paul Miller, Fred Corsie and the eventual winner, Eddie Barnett, swam with the ba' through the mouth of the harbour and into the Basin where hundreds of folk awaited to enjoy a unique experience.

Through a Hotel

On Christmas Day 1948 the Doonies managed to push the scrum to the back of the Albert Hotel. This is the story recounted to me many years later:

> The first window on the east side was the owners' bedroom. At this stage Jim Crisp (Doodle) and his cousin Hughie Marwick were holding the ba' and Hughie said 'Come on Doodle, we'll go in through the window' (there were no barricades up). The window was a 3 feet sash window with an astragal down the middle, and Hughie went head first through the lower half without a scratch. When the rest of the scrum heard the glass break they rushed in through the front entrance of the hotel. Inside, Tommy Brough met Hughie at the door of the bedroom and they wrestled under the bed for the ba'. The scrum pushed the ba' through the corridors of the hotel, into the kitchen and out the back door.

My informant, Dan Grieve, as ever an active participant, recalled that there did not seem to be much damage to the hotel, and certainly the owner, John Ballantyne, never claimed compensation.

A Car is Used

We have already heard how on one occasion a horse was used to carry the ba' Up-street,[4] and during the Youths' Christmas Day game 1900 Uppie operations were for a time directed from horseback! The enthusiastic horseman was called

[4] Men's Christmas Day game 1879, see Chapter 3.

Newlands, and his efforts soon earned him the title of 'General French'.[5] In the Christmas Day Ba' 1953, a car helped to seal the victory following a successful bluff. After nearly three hours, the game ran into confusion when it was discovered that the ba' was no longer in the scrum in Albert Street. The players scattered, some rushing in different directions while others stood about, perplexed. In the fading light, Jim Wilson, one of several Uppie players at the centre of the scrum, had backed out with the ba' under his arm and dashed up the Strynd. He ran along Copland's Lane and across Palace Road to the Congregational manse. He was met at the door and was told that as the minister was recovering from a severe heart attack he could not be disturbed. Nothing daunted he boldly walked back onto Palace Road and, bluffing several waiting Doonies into thinking he was on their side, sent them off towards Victoria Street on a wild goose chase. Running into Thoms Street, he was given a lift in an Uppie's car and driven to New Scapa Road, where he cut back across gardens and touched the ba' on the wall at Scapa Corner.

On Christmas Day 1955 a car played a major part in deciding the result of the Boys' game. This contest was going in favour of the Doonies when a loose maul occurred opposite the Customs House. The ba' was thrown and kicked up Laing Street and Mill Street to The Willows where another loose maul occurred, before a young Uppie, Eric Kemp, lifted the ba' and ran to the top of White Street. Tumbling into a passing motor car he escaped from his pursuers and was driven along Croys Loan (George Street), down Clay Loan and into Manse Road. Thence he made his way to Sandison's Corner, ceremonially touched the wall and stood there somewhat forlorn and quite alone. A butcher's van picked him up and set off via Glaitness Road and Finstown to Hatston housing estate. Finding a crowd milling round his home, back into Kirkwall went boy, ba' and butcher's van, and there by an odd coincidence they came upon the very same car in which the first break had been made. Transferring to it, Master Kemp was taken to a house in Orphir where the ba' was secreted, and it was nearly midnight before he was driven once again to Orphir to collect his hard-earned and much-travelled prize.

Cross-Country

The New Year's Day game 1960 is an interesting example of the roundabout route that a contest may take. Initially play had been conventional, but after an hour on Broad Street a Doonie smuggle took the ba' down Tankerness Lane,

[5] *O*, 29 December 1900. Major-General (later Field Marshal) Sir John French was a senior cavalry officer in the Boer War then being waged. Subsequently he took the British Expeditionary Force to France in 1914.

West Tankerness Lane and into the Peedie Sea. Doonie players surged across the water to within a few yards of the Ayre Road, and then came disaster for them. A mishandling swung the tide of fortune, and resulted in the pack surging back across the water to the bank just below the Pickaquoy playing fields. Through hazards of broken glass, rubble and a barbed wire fence the mêlée erupted onto the tarmac car park. The game surged and whirled in all directions, the tugging, heaving mass of men burst away again, and an attempt was made to re-enter the Peedie Sea by floating the ba' through a culvert. The ba' stuck inside and players had to crawl in to retrieve it. Thereafter the heart of the scrum convulsed in a muddy duck pond and players had to be pulled clear of the clinging 'iper'.[6] The game then swept over a turnip field at the back of the County garage and continued to Glaitness Road, High Street, through a garden, across a field at the side of Balfour Hospital and into Hornersquoy, the Neukatineuks and New Scapa Road, where it fetched up against the Uppie goal. This four hour struggle came to an end after the scrum had been pushed past Mackinson's Corner and some yards down Main Street when it was discovered that the ba' had been smuggled away to the Uppie winner.

Fluctuating Fortunes

One of the remarkable things about the game is the way in which fortunes can change, and there are numerous instances of a smuggle or the appearance of reinforcements turning imminent defeat into victory.

On New Year's Day 1881 the scrum was nearing the Clay Loan before Doonie reinforcements swung the tide of battle their way. In the Boys' game on Christmas Day 1919 the Uppies had taken play along Victoria Street and down a close to Junction Road. There one of the Down-the-Gates wormed his way out of the ruck, and rushed along Union Street and up the Clay Loan, this manoeuvre resulting in the ba' being carried to the harbour.

The furthest Up-street an eventual Doonie victory has gone was in the Men's game on Christmas Day 1935. Initially an Uppie surge was halted at the entrance to Victoria Street, and after two and a quarter hours' play the Doonies had taken the scrum down to the Big Tree. By half past four, play had returned to Broad Street and thereafter the Uppies made progress down Post Office Lane and slowly along Junction Road. Just before six o'clock the game had almost reached Union Street, when in the darkness, and as a finale to a very thrilling contest, a Doonie successfully smuggled the trophy.

[6] Black ooze, mud.

The Uppies, too, have several times dramatically turned the tables on their opponents. On New Year's Day 1960, a smuggle by the Doonies took the ba' up Broad Street, down Tankerness Lane and West Tankerness Lane, across the Peerie Sea and to within a yard or two of the Ayre Road. Just when success was in their grasp a Doonie mis-throw enabled the Uppies to take the prize back across the water to Pickaquoy, and eventually to their own goal. This is described in detail earlier in this chapter, under the heading 'Cross-Country'. What was perhaps the most extraordinary change of fortune occurred on New Year's Day 1966: this is described in the following section.

Dramatic Smuggle

The Men's New Year's Day game 1966 proved unique in that a smuggle took place just as the ba' was being thrown into the harbour. Only one of the previous eleven Men's Ba's had gone Up-street and the Up-the-Gates were determined to make amends. Certainly at the start everything was set fair for their success, and within half an hour the ba' had been forced twenty yards up Victoria Street. With the arrival of Doonie reinforcements there was then a period of mauling rough play and the mass of men, which at this time numbered well over 100, looked as though it would debouch back into Broad Street. Suddenly, an Uppie smuggle took the ba' up Irvine's Close at the top of Victoria Street, round the back of the Bishop's Palace into the Watergate, past the police station and as far as the junction of Buttquoy Place and Buttquoy Crescent. There the breakaway was halted, and a small group formed, soon swollen by other players arriving on the scene, including those who had rushed to the Uppie goal at the Old Castle. Play slowly went downwards, through the Watergate, where for a period the pack was lodged behind some unpleasant railings, along Palace Road and back into Broad Street. The game continued to be a hard uncompromising struggle, but the Doonies now held the upper hand and the exhausted scrum eventually erupted into Harbour Street in the semi-darkness at 4.30 p.m.

Surging across to the steps at the Harbour Office the triumphant Doonies attempted the *coup de grâce* and dropped the trophy over the edge, but the ba' never reached the water. An Uppie, on his knees at the quayside, deftly caught the ba' as it dropped, and doubled up and anonymous, quietly backed out of the mob. Swiftly he made his way walking and running through the deserted streets to the Uppie goal at the Old Castle (aided in the latter stages by a car). In company with another Uppie he symbolically touched the wall with the ba', and both men then drove with the trophy along Harbour Street where they passed searchers for the ba' and thence to the home of the winner where it was safely cached to await his return and several days of celebration. Meanwhile at the harbour people continued to seek in vain the ba'. Some thought there had been a smuggle, others that the ba' had sunk, while others again felt sure that it was lodged in a dark corner of the Basin. Players dived into the water in search of the missing ba', while confusion reigned. Only some time later did the crowd realize that victory had been snatched from the Doonies, and that after two smuggles and three and a half hours of hard fluctuating play the game was over.

The bewildering speed with which the tide of fortune can change is one of the game's fascinations, and the ever-present possibility of the dramatic stimulates and maintains interest to the very end.

The Photographed Fugitive

In the Men's Christmas Day game 1966 an Uppie smuggle at Bridge Street Wynd went awry in Queen Street, and thereafter the struggling mass of men came down St Catherine's Place and to within a few yards of the shore. Shortly before five o'clock as a last desperate fling two Uppies holding the ba' forced it to the ground, and unseen in the darkness it rolled down the slope of the road to one of their players standing on Shore Street. This second smuggle was entirely successful, and unnoticed in the confusion the bystander secreted the ba' under his jersey and ran with the excited crowd part of the way up St Catherine's Place. Choosing his moment he broke away and cut back down Dunkirk Lane, found his way along the shore and up the steep bank to Cromwell Road. Ascertaining that he was not being followed, the fugitive slowed to a comfortable walk and chanced to meet a keen local photographer armed with camera, tripod and flash-gun. Moving together into Mount Drive the photographer calmly recorded the smuggler while little more than 100 yards away frenetic Doonies, jubilant Uppies and confused spectators scoured the shore area. The photo call over, the nonchalant Uppie continued on a roundabout way to the Up-street goal, diverting briefly when he unsuccessfully sought a cup of tea at a relative's empty house. Some time after six o'clock the smuggled and photographed ba' was presented to a stalwart Uppie as a well-merited reward for many years' play.

Two Ba's in the Game

An unusual tactic which occurred on New Year's Day 1876 was the introduction of a second ba', with the result that for a time there were two knots of players. Some onlookers alleged that the ruse was found out, others that the real ba' was smuggled Up-street while others again maintained that it went Down. In any event a ba' was taken to each goal, so presumably both sides were content.[7]

Amusing Mix-up

Sometimes the game debouches into lanes and back gardens, the precise location of the ba' is unknown, and confusion reigns. Players and spectators run helter-skelter in the general mix-up, and this can lead to amusing incidents and an unusual tussle. On Christmas Day 1934, at Gunn's Close the ba' was thrown into a garden and the players spilled in after it. Moving into an adjoining vegetable bed the scrum created havoc before it was finally broken up, the ba' was brought out and thrown up again on the main road. Meanwhile more than half the players and at least 100 spectators rushed to Victoria Street where an alarming rumour met them that the ba' had been smuggled, and was on its way to the harbour. The crowd streamed down to Broad Street where the grave news was that the smuggler had been given a lift by a motor-cyclist and was heading out the Ayre Road. The pack set out in pursuit, and an innocent incoming motorist was stopped and ordered to surrender the ba'! Then 'for some minutes the crowd patrolled the Ayre Road and Harbour Street, and was coming to the conclusion that all was over when a courier came hastening down Junction Road to impart the startling news that the game was still going strong in the neighbourhood of the Crafty. The hoaxed crowd, with renewed enthusiasm, proceeded to the scene of combat, where a sadly depleted gallery was watching two reduced sides fighting for supremacy at the Laverock Creamery. There were less than thirty players, about fourteen aside, taking part in the game,' which was won by the Up-the-Gates.[8]

Simulated Injury

A clever and unusual tactic occurred on New Year's Day 1901. Play had reached the doorway of what was then known as Charlie MacGregor's shop – the last building at the top of Broad Street. An Uppie, Bob Nicolson, pretended to be injured, and as he stood in the doorway clutching himself the scrum ground past. Play continued some yards away, and unnoticed, Nicolson, another stalwart Billy Wick, and the ba' went their unmolested way to the Uppie goal. Incidentally when these two players were proceeding along Victoria Street a lady came out of her house and casually enquired about the location of the ba'.

[7] *O*, 8 January 1876 and *OH*, 5 January 1876.
[8] *OH*, 2 January 1935.

Nicolson nonchalantly lifted his jersey, showed the trophy and said, 'The ba's right here.' In a deserted street, with the clamour of the contest 100 yards back, the scene must have been memorable, even slightly unreal.

After the struggle came a most unkind cut, when the players discovered they could neither celebrate their victory nor drown their disappointment. The publicans had decided to have a half-holiday but had given no intimation to the public!

The Ba' that was Never Won

There is a curious story told about a Ba' in the dim past in which the orb was never taken to either of the goals, and the tale revolves round the friendship of two men – an Uppie and a Doonie. It seems that in mid-afternoon the Doonie slipped away unnoticed with the ba' and his Uppie friend, who arrived late, chanced to meet him in Mill Street. Neither man would betray his Ba' loyalty but neither wanted to endanger the lifelong friendship, so they agreed to hide the ba' and lose it forever. This they did, and that Ba' was never finished. The story is given a tinge of authenticity by the fact that many years ago a very old four-panelled ba', partly decomposed, was found hidden in the rafters of a stable in Kirkwall.

The Ba' that Disappeared

Apart from being a very long struggle – the actual contest finished at quarter past six – the New Year's Day Ba' 1957 has another claim to fame in that after five and a quarter hours' play the ba' vanished. From the throw-up the scrum moved down Post Office Lane and after two hours it had reached the gas works on Junction Road. For a short time the location of the contest was a tiny coal cellar, whence the ba' was pushed past Castle Street and down to Peace's wood yard (now the Post Office). Here the Uppies staged a tremendous revival and slowly play was forced up to the Crafty. Then the ba' vanished, and it transpired that an Uppie youth had got hold of it, and in the darkness secreted himself on the first floor landing of a house in Victoria Street. Later he was joined by a friend, and they crouched there hidden from the searching players who once entered the house. Eventually, about 7 p.m. when the hue and cry had died down the youths slipped out and made Up-street. Then, seeing some unidentified players in Junction Road they thought discretion the better part of valour, and carried the ba' to Jim Harrison, the man who had made it in his shoemaker's shop in the Strynd. Later that night Jim Harrison ritually concluded matters by touching the wall of the Uppie goal with this trophy.

Sustenance for the Scrum

On Christmas Day 1948 the Atholl Café in Albert Street boasted a large plate glass window, behind which were displayed cake stands laden with fancies. The only barricade was an old broom handle, and as the body of men arrived at the café, the handle and the glass broke. Doonie stalwart Johnnie Walls put his hand through the broken glass, picked up a plate of the tempting cakes and handed them to friend and foe alike. Then he shouted to the owner David Spence who was inside, 'Min, gae's a drink o water', to which David replied 'I'll dae better than that, I'll gae ye milk.' Holding a large jug and standing on a chair at the window he poured several pints of milk into the mouths of the thirsty players.

As play went down in the Men's Christmas Day Ba' of 1985, George Stevenson, Vice-Convenor of the Orkney Islands Council, and two of his friends standing in Bridge Street shouted up to Robert Miller, of Scott & Millers, wine merchants, that they were thirsty. Robert did not dare open his house door because of the proximity of the Ba', but generously lowered from his window on the third floor a substantial quantity of whisky attached to a rope and invited them to quench their thirst. The bottle was emptied without delay, and equally swiftly retrieved; all this with the heaving pack some five yards away.

Foreign Visitors

On Christmas Day 1984 the Doonies frustrated an Uppie smuggle in the lane between Templeton's and Boots and rushed the ba' to the Basin. Meanwhile a sizeable scrum swung Up-street and was being played without the ba' at the Tourist Office on Broad Street, whiles the Doonie winner, Brian Anderson, and forty of his supporters ran up Junction Road with the trophy in their midst. The game was filmed by two Belgians. What made the visit special was that one of them had been in Kirkwall eighteen years previously and had played in the Men's Ba', sustaining a broken finger. On this visit as the ba' had been smuggled they could not film the end of the game. To make amends Billy Stephen, with whom they were staying, gave them his Men's ba' and they proceeded to Hatston slipway and made a dummy run down the jetty. Alas in these contrived proceedings the ba' carrier slipped on the wet seaweed and ended in the sea. This made a splendid conclusion to their film.

Dissension at the Finish

The disagreement which often arises at the end of a game, either in connection with choosing the winner or merely because the goal has been reached and the losers are taciturn and disgruntled, can sometimes boil over into a fracas.

On New Year's Day 1859 after five minutes' play the game was over, and the ba' had been kicked into the harbour. 'At this stage of the proceedings, and by way of finale, some of the players, including a lot of navvies, felt disposed to renew the game with the fists, which, however, was entirely put an end to by the crowd closing in and refusing the combatants sufficient room to exercise their pugilistic propensities.'[9]

At the conclusion of the New Year's Day game 1894 the ba' was taken into the Old Police Station at the foot of Wellington Street and thereafter the struggle was continued for a few minutes in the lobby and kitchen.[10]

In the New Year's Day game 1905 the Uppies forced the ba' to Burgar's Bay in only thirty-five minutes. It took another thirty minutes of heated discussion – emphasized occasionally with fists – to decide the champion.[11]

The New Year's Day game 1913 took half an hour to reach the Uppie goal and the real excitement then began with half a dozen claimants struggling for the trophy within the Old Castle walls. More men joined the loose maul, the street wall gave way and masonry and people crashed into the roadway below. By good fortune no one was seriously injured. The door of the Old Castle was forced and the crowd stormed headlong into the dwelling house. The police then took over and Superintendent Wood, aided by Sergeant Tulloch and Constable Manson, managed to put an end to the disorder which had added another half an hour to the length of the game. The eventual winner was Robert Matches 'who according to trustworthy information has played for over thirty years without any award. Before this record the claims of a few beardless youths must surely sink into insignificance'.[12]

On 1 January 1937 play took an hour and a quarter to reach the sea at Shore Street. Thereafter there was a further hour of sustained controversy before the deadlock was resolved and the winner finally selected.[13]

High feelings at the end are by no means confined to men, and the New Year's Day Boys' game 1932 is an outstanding example of this. After the Doonie victory there were two main claimants for the ba' – Johnnie Walls, White Street, and Douglas Thomson, Bridge Street. Amid outbursts of cheering both boys were hoisted shoulder-high by their respective supporters, but when the ba' was taken from the Basin it was handed to Walls:

> Thomson ploughed his way across the shoulders of the crowd and closed with Walls. Pandemonium broke loose and the rival Doonies began to

[9] *O*, 3 January 1859.
[10] *OH*, 3 January 1894.
[11] *OH*, 4 January 1905.
[12] *OH*, 8 January 1913.
[13] *O*, 7 January 1937.

> fight furiously. The battle swung over against the Kirkwall Hotel and for a time the situation looked ugly. Constable Mainland entered the struggle and succeeded in restoring something like order. Animosity still ran high however. Neither Thomson nor Walls was willing to let the other gain possession of the coveted trophy and the ba' was carried to the edge of the Basin and flung into the water a second time.

Although hampered by heavy rubber boots Walls dived in and began to swim towards the floating ba' which was about twenty yards out. Suddenly another claimant entered the lists: this was Billy Moodie, St Catherine's Place, and he too dived into the water. A race to the ba' now took place, Moodie won and made his way back to the pier steps pushing the prize in front of him. It seemed that Walls' great effort would be to no avail, but two youths then arrived in a rowing boat, took the ba', and hauling the exhausted Walls aboard presented the prize to him.[14]

One cannot help feeling a certain amount of sympathy for both Thomson and Moodie, who had success within their grasp only to have it snatched away, and it would be pleasant to record that both duly won a ba' at a later date. This was not to be as shortly afterwards they reached the age limit of fifteen.

At the end of the Boys' Christmas Day Ba' 1937 there were six young Doonies swimming vigorously in the Basin, each making determined efforts to obtain the trophy.

Another remarkable Boys' contest took place on New Year's Day 1975, not least because of the time it took to determine the winner. After a 10.30 a.m. start it took little more than half an hour for the actual game to be concluded. This included a delay of some minutes at the West Pier slip where the ba' ran loose, and as it had not been immersed in the sea, a young Uppie girl, in a gesture of defiance, gained a brief respite for her side by throwing it back over her head to the Kiln Corner. When the ba' had been retrieved from the water six claimants declared themselves and a fresh extended struggle eventuated. All of the candidates had reached the age limit and had played their last Boys' Ba'. They were Jack Leslie, Frank Campbell, Ewen Donaldson, Alan Work, Mark Smith and Stewart Pottinger. The argument raged along Harbour Street, Bridge Street, Bridge Street Wynd and into Mill Street. None of the lads was prepared to concede and the dispute was concluded shortly after 1.30 p.m., some two and a half hours after the contest itself had finished and more than three hours after the start. Stewart Pottinger was declared the winner and thereafter, good humour having been re-established, a

[14] *O*, 7 January 1932 and *OH*, 6 January 1932.

number of the boys proceeded to join their seniors on Broad Street. However, the longest tussle occurred a year later on Christmas Day 1975, when an Uppie victory was achieved after three and a half hours of play. Indeed the struggle was taking place at the foot of the Clay Loan (with two young ladies right in the centre of the scrum) while the Men's Ba' was being played on Broad Street and spectators commuted between the two.

Ill-tempered Ba'

The Christmas Day Men's Ba' 1998 was violent and disturbed throughout by gusts of gratuitous violence. Even before the game started there was a series of scuffles on Broad Street. As the game progressed into Victoria Street a number of people were so perturbed by the fracas that they departed the scene. The hooliganism was particularly reprehensible as over the years the Ba' Committee had held meetings with schoolchildren explaining the game and encouraging them to play in the right spirit – hard but fair. On this day manifestly a poor example was set for the younger generation. The situation was to a considerable extent retrieved the following week when Up-the-Gate winner Brian Kemp very sensibly prefaced throwing up the ba' with a short speech exhorting players to return to the traditional Ba', played in a sporting fashion. Brian had been so concerned at the fisticuffs that he had considered making a personal protest by declining the honour. He thought better of it and used the occasion to encourage 150 players to play in a manner that ensured the future of the Ba': 'Ba' players, the game is not a war; please behave like sportsmen and set a good example for the Boys to follow; the Ba' is part of Orkney's heritage so ensure that we pass it to the next millennium in capable hands for future generations to enjoy.' The speech was warmly applauded and had the desired effect, subsequent Ba's exhibiting little unprovoked hostility. Despite the unusually high level of aggression a spokesman for Orkney Health Board reported that very few injured players appeared for treatment that day at Balfour Hospital.

Awarded 'In Absentia'

The first time on record that the ba' was awarded *in absentia* was on Christmas Day 1935. D. D. Marwick, latterly Head Postmaster at Kirkwall and for many years a stalwart Doonie, had to stop playing at five o'clock to return to duty. A long, fluctuating game was eventually won by the Doonies at six o'clock. After the scrum had reached Mackay's furniture stores on Junction Road, and in what seemed to be easy striking distance of the Uppie goal, a smuggle got the ba' away, and it was carried to the Doonie goal via the Auction Mart where allegedly it was hidden for a time behind a cow. On arrival at the harbour those present unanimously awarded it to Mr Marwick, to whom it was taken.

Meanwhile at the Crafty the main contingents fought on, unaware that the ba' had been spirited away. About 6 p.m. the news filtered back, and the players dispersed, Uppies empty-handed and disconsolate, Doonies tired and jubilant.

In the 1969 New Year's Day Men's Ba' there were three claimants to the trophy. *The Orcadian* reported: 'Round and about the Harbour Office went the argument looking just about as big as the game itself. Eventually it fetched up against the sea wall in and out among the parked cars. For a time, even, it looked as if it might be going into the sea again.' Andy Rendall, the most favoured claimant, could not be there to claim the ba' himself as he had sustained broken ribs playing for the Doonies on Christmas Day. Half an hour later his supporters won the day, proceeded to his home and presented him with the trophy.

Tatties and Herring

A firm belief in Kirkwall has been that a win for the Up-the-Gates brought heavy crops and a good harvest, whereas successful fishing followed a Down-the-Gate victory. For twenty-nine years – between 1846 and 1875 – the Ba' went Down (three Christmas Day games did go Up-street, but at this time *the* Ba' game was that played on New Year's Day) and then on New Year's Day 1875 the Uppies broke this long run by means of a smuggle at the Brig. Later that day an old man was heard to remark that as it was 1846 when the potato blight first appeared in Orkney, 'we'll surely hae guid tatties this year, after the ba's gaen up.'[15]

An old rhyme goes:
Up wi' the ba' boys,
Up wi' the ba',
An' ye'll get cheap meal,
An' tatties an' a'.

On the other hand for the Down-the-Gates, success brought the promise of an abundance of herring.

Over the years the words varied. Around 1900 at the time of the war in South Africa a reference was made to the Boer leader in the battle cry of the Up-street boys:

[15] *Northman*, 9 January 1875.

Up wi' the ba' boys,
Up wi' the ba',
Doon wi' auld Kruger,
An' up wi' the ba'.

The Boys' Christmas Day game 1902 was played in a downpour, and with rain streaming from her face an Uppie girl supporter took what shelter she could in a doorway. Resolutely standing there, as the Ba' went steadily past towards the harbour, she bravely sang:

Up wi' the ba' boys,
Up wi' the ba',
An' ye'll get cheap meal,
An' tatties, an' a',
Then push, shove, and push, boys,
Push, shove, and push,
The Shories are a' drookit,
But ye're no weet ava.

Part II

The Lore of the Ba'

12

Prose and Rhyme

Some interesting articles and poems on the game have been written over the years, and I have thought it worthwhile to reproduce a few of these in this chapter.

From Maelstrom to Dead-lock

In his book *Summers and Winters in the Orkneys*, written in 1868, Daniel Gorrie, who was at one time editor of the *Orkney Herald*, describes the game thus:[1]

> In the winter season the only out-door recreation which finds general favour is the old game of football. From time immemorial it has been the custom in Kirkwall for the inhabitants to take part in this boisterous game on New Year's day. Regularly as the day recurs there is a gathering of the populace intent on preserving one curious and time-honoured custom from extinction. The game – which should have ended with the era of cockfighting – is virtually a trial of strength, of pushing and wrestling power between 'up the street' and 'down the street', the grand object of the belligerents being to propel the ball to one or the other end of the town. Broad Street, where the struggle commences under the shadow of St Magnus, becomes the centre of attraction about noon-tide. Sailors and porters arrive in formidable force from the purlieus of the harbour, tradesmen gather in groups, and even hoary-headed men, feeling the old glow of combative blood in their veins, hasten to the scene of anticipated contest. At one o'clock a signal pistol-shot is fired, the ball is tossed into the air from the steps of the old cross, and around it, as soon as it bumps on the ground, there immediately gathers from all sides a dense and surging crowd. The wrestling and struggling mass

[1] D. Gorrie, *Summers and Winters in the Orkneys*, 2nd edn, pp. 27, 28, 29.

> sways hither and thither, sometimes revolving like a maelstrom, and at other times stationary in a grim dead-lock. At intervals, the ball, as if flying for dear life, makes a spasmodic bound from the crowd; but a sudden headlong rush encloses it again, and so the struggle continues as before. For onlookers it is exciting to observe the fierce red-hot faces of the combatants, while the only appearance of good-humour displayed is a grim smile flickering fitfully across an upturned visage. It is curious also to note the eager, uneasy motions outside the revolving ring, of men long past their prime, who were wont to be in the centre of the crowd in other years. Heavy knock-down blows both foul and fair are freely given and received. The struggle seldom lasts much longer than an hour, and when the seamen and porters win the day, they place the ball, as a trophy of conquest on the top-mast of the largest ship in the harbour. It seems odd that a boisterous pastime like this should continue so long in an otherwise peaceable town; but the authorities perhaps act wisely in declining to interfere with old use-and-wont. Indeed the Provost and Bailies of the Royal Burgh appear to take a lively interest in the proceedings, which they rightly regard as a less eccentric celebration than the tar-barrel bonfires that illumine the streets of Lerwick at the festive season . . . Advantage was sometimes taken of the New Year pastime of foot-ball to pay off old scores when people harboured a grudge at each other.

The New Year's Day Ba' o' Auchty-Twa

The author of the poem of this title, Charles MacGregor JP, was working in Glasgow in 1882, and so did not see the game. He obtained both description and detail from a brother's letter. The words can be sung to the tune 'Bailie Nicol Jarvie's Dream'. It is noteworthy that in its halcyon days, as now, the Ba' was supported by representatives from all classes of society. For example, Emerson was a doctor, and Gold was the factor of the Marquis of Zetland's estates.

I wonder if a revisitation by the rugged enthusiasts described by Mr MacGregor occurs on Christmas and New Year's Days. Perhaps if one looks closely it may be possible to glimpse the wraiths of great Ba' players of long ago lining the kirkyard wall at the stroke of one o'clock. Only the gargoyles hear the thin cries of encouragement and support, and the rough-hewn phantoms, disappointed by their perception of the game's lack of fire and abandon, grow restive. A bearded, gnarl-handed champion flits across the Kirk Green, mingles with the crowd and adds his spectral exhortations to the strident shouts of the onlookers. Then, unheeded and a little sad at present day standards, he melts away disconsolately to reminisce and relive with his shadowy companions the Ba' o' Auchteen Auchty-Twa.

1. 'Twas in the auchteen hundredth year
O' grace and auchty-twa, man,
A bluidy battle, sair and teuch,
Did rage a' for a ba', man.
Brave heroes met on ilka side,
A' there to fecht what e'er betide;
Auld man and loon,
Frae up and doon,
Auld Kirkwall toon,
Did gather roon
The Cross on New Year's Day, man.

Chorus Bold Up-the-Gates hip hip hurray
Press on and clear the way men
Think on your vows by faither's banes
And shout for Burgar's Bay, men.

2. The Up-the-Gates ha'e made a vow
Their honour to redeem, man;
They've marshalled men frae hill and dale
Sware a' by faithers' banes, man.
They gathered in the auld kirkyard
On Hogmanay, and ghosts were scared;
The de'il himsel'
Did look and quail
And wi' a yell
He left them makin' vows, man.

3. St Magnus tolled the battle hour
The signal's fired and a', man;
And Norsemen close in fearfu' wrath,
And mony heroes fa', man.
Wi' pride o' ba' stock lineage
In hottest battle a' engage;

Wi' bated breath,
In deadly wrath,
They fear nae scathe,
But mock at death –
A' dare tae do or die, man.

4. Guidwives are greetin' for their men,
And lassies for their lads, man;
Oot owre ilk window auld wives look,
While bairnies greet for dads, man.
Men pant, and threat, and growl and groan,
The wounded lie and bleedin' moan;
A fearfu' scene
To southern een,
Wha ne'er had seen
Sic warfare keen
In Scotland's realm before, man.

5. There's lawyers and there's magistrates
And doctors there I saw, man;
And fishermen and bankers, too,
And tinkers there and a', man;
The battle raged twa hours and mair,
And mony eyes were blackened sair;
And faces hashed,
And noses bashed,
And legs were smashed,
And windows crashed,
And wa's were knockit doon, man.

6. The doughty Sinclairs fought wi' might,
The Firths did rare pluck show, man;
The Fletts, and Muirs, and Liddles, too,
McQueen's, and Reids, and a', man.
Bold Walls, and Fox, and Mathieson
Led by gallant Emerson;
Did hack and slay,
And cleave their way,
Through bloody fray,

To Burgar's Bay,
Whaur auld wives grat wi' joy, man.

7. The warlike Broughs did muster thrang,
But split in fractions twa, man;
The Younger chieftain sairly rued
He didna' bide awa', man.
The noble Peace and valiant Spence
Parried blows by skilfu' fence;
But soon they reeled,
And forced to yield,
They left the field,
Their doom was sealed,
And in dismay ran home, man.

8. Determined Shearers ground their teeth,
And fought like tigers mad, man;
The Irvines and the Chalmers's
Looked waefully and sad, man.
The Davidsons and Seatters growled,
The Golds and Hourstons darkly scowled;
But when they saw
Their best man fa',
They ran awa',
Nae mair tae craw,
O' valorous deed in war, man.

9. Macgregors fought wi' lion mood,
Wild Saunders slashed and slew, man;
But Nicolson, aboon them a',
Was resolute and true, man.
The battle closed at Burgar's Bay,
The Up-the-Gates ha'e won the day;
Loud cheers were raised,
And heroes praised,
Great bonfires blazed
The de'il amazed
And terror-struck, flew hame, man.

Hogmanay and the New Year's Ba' in Kirkwall [2]

The following poem is by a distinguished Orcadian, John Mooney JP FSA Scot. (1862–1950). He was one of Orkney's leading historians in the twentieth century and a founder member of the Orkney Antiquarian Society to which he contributed numerous papers. A man of vast learning and a Town Councillor for many years, in 1945 he was made a Freeman of Kirkwall. His published books include *Eynhallow, St Magnus Earl of Orkney, The Cathedral and Royal Burgh of Kirkwall,* and *Charters and Other Records of the City and Royal Burgh of Kirkwall.*

'Tis Hogmanay in Kirkwall toon, within the rocky shore,
Whar beat the wild tempestuous waves wi' angry sullen roar,
An' seem as on the massive cliffs they dash wi' micht an' main,
Tae bid fareweel tae the auld year, which ne'er will come again,
Which gangs awa' wi' friendship, wi' pleasure, an' wi' woe,
An' leaves us tae reflect on things that made wir hairts tae glow.

The hoor o' twal is comin' fast, the throng gang up an' doon
The lang an' narrow windin' street that is in Kirkwall toon,
Their lauchin' voices rend the air as merry they a' seem
Tae taste the new-sprung rivulet that adds tae Time's lang stream,
Which carries us an' a' oor race upon its surface wide,
Like feathers frae the seabirds breast alang the flowin' tide.

Up, up the street quick come the mob wi' bugle an' wi' drum,
An' pleasures seem rife i' their hairts, by their lood joyfu' hum,
They flock aroun' the Market Cross – that cross grown auld wi' age,
Roun' which in days noo lang syne gane, fierce conflicts aft did wage,
Whaur stubborn men o' true Norse bluid repelled the numerous foe,
An' on the narrow stony street laid all invaders low.

That wee auld street that ance did see proud Patrick's haughty sway,
An' felt the warm tricklin' bluid frae warriors as they lay
Wi' forms defigured an a' aghast, but hairts still brave an' true
An' vengeance i' their tameless breasts began tae rise anew; –
That wee auld street whaur ance there stood great Cromwell's michty force,
Tae scatter the posterity o' the brave and fearless Norse.

[2] J. Mooney, *Songs of the Norse, and other Poems*, 1883.

Wi' beatin' hairts the crood stands still tae hear the clock strik twal,
When tae the year that is unborn Auld Time sends forth his call;
The hoor noo strik's, the year is fled, anither taks it place,
An' thus afore the cheerin' crood there died a twal month space.
Vocif'rous greetin's rend the air in every hairt is glee,
An' instantly true frien's step forth, 'A happy year tae thee.'

The trumpet, bugle, drum an' a', their martial notes doth sound,
An' send their New-Year's greetin' shrill thro' a' the air around,
Which fills the breasts of ancient bluid wi' pride o' Vikings auld,
An' sends a thrill thro' some one there which aft has felt the Scald
When he heard the wild tumultuous shrieks ring from the Norseman's fray,
When fichtin' on a savage shore whaur warriors laid the way.

The nicht went on an' nothin' passed but sports o' youthful kin',
An' onyone wha seen them there wad think the fierce auld line
O' warlike men are dead an' gone wha ruled the rollin' wave,
An' proved themselves in spite o' a' tae be baith bold an' brave;
But we'll soon see if they are dead, an' if they are nae more,
An' see if none possess their hairts in Orkney's sea-washed shore.

Why thrang the crood alang the street as one o'clock draw nigh?
An' why sic eager glances frae mony a flashin' eye?
Why speak they sae defiant in sic a wee auld toon,
As on its sma' Norwegian street they walk baith up an' doon?
They really seem excited as they gang in bodies twa.
A warlike hairt there seems tae beat in breast o' ane an' a'.

Great joy abounds in every hairt because they're a' aware
That somethin' grand is just tae be in which they a' will share:
These forms o' Norse appearance wi' voices shrill an' clear
Are preparin' for the usual game they play at the New Year –
The gude auld game, the true auld game which we hope will never fa' –
The game beloved by northern hairts – the Kirkwall New Year's Ba'.

Noo larger comes the flockin' crood, the clock will just strik' one,
An' a' aroun' the Market Cross they soon begin tae stan';
A robust figure mounts the steps, the mob begins tae cheer
In notes as shrill as when they bade farewell tae the auld year;
He draws frae oot his loosened coat a roun' thing black an' sma',
An' lood an' fiercer cheer the crood for they see the New Year's Ba'.

One! strik's the clock, the ba' is pitched amang the fierce-like men
Wha' seem tae brace their ev'ry nerve an' a' their courage strain;
A darin' an' a warlike rush is made by each bold side,
An' they seem tae love that savage game an' play at it wi' pride; –
Each charge at each wi' fearless hairt an' mony a' wild hurrah,
Blow follows blow wi' vengeance wild for a wee bit corkie ba'.

Why do they play in savage way, like vengeance on the wing,
An' kindred ficht in sic a style for sic a simple thing?
Tae see a toon like Kirkwall divide itsel' in twa,
An' ficht wi' fierce an' earnest hairt for a wee bit corkie ba'!
E'en if they were in battle they could na better ficht
To save their land frae foreign foes or show a better micht.

We easily can ascertain why their hairts sae boldly glow,
Why they rush wi' ardour, fierce and keen, wi' savage shout an' blow, –
We know they are descended frae the Norse o' ancient times
Whose glorious an' gallant deeds we read in Runic Rhymes;
Then we should sing an' a' be prood, because in Orkney old
The noble hairts o' Vikings brave beat in her sons sae bold.

The sailors brave wha steer their ships as sea-kings used to do,
Are fichtin' hard wi' vigour fierce, and rushin' thro' an' thro'
The furious mob o' shoutin' men, whase looks bespeak their rage,
As wrathfully they rush at each, an' ane an' a' engage
In conflict, fierce an' savage like, sic as one never saw,
Tae drive doon the street that envied thing – that little corkie ba.'

On the ither side the 'Up-the-gates,' whase blood is at its height,
For up the street are strugglin' hard wi' vengeance an' wi' micht;
They wish tae shaw tae those aroun' wha earnestly look on,
That they will ficht for up the street, the side o' which they're fon'
So in they dash an' boldly try tae shove alang the wa',
Determined that the 'Up-the-gates' shall win the New Year's Ba'.

Behold, here comes a band o' men, straight for the ba' they go;
Their eyes o' blue are sheddin' forth a' wild an' darin' glow;
Their very teeth are firmly clenched an' fierce-like is their gaze
Resemblin' much the Vikings looks in ancient warlike days –

The strongest man o' a' the gang well known by ane an' a' –
They are the Scapa Champions wha always win the ba'.

The ficht is fierce, baith sides are strong, an' equal hairts abide
Within each brave an' darin' man wha is fichtin' for his side;
Yet the 'Up-the-gates' are gainin' ground, they drive their foes before,
An' force their way up Broad street brae wi' warlike whoop an' roar;
While manfully the 'Doon-the-gates' endeavour weel tae caa
Their enemies for doon the street, that they micht win the ba'.

In spite o' sic resistance bold, up o'er the brae they're ta'en
An' driven quick up the sma' street by these exultant men.
The bravery an' the darin' o' the 'Doon-the-gates' can't stay
The rushin' o' their enemies, wha fiercely force their way;
An' mony a' ane is trodden doon, an' crushed beneath them a' –
Oh! sic a wild an' furious ficht for a wee bit corkie ba'!

The 'Up-the-gates' hae forced their way near tae their boundary,
An' seein' that they're won sae far, their hairts do bound wi' glee –
But noo a fearfu' ficht begins, sic as was never seen,
For twa' lang hoors they struggled hard an' fought wi' vigour keen.
Nae stranger wha micht seen them then, could venture forth to say
That cowardice was in a hairt wha at the ba' did play.

Each side fought long an' bravely, determined not to yield,
An' every ane o' a' those men strive weel their fame tae shield;
But up, in spite o' a' their waurk the ba' is sure tae go,
Altho' opposed by fearless men frae whom the blood does flow;
So up the toon an' oot the road the ba' is boldly ta'en
Unto the grim and thackit hames o' the brave Scapa men.

Oh! may great bards in Orkney rise, tae sing o' Orkney's fame
An' set the hairts o' a' her sons wi' patriot lore aflame,
That land in which sae mony deeds o' warlike times remain
Hidden in dark obscurity – the acts o' gallant men:
An' sing o' the relic o' the past, which should be loved by a' –
The only thing o' ancient kind – the Kirkwall New Year's Ba'.

The Ba'

David Horne Senior[3] was the author of *Under Orcadian Skies* and *Songs of Orkney*, from which this verse, 'The Ba'', comes:

If you love a democratic, acrobatic, half-aquatic
Game of football, with ten rules, or none at all,
Then you'd better take a train, then a boat to cross the main,
And land on New Year's Day at Old Kirkwall.

Put on your cast-off clothes, and if you love your toes,
A pair of seaboots helps in the stramash;
Throw all your dignitee away into the Peerie Sea;
Don't bring your watch, though none will steal your cash.

Then take your proper place, minus frock-coat and sleek 'lum',
On Broad Street nearing one, and keep an eye
Upon the crawling clock; when it rings you'll get a shock!
Up leaps the Ba', and then it's do or die!

For the game may last an hour, yet it's far beyond the power
Of mortal man to give an estimate;
It may run for half a day, or ten minutes end the fray
In favour of the Up- or Down-the-Gate.

Up and down the narrow street, where 'carts tremble when they meet',
The conflict rushes on just like the tide;
You feel your heart will burst (when you're sane the game is curst),
But you're caught within the maelstrom's giant stride.

The Doonies all push north, while the Uppies, topsy-turve,
Strive to take the precious leather to the south;
The one goal's Kirkwall Bay, the other, lackaday!
Is a ruined castle, gnarled and uncouth.

But, ah! the motley crowd! tinkers, tailors, humble, proud;
Doctors, lawyers, with a woman here and there;
A father and his sons; enthusiastic little ones;
A grandad who has left his easy chair.

[3] D. Horne, *Songs of Orkney*, p. 50.

Where is the famous ball? Well that's often hard to tell,
But it's somewhere in the middle of the throng,
Where the steam uprises most. Yes, sometimes it does get lost.
But just listen to the magic of its song!

For this democratic crowd, with its tall and small and bowed,
Hums a song of splendid joy and ecstasy
That is heard by every man, every station, every clan –
'Tis the proud, imperious summons of the sea.

You can hear its breakers roar, as they did in days of yore:
None resist it, neither high nor low degree;
They're obedient to the call of this New Year's festival,
To this thousand-throated summons of the sea.

No! there is no referee; there's no need, as you can see;
A thousand men may play, or they may not.
You may push just as you like; well, you mustn't ride a bike,
But there's one thing that must never be forgot:

For in this democratic, acrobatic, half-aquatic
Game of football, with ten rules, or none at all,
You may jettison good sense, and to everything be dense
Except straight play, or then you'll get a fall.

The Vikings, brave and bold, with their helms of burnished gold,
Played this game in days now hidden in the haze;
And our ancient minster brown, overlooking Kirkwall Town,
Agrees that men don't change their little ways.

* * * * * *

Young people are particularly interested in the Ba' and this is exemplified by Jane Skea, aged fifteen, in a delightful poem published in the December 1994/ January 1995 issue of the *Orkney View*:

They gather there at one on the dot
The Uppies and Doonies a gruesome lot
The men are savage around one small ba'
Doonies tae the Basin Uppies tae the Wa

Dependin on whit side o' the Market Cross y
Decides if yur an Uppie or nae
If you're brought up on the left yur down-the-gates
Brought up on the right yur up-the-gates

The Doonies hiv tae reach the Basin
When it's in there's no more chasin
The Uppies hiv tae touch the Wa
To get to either end is the object o' the Ba'

Both sides might meet the night before
To discuss their tactics and make up more
To this game there is no laa
When the Orkney men play the Ba'

If it's a bonnie day hundreds appear to spectate
To support their sides whether it is glory or fate
Great excitement is caused by the Ba'
Whether it's in the Basin or touchin' the Wa

Wives and friends all stand by for sure
Wae a bottle o' whisky as a cure
A dram for both external and internal use
Could be better known as the Ba' juice!

The Ba' takes over Christmas and New Year's Day
Dinners are postponed for this play
Wives and children have to suffer the moans
Of their husbands' and fathers' aching bones

The ba's thrown up there's an almighty roar
It's the beginning of an eight hour fight or more
The men are savage around one small ba'
Doonies tae the Basin Uppies tae the Wa'

The Brutality of the Ba'

The following is by David Horne Senior:[4]

> If you happen to be a stranger to Kirkwall town and wish to take part in the New Year's Day Ba', there are two simple rules to be observed. Firstly, dress yourself up in the oldest and most worthless rags you can muster. Strictly speaking, this rule is quite optional. If you care to don an evening suit and tall hat, nobody will object, least of all your tailor. You may dress in a sack if you like. Nobody cares. Either way will cause no comment today, but would decidedly do so tomorrow. Secondly, take your stand in the middle of Broad Street immediately opposite the Market Cross, a few minutes before one and on the stroke of the hour you will have mastered the rules, science, and spirit of the game. If good luck favours you, you will emerge from the contest a couple of hours later, flushed, enlightened, unrecognisable, and breathless, from which it will be seen that the mysteries of the Ba' are much more easily mastered than the intricacies of the Tango.
>
> Speaking for myself, I am an old and seasoned inhabitant. My candid opinion of the ba' is that it is a silly, brutal degrading spectacle, which ought to be done away with. Why the Authorities permit it is a mystery that can never be cleared up. There is neither science, rules, sport nor anything else in it. None! It's perfectly disgusting.
>
> As I said before, the correct dress to don for it is your oldest, most worthless rags. You will consequently surmise, and you will be right, that seeing I am wearing this new suit and new shoes, I, for one, do not intend making an exhibition of myself. They are flimsy things, but I have put them on in deference to the holiday spirit.
>
> Downright silly it is to see such a crowd of otherwise decent sensible, law-abiding folks gather to watch a contest that would rival a bull fight in sunny Spain. In fact, were it not for the splendid opportunity it gives me of seeing so many of my friends, I should not have stirred a foot from the inglenook this dull winter day.
>
> It wants ten minutes to the hour as we take our stand on the parapet wall opposite the Cross. The waiting crowd, which up till now has been somewhat meagre, grows silently. A couple of minutes to one, and all eyes are turned expectantly to the old gilt dial of St Magnus. We await the last remaining seconds in impatience; but the clock has seen quite a lot, and is in no hurry. A bunch of stalwarts, most of them coatless and hatless,

[4] D. Horne, *Under Orcadian Skies*, p. 19.

gather in the middle of the road. Veterans – 'Uppies' and 'Doonies' – are there. Amid so much talent it would be invidious to mention names. 'Up wi' her!' they cry impatiently, but the enthusiast who holds the ba', as he stands on the old Cross, waits until the hour is tolled solemnly out, and then we see the shining leather sweep through the air, and disappear until the game is over. The stalwarts also vanish, and in their stead a mob of ancient Vikings push and jostle each other as if they were bent on mutual destruction. They surge towards the Old Hall door and stick like burrs around it. A cloud of steam rises from the struggling mass, and grows in volume as the struggle proceeds. After all there is only one rule: Be there at one o'clock. Five hundred men may push on one side, and ten men on the other. Nobody objects. Boys of fourteen stand on the side, and at length venture in; ancients of the city push, feebly, it is true, but with all their might; women – old and young – urge their menfolks on, and are often engulfed in the maelstrom.

The ba' crews up slowly for a few yards, and, in spite of the little brae, the 'Uppies' force their opponents onward towards the south. Fresh men on both sides enter, just for a mere push, and remain for the rest of the game. Suddenly the heart of the thing collapses and melts away into nothing, but in a moment more regains larger proportions than ever. A yelling conglomeration of perspiring humanity – tinkers, tailors, soldiers, sailors, doctors, lawyers – representatives of every grade of our small community almost – lurches dangerously towards the parapet wall. The uninitiated shudder, as well they may, for visions of broken legs and arms, lint and bandages, rise vividly before them, but the audience looks on with complete indifference. They are concerned with the fortunes of the ba.' Marvel of marvels! their splendid optimism is justified – no bones are broken. The players push on, regardless of the fact that they are being squeezed out of shape on the low wall. But stay! Hands and voices are raised: 'Back! back!' rings out over the hubbub. The game halts for a few moments and a limp bundle is dragged out of the mass. He is covered with mud, his clothes are in tatters, and although I quite probably know him in everyday life, I must look twice ere I know him now. His face is lividly purple, his eyes, or what can be seen of them are strained and wild looking. He breathes with effort. In a couple of minutes he is away again as enthusiastic as ever.

But stalwarts there are who are not 'in the ba'.' You can easily recognize them by the look of intense excitement on their faces, and by the fact that they have on their best clothes. Mrs. Stalwart and, it may be, some of the young stalwarts are with them, but flesh and blood has its limits.

As they see quite plainly that their side – whichever it may be – only requires the assistance of, say, half a dozen fresh men, they leave their womenfolks and break away just as they are, and in turn become merged in the struggling mass. Neither age, nor sex, nor rank, nor silk hat, nor white waistcoat, nor swallowtail coat, nor any other thing is able to keep a true Kirkwallian out of the ba' once he thinks his side is in desperate straits. The only way he can keep out of it is either to ascend Wideford Hill or go round the Head of Work while the game is in progress. Strangers even, have been known to take a plunge in the excitement of the moment. But for supreme ecstasy give me the face of an old Kirkwall boy home on holiday as he is swept into the mêlée.

The ba' at last reaches MacGregor's corner, one of the keys to the stuggie lad; Jacky Miller, another 'doonie' leading-light; Davie Logie; successful effort and slowly turn the tide to the gateway of Tankerness House. It seems the ba' will end in the 'Basin' after all! Really it is a thousand pities to see it go like this. Just a few fresh men and the tide can be turned, 'Come on boys!' I cry. 'Just a shove and we'll do it! Up with her, lads! Hurrah!' In spite of all I've said, I'm not the man to see my own side lose for want of a little help (for I'm an 'Uppie'). Some other day the ba' may be pushed into the Harbour and hoisted topmast high by the 'Doonies', but not this day if I can be of any use. And you can't blame me. A lot more follow my example, or I follow theirs, and we manage by heroic work to regain lost ground and get the ba' through into Victoria Street. The railings of the National Bank tremble beneath the strain, but eventually we pass all danger points and land at the old Castle – it used to be Burgar's Bay – whence I emerge breathless, but jubilant. 'Is this your hat?' enquires a friend, holding a lump of mud gingerly between finger and thumb. It may have been anything for aught I can say, but now it resembles nothing with which I am familiar. Never mind! To be hatless is quite the fashion nowadays and, after all, I am merely anticipating summer by a few months. I look at my watch. It is now three o'clock.

Of course, it sometimes happens that an occasional drunk wanders into the fray, but he is soon expelled. In the excitement rows occur, but, as a rule, the police take no notice. The crowd deals with them and should things appear to be getting out of hand, there are men able and willing to quench any small disturbance with crushing effectiveness.

Yes! I'm afraid my clothes are past their first youth, new though they may be, and the less said about my shoes the better. But stop the Ba'! Nonsense! I freely admit there is no science in it – no rules, no skill

– nothing but the primitive joy of 'carefree activity' – yet it is carried through in a very sporting spirit with a few exceptions; and, again, what would New Year's Day in Kirkwall be without it? What about my clothes and my dignity? My dear sir, these considerations are non-existent on New Year's Day. There is no dignity but that of good humour. Talk about the call of the wild! Why, it's not half so powerful as the call of the New Year's Day Ba.' Brutality, indeed!

200 Men's 200 Minute Battle for 38-year-old Ba'
Alie Groundwater Takes 'Her' Home

David Horne Junior (the well-known sports writer 'Cubbie Roo' and son of the David Horne previously mentioned) did a great deal to stimulate and maintain interest in the game after the Second World War. He was present on every occasion, noting names and the most minute details of play. His article on the New Year's Day Ba' 1947 is typical of its kind, and well worth repeating:[5]

> New Year's Day was fine and dry, but in the afternoon a strong wind was blowing. Atmospheric conditions were such that no steam rose from this monster ba'. A large crowd lined Broad Street – reminiscent of pre-war years.
>
> The actual ba' was gifted by Willie Harrison, who won her on New Year's Day 1909. Now she shone like new – for all her thirty-eight years . . . She had been previously proudly displayed in the window of James Turfus (St Olaf's Stores).
>
> Again we 'felt' the silence, when the clock struck one – and Willie Harrison threw her up, to the waiting anxious players – the light of sweet anticipation shining in every eye . . . But Willie slightly miscalculated his throw. The ba' fell short – to roll tantalisingly on the road, towards the Cathedral side of Broad Street. Davie Keldie, amateur weight-lifter and footballer, was first to get hold of her. He kept a grip of her for some time . . . the players closed in. And the fight was on . . .
>
> It was early evident that this was going to be no ordinary ba' – the sides were pretty evenly matched – with slight odds on the 'Uppies'. They had more men and weight, but the slope of Broad Street balanced the scales for the 'Doonies'.
>
> I saw Provost Flett – on Broad Street – looking 'nippy' to keep out of the way of a sudden 'rush' to the Post Office Lane. Our first citizen

[5] *OH*, 7 January 1947.

would fain have liked to have had a go, I thought. Ex-Treasurer Albert Maxwell watched the ba' with dancing eyes too old now for the game. Albert was a good 'doonie' in his day. (This I have on the authority of an old-time ba' player.)

'Peem' Inkster had to be extra careful this afternoon – he was looking after something doubly-precious at this time of year – for a 'doonie' player . . .

TERRIFIC PRESSURE

A few navymen played doon – one wearing a perfect 'Players' Cigarette' beard . . . The ba' started to crawl up street, along the low Cathedral wall – up as far as the Market Cross – then over to the Town Hall door, where she stuck for a full half hour . . . Drum Major Edgar Gibson was prominent for the 'uppies' – dressed this time in battledress, both arms held aloft – directing play . . . Some players were even smoking . . . The pressure in the centre must have been terrific. Johnny Hourston, in his old Home Guard battledress, a grin of enjoyment on his face, was there; and his brother Jim in navy dungarees. Both helped lead the 'uppies' to the Old Castle. The 'doonies' had no one comparable – except 'Pingo' Dave Kemp, senior. 'Pingo' was a dangerous man to the 'uppies'. Most of the Christmas Day stalwarts were out except a few who were 'bedded down for the day' – after Hogmanay . . . Others arrived late on the scene. And boys in their teens even lent a hand . . .

JUST IN TIME

'Tusker' Ross – just home in time – was there and young Davie Fox the footballer; Cecil Simpson – the plumber; Jim Kelday, junior; 'Tucker' Binks; 'Tiny' Leonard; 'Tomo' Leonard; 'Cakki' Flett; Tom Foubister of the Highland Park and young Tom; Bertie Craigie of Warren's Walk; Douglas Wood, the County Clerk, appropriately dressed and doing manfully; Big Robbie Robertson, directing operations from outside and occasionally adding his weight; Jimmie Harrison, son of the ba' donor; the one and only Bill Annal, who took a hefty clout on the mouth in Broad Street and didn't even stop talking; young Jock Robertson; Jim Flett of 47 Victoria Street; 'Tara' Shearer; Jim Laughton, the dealer; 'Alie' Findlater, yachtsman; Jock Price; tough Bill Sinclair o' Smerquoy; Steve Twatt fae Lingro; Ronnie Park, specially in from his farm in South Ronaldsay; old Arthur Robson from the Highland Park; 'Fluker' Bews; 'Fatty' Linklater, who played hard and well; 'Dooie' Craigie; Ian Cooper;

'Rastas' Johnstone; 'Chuffie' Muir; John Donaldson, who never even lost the shade in his hair; 'Ginger' Cromarty; Davie Keldie; Freddy Grieve; Big Jacky Watson; Dod Donaldson, who got his breeks torn and sent for a new pair; Billy Jolly, junior; John Craigie, the docker; 'Tucker' Miller, who lost a shoe and thought he'd lose his pants; Davie Marwick of the Post Office, dressed for the game, a hardy veteran; Andy Wilson; Bob Kelday; 'Haco' Muir; young Alex. MacEwan of the Sea Cadets; Big Harcus off the *Sigurd*; 'Patsy' Callighan – he nearly lost his flannels; Young Charlie Smith, a chip off the old block; Ian MacKay; 'Bricky' Bews; 'Tamo' Wylie, who specialised in a right hook; Tommy Hourston, younger brother of John and Jim, still wearing his prairie cap; 'Doodles' Crisp and young 'Doodles'; Arthur Borwick o' Tafts; Ernie Scollay, who tore two leaders in his ankle; 'Gussie' Harcus, the man who started out with a clean white sark and finished with a 'sweat-rag' round his neck, the tan of Burma and India still on him; 'Chooker' Bews; Ian Fraser, the electrician, who played like a hero; Bill Muir; 'Alie' Groundwater, who did a day's work before ever he went in the ba'; David Bews (Tia); 'Sleepy' Harcus, minus his watch this time; Freddy Cooper; 'Geesh'; Bobby Sinclair; Steven Brodie o' Sunnybank; Tommy Brough, a tower of strength to the 'doonies'; Sandy Brodie o' Sunnybank; 'Polo' Shearer; Verdun Harcus, a stuggie lad; Jacky Miller, another 'doonie' leading-light; Davie Logie; Sidney Cooper, home on leave.

RORIE QUINTET

The five Rorie boys were there – Gordon, Albert, Theo, George William and Bill (with a cracked rib), and 'Dano' Grieve, a rugged lad; Big-Drummer Langskaill, hoping the ba' would go doon; Young Johnny Walls, slightly late; Jim 'Duck' Wylie and Andy 'Duck' Wylie; Alex. Webster; 'Dump' Linklater, with three bruised ribs from Christmas Day; his elder brother Harald; Geordie Borwick; Young Muir of the Hotspurs; 'Dooda' Mowat; 'Juice' Ross; 'Thug' Kelday; Jackay Monkman and Jim Monkman; John Cutt; 'Willick' Schollay, a never-say-die trier; Rognvald Keldie; Thorfinn Keldie, the footballer; Andrew Thomson; Douglas Thomson, a gymnast; Gordon Sandison of the Salvation Army; 'Waltie' Scott, a dour fighter; 'Pip' Philips from the Air Ministry, feeling 'breeksed' by now I'll warrant; young 'Pingo' Kemp; Jim Miller, Post Office; 'Beefy' Johnston, son of 'Big Dano'; Charlie Fraser, the goalkeeper and swimmer; young Robert Muir from the Ayre Mills; 'Titta' Marwick, ex-P.O.W.; John Sinclair, joiner; 'Buster' Bews; MacLean the weaver; Alan Rosie; Pat

Thomson from South Africa; Alan Borwick; 'Sonny' Yule; young Jacko Flett, the farmer; Gordon MacGillivray; Charlie Thomson, ex-P.O.W.; 'Pottie' Pottinger; Sid Watson; Bill Stanger; Scotty Harcus of Glaitness; 'Moosie' Sutherland; Jim Thomson, the printer from Stromness; Peter Leslie, ex-P.O.W.; Watty Lobban; Geordie Cook; Harry Peace; Jim Mackenzie; 'Cheemo' Cooper; Davy Walls; 'Swick' Swanney and his father Jake; Jacky Herdman; Malcolm Heddle, without his specs; Bob Johnstone, the plumber; 'Horrie' Thomson; George Currie; 'Nipper' Sinclair, wishing he were younger; 'Pulp' MacGillivray (he'll very likely set-up this report); Davie 'Flash' Walker; Big Bill Bews, the docker – a burly lad; Paterson, the Hotspurs' goalie; 'Square' Andrew Sinclair and twin-brother Geordo; Gordon Lennie; Bryce Swanney; Cecil Walls, the lawyer; Douglas Tait; Staff-Sergeant 'Texas' McColm, who certainly never saw anything like this in Chicago; 'Nobby' Clark, a doughty 'uppie'; veteran Bill Costie, who did his bit; Dougal Stout; Davie Fox, senior; young Gordon Newlands, Boys' Brigade big drummer, only fifteen, yet sticking it out in the middle till the end; 'Pluto' Shearer; Gillie Hercus, in dungarees, minus his cheroot; 'Tullie' Tulloch, still wondering who stood on his ankle, 'Heppy' Sinclair; 'Roostie' Shearer, one of the best; Jacky Scott; 'Toddo' Borwick; Billy Brown, the boxer from Dounby; 'Jocky' Bews . . . And there were many more.

DING-DONG STRUGGLE

Slowly the ba' edged upstreet to slip as far back again. A rush to the middle of the road. Two men detached themselves and streaked doon the street like hares – 'Dano' Grieve and Jacky Watson. They got as far through the stunned onlookers as Pat Gorie's grocer shop. Young Jim Kelday of 47 Victoria Street dashed after them, bringing 'Dan' to the ground. Jim got a cut lip for his pains. And the game began all over again – up to the Market Cross – across the street to the Town Hall. Once more up to J. & W. Tait's. Slowly she crawled to Tankerness House. 'Fatty' Linklater smuggled her into the cellar. And the bulk of the players lost the ba.' But 'Fatty' couldn't get her away. Down Bain the painter's close she went. Everybody rested for a while. Out again, back and fore, up, down and across the street. Then on to the road at the bottom of Palace Road. Here Linklater made a determined sprint down the street, but he was 'downed' by Davie Horne. Veteran 'uppie' Bill Costie and young Jock Robertson got the ba' away. Again we were 'As You Were.'

OFF BROAD STREET AT LAST

It was now after three o'clock. The 'uppies', with a tremendous effort, every man available lending a hand – Police an' all – got the ba', despite the stubborn 'doonies' to the top of Tankerness Lane. Jacky Scott, got her out, kicking her down the lane. 'Dano' Grieve, Jacky Miller, Alex. Webster, Willick Schollay took turns to keep her going. Players with tired feet and punished bodies with laboured running chased the ba' across the Back Road, past Leslie the millwright's up Great Western Road. Ian Fraser outdistanced the field, kicking the ba' in front of him. Then he picked her up, running until he could run no further. So he threw her ahead where she rolled forlornly on the triangular piece of waste ground where Great Western Road meets 'The Road to Lord Knows Where.' Bryce Swanney then got hold of her and threw her back on the road – but not quite far enough for the 'uppies.' Big Bill Langskaill grabbed her.

With 'into the sea wi' her boys' Bill bunged the ba' into the Peedie Sea. Sandy Brodie, 'Dump' Linklater, Sidney Cooper, Jacky Scott, Ernie Schollay, a sodger and some others, went into Kirkwall's own pleasure lake to be (?) the stink unheeding. Eventually Sandy Brodie, that dogged 'uppie', retrieved the ba' and threw her on dry land again. But 'Thug' Keldie, rubber boots and all, snaffled her. He ran, rugby fashion, doon the way. Making some progress, he soon saw it was hopeless, so threw her up again where she brought up opposite what used to be 'Maggie' Gunn's house – now the home of Orkney Builders Ltd. (Alfie MacKay). Tireless 'Alie' Groundwater pounced on her. And the strife began all over again.

DOONIES STILL DOGGED

It was getting dark and the 'doonies' would still not give in. The 'uppies' watching every opening for a 'doonie' smuggle, moved the ba' up Great Western Road towards the corner. It seemed as if she would go into Corse's field at the slaughterhouse. Now she went faster, pulled as well as pushed, past the slaughterhouse up by the Crafty. A scrap nearly materialised hereabouts, but the parties concerned were quickly and quietly collared – and that was that. Would that the United Nations could settle their disputes likewise?

Along the Crafty wall – nearly over it ('Dano' Grieve again), but she's safely past the opening now – across the road as far as the bottom of Union Street. She MUST go up now – no matter wha' wins her – she MUST GO UP! And up at last she goes. Was there ever a ba' which

> stayed on Broad Street for two and a half hours, yet ended at the Old Castle? There's nothing much wrong with the 'guts' of Kirkwall's young men of today.
>
> WHA'LL GET HER?
>
> 'Wha'll get her', Davie Logie, old-time ba' player got on top of the Old Castle Wall, but 'Alie' Groundwater was the man in possession. Possession is nine-tenths of the law (and of the ba'). 'Alie' was lifted, ba' (which was by now slightly damaged) and all. He held the ba' aloft for all to see, amid prolonged cheering, proud forty-two year old winner of the 1947 Men's New Year Ba'.
>
> Last week I asked some pertinent questions regarding the ba'. They have been well and truly answered. The Spirit of the Vikings still lives. This game of guts and backbone goes on. The ba' will never die!
>
> Some of the men who held the ba' for a time were – Dave Fox, jnr, 'Chuffie' Muir, Ian Fraser, Ernie Scollay, Verdun Harcus, John Donaldson, Cecil Simpson, 'Fatty' Linklater, 'Dano' Grieve, 'Alie' Groundwater, 'Ginger' Cromarty, Davie Keldie, Tom Brough, and Freddy Grieve.
>
> A certain old-timer, who has seen every ba' for the last sixty years, was of the opinion that this New Year's Men's game was the toughest he had ever seen.

Another wonderfully descriptive report by David Horne was of the Christmas Day Men's Ba' 1948 contained in the *Orkney Herald* of 28 December. At 1.30 p.m. in brilliant December sunshine the ba' was at the Big Tree when in David's own words 'today the ba' has the smell of salt water':

> Uppie 'Titto' Linklater, coalman, strives to stem the tide. More faces – Andrew Thomson, 'Tiny' Leonard, plumber; Ian Smith, coalman; young 'Banffie' George Ritchie; Alan Wylie; Dougie Campbell.
>
> She's at MacDonald's the butchers, and is getting 'coorser.' Many more doonies who had not intended to take part, here lend their weight.
>
> Five minutes more and she's at Morgan's the jeweller's and then bounds across to Boots, the chemists' (Wright's). A B.E.A. 'plane flies low overhead to get a good view. Several players fall, but are quickly pulled to their feet by willing hands.
>
> There is no 'smuggling' – no lightning 'break-aways'.
>
> She reaches the Atholl Café railings and we notice with forebodings that Davie does not have his windows very strongly barricaded.

Sutherland Taylor's son Sid is there; Bobbo Sinclair from the Cheese Factory; Peter Johnstone; young Arnold Russell from Cannigall who was in the boys' ba'; big Hercus, the Edayman off the 'Sigurd'; old ba' player Peter Hercus, wistfully looking on; Jeemie Maxwell, who spent some years 'down-under.'

She stops with a bump at the Albert Kinema. I run upstairs to lean out of Dougie Shearer's window for a bird's eye view.

Old doonie stalwart Bill Lennie is a keen onlooker. Dennis Linklater of Bill Reid's is in the thick of her; big 'Danno' Johnstone fain would have a go; Russell Croy, of the Rovers, sticks in with the best of them; Jim 'Pluto' Shearer; 'Pym' Sinclair; George Robinson from Aim's Buildings.

A rumour goes round that she's been pushed through one of the Albert Kinema's windows – but it's only a ruse.

Jacky Crisp, docker, is playing today, and Davie Wylie; Billy Peace of Picky; young Pat Baikie and Alan Rosie the linesman.

Two o'clock. Back to the Atholl Café. There is little pressure in the middle, however, for all her size. Down to the Dundee Equitable.

Then Jimmy Monkman breaks clear and runs off with her down-street – doubling on his tracks, but he's caught and she's back at the Dundee.

Sammy Bews, policeman, off-duty, is pushing down. Up she goes a bit again.

Our forecast is correct. A window of the Atholl Café goes in with a tinkle of falling glass and a player hands out a plate of fancies to the crowd. Soon home-bakes are being handed out indiscriminately, a wag remarking, 'Shae disna waant tae go bye the Atholl. Davie's fancies are too good.'

Over to the Picture House again. Here footballer John Donaldson gets her away but the street is too packed to go far. More kent faces are seen. David Bews, apprentice joiner; Gordon Muir of the Auction Mart; Alex Wilson of the Power Station; Bob Gunn, docker, and John Sinclair, joiner.

Steam rises. Back to the Atholl. Over to J. & J. Smith's – oldest draper shop in Kirkwall.

Jim Miller of the Post Office helps at the edges. 'Blurt' Rosie is there and young 'Juker' Bews; 'Bobbo'Thomson and young Bob Gunn.

Policeman Sammy Bews lifts out splinters of glass from the broken window. The cold wind makes the spectators shiver.

More tinkling of glass. Another café window is broken. The time is 2.20 p.m. Up she goes again to Wright's. Jocky Sinclair gets the soles and heels torn right off his shoes. The shrill cries of the bairns, 'Come on the uppies' and 'Doon wi' her, doonies' never let up.

Jim Bews, the Shapinsay footballer, pushes doon; Bob Muir is there and Dougie Leslie; Fred Johnstone; Gordon Cooper, the milkman, still wearing his cap; Ian Fraser, redoubtable young uppie; George Louttit, docker, trombone player and lover of 'swing'; 'Tullie' Tullock, Ford's Orkney agent; schoolboy David Tinch; Bill Rorie.

She's back at J. & J. Smith's.

Here Alan Rosie is lifted bodily over the heads of the uppies. Up to the café again; across to Wright's. Up to Morgan's in short, quick rushes.

More players are discerned. Arthur Borwick of Tafts; Tom Foubister of Croy's Garage; Billy Barnett; Ian Swanney.

A man from Banffshire, who has been playing up valiantly, thinks the game terrific but that the folk south should be told more about it. 'Rugby is nothing to this,' he says.

It is a quarter to three.

Three Hatston soldiers in their best rig enter the game and play down. Over to the Kinema and 'Pingo' senior nearly works the oracle. Up the close between the café and Groundwater's shop. Someone loses an iron heel. Listen again to the 'song of the ba'.'

Further up Groundwater's close for a rest. 'Ginger' Wylie from Burgher's Bay – still with only half-a-shirt – does his stuff; an Edinburgh girl student excitedly cries, 'Up wi' her, uppies.' Another uppie girl supporter remarks, 'My I wid love to gae a push.' And in she goes and puts her wish into action.

Big Bob Craigie the policeman is caught in a doonie rush and momentarily loses his hat – but enjoys the fun.

She's down at Leith's the butchers. Enters the opening between Davie Nicolson's and Flett's Home Bakery. A welcome rest for a breather and smoke.

Johnny Walls, his throat parched, says to Davie Nicolson (through the window), 'Gae's a drink o' watter min.' Which was the best joke of the day.

Out with a rush to Hourston's the jeweller's; across to the bakery; down the 'Orkney Herald' Lane a bit; along to Drever & Heddle's. Time 3.10 p.m. Over to Turfus's; back to Drever & Heddle's; some bairns are on the wall there and are hanging on to the railings.

A high-pitched wail and they disappear as part of the railings fall into the courtyard, but nobody is hurt. More for the Council to put right.

Moving down, she turns into 'Porky Horne's Lane' and sticks for a minute. As she passes the bacon-curer's, Sgt. Vickers (Hatston) – who had been all dolled up in his kilt but who wanted to 'have a go' and borrowed a pair o' breeks – shouts, 'A pound of ham.'

Past the Albert Hotel, through the narrow lane at the back. She stops – and the third window-pane goes. A yell, 'She's in the hotel.'

The game breaks up. Folk run here, there and everywhere. Nobody knows where the ba' is. Too bad for the doonies if she should go up after all.

Gerald Eccles runs up the Back Road, shouting 'She's awey upstreet. Doodles Crisp has her.' But the doonies are not to be deceived. I enter the hotel to find out where she is. 'She wis here but she's no' here noo.' A couple of doonies also enter but can't find her. We come out. The ba' is raging as fiercely as ever at 'Long' John Miller's show-room window.

'Doodles' – I find out later – went in through the broken window shoulder first, after having thrown in the ba' first. Jocky Sinclair caught hold of his feet as he lay over the sill.

Then he let go and the last he saw was 'Doodles' wrestling with Tom Brough on a bed for possession of the ba'.

Edwin Work, the ironmonger, is in her; and Jim Kelday, former butcher, now G.P.O. linesman; Jim Duncan, postman; young Billy Grant from the Ayre Mills; Dod Donaldson, the butcher, and eldest son George, the swimmer; John Flett of P. C. Flett & Co.; Billy Cooper, the baker; Billy Wilson; Leslie Leonard; and many, many more, the names of whom have slipped my memory.

Time 3.40 p.m. It is getting dark but still the uppies will not give in. But the writing is on the wall and the ba' will soon be in the water. And not a single uppie will grudge the doonies their win.

Long John Miller is caught here but likes it and decides to stay where he is. She makes for the Basin. A rush round the Kiln Corner at breakneck speed – towards the iron railings at the harbour. I jump aboard a fishing boat tied up at the West Pier. The tide – fortunately – is out and there is only a few feet of water.

Down the small slipway from the head of the West Pier she goes with a rumble of tired feet. The players can't stop in time. They waver on the edge of the slipway and there is a hush as first one, and then another, tumbles or is pushed into the sea until, with a mighty splashing of water and spumes of spray, there are close on twenty bobbing up and down in the icy-cold Basin, the ba' somewhere in their midst.

Tom Brough has her but Danno Grieve wants 'Tucker' Miller to get her. There is some squabbling. She is thrown up the slipway to be caught and handed to the happy 'Tucker,' who is at once shouldered high up the slip to the harbour Front. The score or so droukled players squelsh and chirp their way home, leaving a trail of salt-water behind them, and the rest of the players and spectators go home, too, to waiting dinners – the lucky few to hot baths. And none of the men who took a dip will even get a cold, far less catch pneumonia. They're tough, mighty tough in Orkney.

The time is ten minutes to four o'clock. The 1948 Christmas Day Men's Ba' is over.

FIG. 87: Gouache painting by Gordon Henry.

13

As Others See Us

Early Reporting outside Orkney

Some early reports from the nearby *John O' Groats Journal* are given in Chapter 14, 'Early Records of the Kirkwall Ba''. By the 1880s word of the Ba' had spread as far as England, presumably via trawlermen. The *Hull Eastern Morning News* of 4 January 1882 reported: 'At Kirkwall, Orkney, the great event was a football match played in the street . . . Merchants, doctors, bankers, magistrates, town councillors and tradesmen were all engaged, either as skips or players.'

The *Pictorial World* delivered itself of a quaint article in January 1883 averring that on New Year's Eve the contesting sides were selected in a church – presumably the cathedral:

> The New Year's Day Ball – old customs survive among primitive peoples. For centuries past the inhabitants of Kirkwall, capital of the Orkney Islands, have been in the habit of meeting in the church on the eve of the New Year, and then and there arranging the sides for a football match on the following morning. This year was no exception to the rule. The male population of the town met at the Market Cross and dividing themselves into two parties (sides), began a general and active football match. Those living above the church strove to get the ball into their own district, while those residing below it did their best to drive it into the sea. The above-church players were, I believe, successful, all the women and girls the boys and the children witnessing the melee.

Confusion Down Under

Harry Clouston, a New Zealander of Orcadian extraction who was hiking round the world, played in the Men's Ba' on New Year's Day 1933. At the conclusion of the game several spectators declared that the ba' should be awarded to him (see

FIG. 88: A cartoon of the Ba' featured in the 1987 Orkney View calendar. It was created by Harald Nicolson.

Ch. 10). In 1937 he published a book, *The Happy Hobo*, which revealed that such an accolade would have been misplaced. Having been recruited by the Up-the-Gates he had not appreciated that each side played towards its own goal:

> This much I knew, that as a staunch supporter of the Uppies it was my duty to help throw the ball into the docks at the bottom of the town, the territory of the Doonies, and to prevent the Doonies from carrying the ball into a field at our, the upper end of town. It seemed simple enough ... two hours after the start of the play we had, at the expense of great effort and some of our clothing, propelled the ball to the side of the docks. Our opponents put up an admirable last stand. I should have done the same in their position, because in front of them the Uppies, like the heathen, raged furiously, while behind them was the chilly water of the docks. The cheers that rang out when eventually we tossed the ball over the pier, and with it many of the Doonies, must have echoed all through Kirkwall.

The Down-the-Gates had no idea that they had a staunch Uppie playing in their ranks!

FIG. 89: The late R. T. Johnston (Spike) was a popular local cartoonist whose humorous look at life was featured in the *Orkney Herald*.

Exile's Christmas Card Message

Our traditional street game is an enthusiasm that is understood and appreciated by Orcadians everywhere. Most people in Kirkwall and many who live in surrounding districts are true believers. Expatriates return to play and to watch, while exiles avidly follow the fortunes of the game, their interest undiminished by distance.

At the festive season the Ba' is never far from the thoughts of Orcadians. Even when abroad Orcadians maintain an avid interest. On New Year's Day 1946 in North Africa, two Seaforth Highlanders, Johnnie Walls and George Currie, sat under a cloudless sky in bright sunshine having a convivial dram. Johnnie turned to George and with fine humour said 'Min, hid's a fine day fur the Ba'.' Draining his glass George replied, 'Buey, hid shur is that'.

At Ba' time numerous telephone calls and letters examine and widely transmit incidents and results, and there is some communication and viewing via the Internet. For many folk in Orkney and far beyond there is an ongoing chemistry between the Ba' and its adherents that never fails to quicken the pulse.

The following tongue-in-cheek message was composed by Bill Wilson, a stalwart Doonie for many years and winner of the Men's Ba' on New Year's Day 1961:

Me Freends I hope this Yuiletide season
Thoo've sherly reached the age o' reason,
And at thee fireside gether roon,
Instead o' trampan doon the toon.
Tae get involved wae a' the rabble
And efter cork and hide tae scrabble,
And gettan keeked and maybe bit
Displays an awful lack o' wit!
My friend, the quiet simple pleasures,
The peaceful day at home one treasures,
The cosy seat before the fire,
To better this one can't aspire,
A Happy Ne'er Day Fae A Liar!

Orkney Holds Savage New Year Rite: Mass Mayhem Called Ba' Rages Four Hours in Streets

This was the headline for an article on 2 January 1970 by Fernand Auberjonois, European correspondent for the *Blade* newspaper, Toledo, Ohio.

He produced a lively report:

> Once thrown, the ba' seemed to disappear into the swirling, pushing, steaming, kicking, groaning mass of humanity and was seldom seen again unless one of the players, assisted by supernatural beings, extricated himself and ran . . . For most of the play, however, the male population of Kirkwall is knitted into a giant knot. They say that in the eye of the storm, the fighting is merciless . . . As the swarm of contestants inched its way along the walls and the boarded-up windows, exhausted men collapsed under a sign reading 'Season's Greetings.' One test of sheer stamina took place in a recess outside the gents' conveniences. It followed a brilliant 'smuggle' by a short, bald man, one Mr Findlay, who carried the ba' down narrow alleys and across several high walls separating half a dozen gardens soon trampled by the shouting crowd of pursuers . . . All the while, sympathizers, relatives and onlookers stood by ready to comfort the wounded with a dram of local brew strong enough for both external and internal use.

The View from Stromness[1]

Even Stromnessians such as George Mackay Brown have appreciated that Kirkwallians are called to a unique tradition:

> I usually think, sometime during the course of January the first, about the strength and endurance of the men of Kirkwall. One assumes that, like the men of Stromness, and every other town in Scotland, they have brought in the New Year with revelry, and carried on with the first-footing till 4 or 5 or 6 in the morning.
>
> For all the other townsmen in Scotland the rest of the day is spent in sleep and heavy eating and a kind of muted visiting and welcoming. Not for the men of Kirkwall. Under the Market Cross 'the Ba'' is thrown up and Uppies and Doonies, Earl's men and Bishop's men, meet in a furious onset. Compared with it, rugby is as correct and mannered as croquet. I have, only once, seen the pall of steam hanging over the motionless scrum at the top of Tankerness Lane. How, the men of other towns must ask themselves, can the Kirkwallians do it, on the day after Hogmanay? What fire in them – what iron – compared to other men? If it was all over in an hour, the heroism would still be there – but I read that the 1976 Ba' went on for eight punishing hours! Supposing the ba' goes 'doon,' there is

[1] *O*, 5 February 1976.

FIG. 90: Christmas Day 2002. Dr Tim Wright captures the atmosphere.

an extra element of bravado, for the sweating steaming weary (probably hungover) players plunge into the winter waters of the harbour.

As a Stromnessian, born under Brinkie's Brae, I forget ancient rivalry for two days a year and waft a tribute over the Orphir Hills to those brave warriors.

Freud, English Soccer and the Ba'

The following is extracted from an article by Andrew Anthony in the *Weekend Guardian*, 23–24 December 1989.

> The game, well more a free-for-all actually, dates back to the middle ages when the men-folk played out something of a fertility rite at weddings. What Freud would have seen as a primordial quest for sexual identity has now evolved into a traditional festive event between the Uppies and Doonies . . . it's probably no more dangerous than your average Arsenal-Norwich match. For those who join the fray there is the opportunity to indulge in Machiavellian tactics (like hiding the ba'), rich skills and camaraderie. And there is the chance of winning the supreme accolade – individual winner of the Ba' game and the award of the ba' itself – a sort of Man of the Match award minus the champagne . . . Be warned, though, it can take anything up to eight hours before a goal is scored – again, not unlike live televised soccer.

Better than the Old Firm

From an article by Ron Ferguson in *The Herald*, 2 January 1998.

> Who is going to win this time? It is looking like the Doonies, winners for the past six years. Then comes an amazing stroke of fortune, which will be talked about for years to come.
>
> Local insurance man Kevin Hancock, who is not playing this year because of injury, is amazed to see the coveted ball bouncing out of the scrum, along the street towards him. He can resist everything except temptation. Does this personable Orcadian know that he is acting out the ancient Sea Mither myth? Does he realise that he is about to pick up a severed Viking head? Irresistible ancient history beckons him as he races through the winding Kirkwall streets, until he reaches the gable end, five hours after the start of the game. The Uppies have won! The wild celebrations can begin.
>
> Old firm, eat your heart out. This is more thrilling than the prejudice-riven events at Parkhead today.

A Spy in the Uppie Camp

From an article by Raymond Travers in *Scotland on Sunday*, 4 January 1998. The author arrived in Kirkwall on 31 December.

> By early evening, I had stumbled upon the Uppies' traditional pre-match team talk in the West End Hotel. There was a hushed silence as one of the heid-bummers called the troops to attention for some tactical analysis. 'Look', he implored, 'Ah don't want tae see any of ye sneakin' aff fur a dram or talkin' tae your burd durin' the game. An' if yer gony huv a fag, huv it in a place ye can still dae some damage, ken.'
>
> This counsel was easy enough to comprehend, but what followed had me quite flummoxed. There were esoteric references to 'dummies' and 'smuggles' and 'zig-zags' coursing around the room. Suddenly, I realised that this game was more than just a lumpen free-for-all.
>
> I was then collared in the bog by four strapping Uppies who enquired, jokingly (I hope), if I was a spy for the Doonies. In the interest of unbiased reporting, I played the neutrality card. 'Nah, I'm an Inbetweenie, mate.' After an hour of briefing and bonding, 50-odd Uppies downed their swally, and repaired home for an early night. Their abstinence was impressive, being Hogmanay.

FIG. 91: Elsie Lennox, a well known illustrator of children's books, produced this cartoon to accompany an article on the Ba' which appeared in the *Nursing Times* in December 1983.

After watching a dramatic four hour game the next day, the author concluded 'you can shove your rulebook where the sun don't shine, Farry, because fitba's coming home.'

Media Interest

In his annual article in *The Orcadian* on 17 December 1998 Bobby Leslie wrote:

> the Ba' continues to generate an interest outside Orkney with numerous requests from newspapers, magazines and tourist organisations. This year contact has come from British Airways' *High Life* and *The Field* magazines, *The Times* and *The Independent*, all wanting various details on the Ba'. *Camping and Caravanning* hoped to include an item in the December edition while a Polish travel magazine *Voyager* made contact for an article on the game. A more interesting letter received by John Robertson was from the Automobile Association asking if there was a requirement for signs to be erected directing people to the Ba'.

FIG. 92: The Doonies v. the Croonies on New Year's Day *c.*1810, by Alexander Carse.

Don't Try This One

From an article in *Outside* magazine, March 2001, by Christopher McDougall, who visited Orkney to experience the Ba' for himself.

After the throw-up, he says:

> I'd planned to play modestly, but now that the prize is within reach, I start toying with a notion that popped into my head after the Fletts' [his hosts] second whisky: *I could win this thing.* Who better to pull off a smuggle? Hardly anyone knows if I'm an Uppie or a Doonie . . . It just takes a few seconds to kill this fantasy. The scrabbling becomes ferocious as the pack presses tight, then still tighter round the spot where the ba' disappeared. Layer after layer of Orcadian is piling on behind me. My legs are twisting beneath me, my feet searching desperately for even ground among the shifting boots and tumbled bodies. Each time the crowd surges, I'm

> completely off my feet, the pressure of the pack keeping me aloft . . . Suffocating, I crane my head above the crowd, gasping for air but taking in only steaming sweat and fumes of scotch. My ribs are being crushed, my arms trapped. One leg is vised behind me. A single phrase starts beating through my mind: 'Not my fight . . . Not my fight . . .' With the next shift I squirm free, hauling myself from the mess to join the bystanders, my head spinning.

The Ba' goes East

From *The Orcadian*, 11 January 2001:

> Professor Norihisa Yoshida has visited Orkney three times to study the Ba', as part of his thesis on street ball games in Britain. He said 'I think the Kirkwall Ba' game should be introduced to the Japanese as a surviving folk football in Britain. In addition, as the World Cup soccer festival will be held in Japan in 2002, I want to introduce your game to the Japanese as a game of the origin of football . . . we have to receive it as the opportunity of understanding more about the culture of football.'

In a subsequent article for *The Goal* magazine, published in Japan for the 2002 World Cup, Professor Yoshida gives a full description of the Ba' game. This short extract suggests that he was impressed by what he saw:

> I saw a ball thrown into the game, more than 100 people milled around in the main streets and lanes, then there was a goal. Every player has a vapour from their body from the cold weather. There were many (more) moments of excitement, and power than I expected.

Part III

History of the Ba'

14

Early Records of the Kirkwall Ba'

The Ba' was considered old in 1863, and on 6 January of that year the *Orkney Herald* said, 'the game . . . is of very old standing'. In the *Herald* 6 January 1883 we find: 'The New Year's Day Ba' has been an institution for centuries in our ancient burgh.' In 1914 George MacGregor wrote: 'The origin of the above annual event began, it is supposed, as far back as two centuries ago.' I am afraid these statements are not substantiated by the facts, which suggest that the Ba' did not exist in anything like its present form much before 1800.

In 'Mass Football Playing in Orkney' (Ch. 16) I will show how football was established in Orkney by the 1650s. It seems highly probable that it had been introduced some time before then from the mainland of Scotland, having spread to Scotland from France, either direct or via England. Hossack tells us that in the mid-seventeenth century in Kirkwall, men and boys played football on the Ba' Lea, which then stretched from the foot of Dundas Crescent to Warrenfield. However, by the last decade or two of the eighteenth century the game was played on the Kirk Green. Indeed, a 'spat at the ba'' on the Green in front of the cathedral was an integral part of every holiday. Although all who wished took part, and the sides were Up-the-Gates and Down-the-Gates, there does not seem to have been any attempt to take the ba' to goals. This was basically still the old type football, which we know had been played in the county since at least 1659 (Burrik, South Ronaldshay) and which had been so popular in Scotland by the early part of the fifteenth century.

No pre-nineteenth century account of Kirkwall mentions the street game. There is a faint memory of a great 'bruilzie' which allegedly occurred in the 1780s. Probably this did not take place (if at all) before 1800, and it is rumoured that 'the still struggling but exhausted players staggered down past what is now St Catherine's Place at 8 o'clock at night, taking the ball along with them.'[1]

[1] *OH*, 4 January 1922.

The evolution of the game to one of competitive street football, with goals but without lifting of the ba', occurred around 1800 or perhaps a few years earlier. This style of fast open play with the accent on mobility, and the ba' mostly kept on the ground, continued until the 1820s.

A colourful incident is said to have occurred after the New Year's Day game 1810. At that time a number of soldiers were quartered in Kirkwall, and playing as Down-the-Gates had contributed substantially in forcing the ba' to the harbour. When the game was over a blacksmith whose smithy was in Main Street challenged the soldiers to take the ba' to the Head of the Town. The challenge was accepted, the soldiers formed into marching order, and with drums beating made their way up through the town carrying the ba'. They met no opposition until Main Street was reached. At this point 'an ambuscade, prepared by the blacksmith, awaited them on their approach to the smithy. In the establishment were some half-dozen brawny sons of Vulcan, and as the soldiers approached, three of these rushed out, each armed with a long bar of iron, red-hot at the one end. These they swung round their heads like an ordinary stick, poked them into the faces of the soldiers, sent them through the heads of the drums, and speedily created a panic amongst the sons of Mars, who were unaccustomed to this sort of warfare. By the time the rods carried by the first three were losing their heat, a like number of men and weapons were ready to take their place. In this way the soldiers were thoroughly routed, and the gallant knights of the red-hot iron had many a good crow over their victory.'[2]

Though there is no written record of the very early games, in 1894 old men could recollect struggles that took place in their younger days. They could also recall stories recounted to them when they were young, and relating to contests in an earlier era.[3] One reminiscence was of a game fought out in the Peedie Sea at high water, the scrum having surged down Broad Street to the beach over which Junction Road now passes.

Another memory was of the Ba' going Down, erupting out of Bridge Street, there being only a small jetty there then, of the crowd falling into the sea and of some people nearly drowning. Visiting Orkney in July 1804, Patrick Neill remarked that although Kirkwall was a place of considerable trade there was no quay at the harbour. 'No, not so much as a little pier at which a boat may land! Passengers from the adjacent islands must either leap into the sea, or be carried ashore on men's shoulders!'[4] It was 1811 before Kirkwall had its first pier – directly opposite the end of Bridge Street – so this game must have taken place between these dates.

[2] *OH*, 6 January 1880.
[3] *OH*, 3 January 1894.
[4] P. Neill, *A Tour through some of the Islands of Orkney and Shetland*. Edinburgh, 1806.

Yet another recollection was how more than once the scene of the struggle was the Long Gutter, which ran along the east side of Broad Street. This would have been prior to 1820.

The first written record of the Ba' is in a letter dated 18 January 1830 from his parents to Henry Leask, residing care of Mr John Reid, at Church Court, facing Gun Dock, Wapping, London: 'their is bein a Great struggle about the foot Ball this year on the Broad Street – nearly four hours – at last carried up-street.'[5] A very early newspaper report comes from the *John O'Groats Journal* of 24 January 1840, which contains a letter dated 14 January from Kirkwall: 'Yesterday was held as old-new-year's day. Men, women and children, turned out to a man, to witness or assist at playing the foot-ball. The "down the gets" won the day after a short struggle. The shops were all shut after one A.M. and the people were on the whole very orderly and sober.' At that time the Ba' was played on 13 January which was New Year's Day according to the Julian calendar. The Old Style persisted in the islands long after the Gregorian calendar had been adopted in Great Britain in 1752.

The *Groat's* Kirkwall letter of 14 January 1845 stated 'Monday was observed as a holiday here' and mentioned that the Ba' contest was 'short but keen'. A letter dated February 1845 from Thomas Campbell, Kirkwall, to David Scott, originally from Sanday but then living near Haddington, said 'I am happy to inform you that the bal went down the Street on new years day. She was not on the broad Street above ten minuts when She was played up the Straind and went in to the Street at Mr Robertsons and then went down to the harbour and was put up to the top of the Brendo and you may consider the Steat of the up Streets as they thought She would never go down again but the down Street players Stood very trusty and determined.' Prior to this the Down-the-Gates had experienced a long run of defeats and their win was unexpected.

When considering the mode of play it is important to remember that up to 1840 or so the game was basically one of street football, and consisted of fast open play. Writing in *The Orcadian*, 7 January 1889, in one of a series of delightful articles entitled 'In the old arm chair', 'Granpa', referring to a period of Up-the-Gate ascendancy in the 1840s and earlier, said that James Mowat and Peter Wick were the great Up-street champions, and the former could *kick* the ba' the whole length of Broad Street. 'Granpa' also stated that in those days no one dared to put their hands on the ba', and that the game was really one of football. He considered that at the time of writing the game had 'degenerated into a rush, push, tumble, smack-your-neighbour, go-as-you-please free-fight, and brute force generally wins.'

[5] Orkney Archives, D1/182/1/11.

Andrew Louttit, writing his boyhood reminiscences in 1917 when he was eighty-seven years old, recalled: 'The tactics of both sides was to get the ball out of Broad Street. At the upper end the approach from this street to Victoria Street, between Reid the bookseller's shop and a draper's on the opposite corner, was very narrow, while at the lower end between Dinnison's Draper's shop and Dr Logie's, the entrance to Albert Street was also narrow. If then the ball could be got through one or other of these openings the game was practically won, as it was rushed along at headlong speed up or down . . . I have known, however, a diversion made. The ball having been got down to Dr Logie's[6] an up-the-gate had got his hands on it and rushed up the Stryne [*sic*] with the intention of working round by some back road, but this endeavour generally failed. The ball was of leather, six or seven inches in diameter, not oval as is the present fashion but round, and stuffed with cork cut very thin. It was thrown up at the Market Cross punctually as the clock struck one. If the up-the-gates were successful I don't know what became of it, but if we, the down-the-gates, were victorious it was kicked into the harbour, then taken out and stuck on the vance spindle of the biggest one-masted vessel lying alongside the pier. Why one-masted vessel I don't know, but that was the invariable custom. It was taken down at sunset, and used during the remainder of the winter in many a game by the young fellows knocking about in Harbour Street.'[7]

The first mention of a Christmas Day game (which had obviously been established for some little time) comes in 1855, when the absence of a Ba' was remarked upon – 'Christmas Day has passed over; but how changed! Not the slightest difference could anywhere be observed in town – not even the usual game at football.'[8] The omission was only for a year, for on Christmas Day 1856 an energetic game took place. The streets were very muddy, so that the appearance of the players 'might have reminded our Tourist of a herd of Zetland ponies gambolling among the treeless forests of their native hills.'[9] In 1866 'in the evening two bands of music enlivened the streets, and the youth of the town joined in the favourite game of football.'[10] At that time Christmas Day was not a general holiday, and this is probably why this game was played in the evening, and often those who played were young lads. Whatever games were played on Christmas Day or on 24 May as part of the Queen's Birthday celebrations (see the last section in this chapter), there can be no doubt that from its inception

[6] James S. S. Logie MD had his surgery in the building at the corner of Albert Street and the Strynd.

[7] *Orkney View*, December 2000/January 2001.

[8] *O*, 29 December 1855.

[9] *O*, 29 December 1859.

[10] *OH*, 1 January 1867.

the Ba' game, and the only one of any importance, was the New Year's Day Ba'. On 4 January 1868 an unknown Kirkwall seaman wrote affectionately to his sweetheart in Holm[11] recounting how he had spent New Year's Day in the town: 'Dear Love . . . next you write you must tell me how you spent your New Year's Day as i shall do to you now i tell you that the first after brakfast was a small interval and then to the foot Ball we had a stiff work but we got her Down street . . . yours, While life.'

The New Year's Day Ba's pre-eminence remained until around 1880 when the Christmas Day game began to achieve some stature. However, Hossack in *Kirkwall in the Orkneys* (1900) says:[12]

> But this old institution, which set all authority at defiance, is obviously sinking into a gradual decline. The first downward step was the starting of a ball on Christmas Day, and now there are something like half-a-dozen balls. This kind of thing tends to make the ball a nuisance, and is certainly killing the enthusiasm so strongly inspired by the old New Year's Ba'.

Nowadays both Ba's have the same standing, and are equally well supported.

Pat Gunn, winner of the Youths' Christmas Day Ba' 1907, had a discussion in 1956 with the *Orkney Herald* who printed the conversation in its issue of 8 January 1957. Mr Gunn was on holiday from Canada and had not seen a Ba' since 1908. Before discussing tactics Mr Gunn threw some interesting sidelights on those games of bygone years. He recalled that at the turn of the century the harbour was full of ships, and conspicuous among the players each year were the men from the smacks and schooners with their cheesecutter hats and blue 'ganzies'. Over from Wideford Hill came the tinkers full of bravado and drink, pushing and shouting and proclaiming most violently to sensitive nostrils, when the players got really hot, their contempt for baths.

When asked how the actual games compared, Mr Gunn said that in the old days there was much more planning of tactics in advance, and a readier response to the directions of acknowledged leaders who guided the game from first to last. The tradition that pushing and pushing only was permitted did not seem to hold, and there was now a certain amount of pulling and elbowing which the old-timers would not have allowed.

To summarize, we know that in its present form the game dates from around 1820; that for approximately twenty years before that there was a competitive

[11] Orkney Archives, D1/88/6/1. The billet-doux came from the Isbister family, Hall of Gorn, Holm.

[12] B. H. Hossack, *Kirkwall in the Orkneys*, p. 465.

Ba' game between Up-the-Gates and Down-the-Gates; that during this period the ba' was kicked or dribbled rather than lifted, agility and fleetness of foot being prime assets; and that for the first eighty or so years of its existence, up to roughly 1880, the Ba' game was primarily associated with New Year's Day.

The Queen's Birthday Bonfire

An interesting custom, observed from the reign of King George I (1714–27) and continued until the 1840s, was the bonfire on the Kirk Green, Kirkwall. This was the highlight of the celebrations to mark the official birthday of the reigning sovereign, and latterly the event was known as the Queen's Birthday Bonfire, after Queen Victoria.[13]

Originally these celebrations had the support of the Town Council who provided help for the bonfire, and in celebrating the King's birthday in May 1726 the Council purchased 3 lb of gunpowder, £2 8*s*., and a tar barrel and peats, £1 10*s*. Indeed the Council considered the occasion one which justified a certain amount of self-indulgence, and on the same occasion they consumed 4 pints of claret and 4 pints of brandy, £9 12*s*., a chapin of lemon juice, 12*s*., 2 lb of fine sugar, £2, and one barrel of ale £6 – a total of £18 4*s*. Scots of public money spent on refreshments![14]

For some days before 24 May the young men of the town collected combustible items, and in their zeal they did not always restrict themselves to items of no value! Indeed it was not uncommon for useful wooden utensils to be included and lie hidden in the mass of materials. An old boat acquired illicitly was invariably part of the pile, in the midst of which was set a tall flagstaff.[15]

The bonfire was touched off as Up-the-Gates and Down-the-Gates mustered at their respective sides, and the scene which followed is described thus by Hossack:

> When the conflagration is at its height it is seen that the middletree, caught in the bight of a rope, is swaying to one side, and loud cheers rise from the successful faction. But suddenly – and very few see how it comes about – the mast is straitened by an opposite pull, and cheers, or rather roars, go up all round. The swaying of the pole turns the bonfire into an open crater; the flame gets freer access to the butt of the stick, which is now burning clearly. But it has lost its support and falls, to the lucky

[13] B. H. Hossack, *Kirkwall in the Orkneys*, p. 465.
[14] W. R. Mackintosh, *Curious Incidents from the Ancient Records of Kirkwall*, p. 177.
[15] B. H. Hossack, *Kirkwall in the Orkneys*, p. 465.

> side. Immediately the unburnt part is gripped by as many hands as there is space for, and off it goes towards its goal, Burgar's Bay or the harbour. But there is a check. A double hitch of chain has been deftly cast over the butt of the pole, and an iron spike to prevent its slipping is quickly driven in by a young blacksmith, waiting his opportunity, and now 'pull baker, pull devil.' Singed garment and burned skin go unnoticed. The heavy end of the mast, sometimes on the ground, sometimes swinging free, goes foremost in the rush, and by-and-by is jammed with the crowd into the narrow court above the head of the town, or plunged, with a hiss, into the harbour.[16]

The occasion was a glorious opportunity for Uppies and Doonies to give boisterous expression to their rivalry, and for the purposes of the contest the goals were the same as in the Ba'. When the bonfire was in its heyday it provided an outlet for the strength and courage of Up-the-Gates and Down-the-Gates, whereas at that time the desirable and successful qualities for Ba' playing were skill, agility and fleetness of foot.[17]

After the mast had been taken to one of the goals the crowd returned to the bonfire and congregated on the weather side. Then while the flames licked up, daredevils would jump into the centre of the fiery circle and out again at the other side. When the blaze had died down the embers were kicked all over the street and the year's revels came to an end.[18]

Latterly the event was organized by the crowd themselves and inevitably it got out of control. Thefts occurred, business was affected and on one occasion a boat stuck in Bridge Street. Traffic was held up for hours. It is not surprising that the same Sheriff Robertson who had tried to stop the Ba' was more successful with the bonfire, and he had little difficulty in having it removed in the early 1840s to Gallowha'.[19]

Preparations for the annual event were elaborate, and as can be imagined the conflagration produced an intense heat. Apparently the removal to Gallowha' was precipitated when the heat scorched paint and woodwork of the houses on Broad Street.[20]

The bonfire was continued in its new location until 1859 when it fell into abeyance. In the years 1856 and 1857 the event had flared briefly, regaining some of its former confused splendour. Practically the entire population of Kirkwall as well

[16] B. H. Hossack, *Kirkwall in the Orkneys*, p. 465.
[17] B. H. Hossack, *Kirkwall in the Orkneys*, p. 465.
[18] B. H. Hossack, *Kirkwall in the Orkneys*, p. 465.
[19] B. H. Hossack, *Kirkwall in the Orkneys*, p. 466.
[20] Orkney and Shetland Miscellany, Vol. 1, Part v, p. 183.

as many others from round about assembled at Warrenfield in May 1856 to witness the spectacle. When the blaze had subsided onlookers vied for pieces of the flag emblazoned 'Queen Victoria' flown from the topmost branches of the tree. There followed a struggle between Up-the-Gates and Down-the-Gates – young and old alike taking part – for the forty-to-fifty foot tree which had been taken from the south, the trunk of which had been burnt through. The Uppies succeeded in taking the tree down Clay Loan and then, as they did frequently, to a house belonging to Mansie Heddle in Wellington Street. The Doonies endeavoured to carry the tree through School Place to the harbour. A game played afterwards and commencing as usual on Broad Street was won also by the Up-the-Gates.[21] The following year there was an even more determined argument over the middle-tree, 'almost the entire male population joining in the struggle'. The location was Gallowha' (presumably again the Warrenfield Gallowha' rather than the Gallowha' at the top of the Clay Loan) and the burning pole was forced down Clay Loan by the Up-the-Gates. On level ground a desperate altercation ensued and it was only after forty minutes of sustained heaving that the Uppies won the day. As can be imagined there was a certain amount of danger at the Bonfire and during the subsequent quarrel over possession of the middle-tree. On this occasion there were two casualties. A young man named Benderman, from Thurso, had his left foot damaged when the pole fell on it, and John Hepburn, a tinsmith, was severely cut below the left eye by a stone. Hepburn's injury was brought about by the dangerous practice of throwing stones at the pole while the fire was burning, with the object of causing it to fall.[22]

In 1858 the youth of Kirkwall gave notice by tuck of drum that they would express their loyalty that night by burning the usual bonfire.[23] That year the middle-tree or 'stick' was won by the Down-the-Gates.[24]

This seems to have been the last bonfire in connection with recognition of the Sovereign's birthday, as the following year the boisterous part of the festivities consisted only of a Ba' which began about 9 p.m. The game ended 'by the ball most unceremoniously bounding through the window into a gentleman's parlour, somewhere at the upper end of the town.'[25]

The celebration itself continued for many years taking the form of a public holiday, in which excursions, volunteer activities and fireworks provided somewhat staid alternatives to the spectacular Kirk Green blaze of former times.

[21] *O*, 31 May 1856.
[22] *O*, 25 May 1857.
[23] *O*, 24 May 1858.
[24] *O*, 31 May 1858.
[25] *O*, 30 May 1859.

Ba' Playing

While the Ba' normally took place at the festive season, any holiday or occasion which brought people together was an opportunity to indulge in the sport. Thus in Kirkwall the Queen's Birthday festivities on 24 May usually included a Ba' game in the evening. The sides were Up-the-Gates and Down-the-Gates, the goals were the normal ones, and the ba' was trucked if it went Down-street.

The records show that on 24 May 1855, 'the two opposing parties commenced a most determined melee',[26] and during the rejoicings in May 1862 the town was very crowded, 'farmservants having come in from the rural districts to look out for a little amusement. The old game of foot-ball was carried on along Broad Street and Albert Street amid considerable uproar.'[27] In May 1869, 'As usual the game of football was stiffly contested on the Broad Street for some time, and ultimately ended by someone more mischievous than the rest cutting the ball.'[28] Again, in connection with the celebration in May 1871, we learn that 'with the exception of a game at Foot-ball and the setting off of some fireworks in the evening the town was comparatively quiet.'[29] The last time the Ba' was played other than on Christmas and New Year's Day seems to have been in connection with the Queen's Birthday celebrations in May 1877 when fireworks were set off on Broad Street and a game of football concluded the proceedings.[30]

[26] *O*, 2 January 1855.
[27] *OH,* 27 May 1862.
[28] *OH,* June 1869.
[29] *OH,* 31 May 1871.
[30] *O*, 26 May 1877.

15

Origin of the Kirkwall Ba'

Sometimes an old custom has its origin in a source we cannot define or know. While it is not put forward as a serious contention, I dare say an origin for the game could be found in folklore such as the myth of the Mither of the Sea. This benign being was a great creative force who gave vitality to every living creature in the sea, and her implacable rival was the evil Teran who was a destructive force. The Sea Mither took up residence in the ocean in springtime, when there was a violent and lengthy conflict with her adversary (thus occasioning the spring gales). Teran was conquered, bound, and consigned to the bottom of the sea. When the autumnal equinox came, tired out by her many good works the Sea Mither was vanquished by her wicked prisoner and took flight from the deep, leaving it for a time under the control of the wintry-faced Teran.[1] As Robert Rendall in his *Orkney Variants* says (naming the creature Terran):

> But luik ye, niver noo in Vore
> Can man hear tell o' Terran,
> Rampagan on the ocean floor,
> For folk are little carean
> Hoo tullyas or brullyas
> Fought wi' the great Sea-mither
> B' swordship gae lordship
> Tae ane or else the tither.[2]

In its annual strife, confusion and turmoil the game is a parallel of the myth, and who knows, perhaps the 'tullya' and 'brullya' of the Ba' originated as a ritual contest at the festive season, based on a thin memory sounding down through the centuries of internecine strife between Teran and the great Sea Mither. Certainly

[1] W. T. Dennison, *Orkney Folklore and Traditions*, pp. 6, 7.
[2] R. Rendall, *Orkney Variants and other Poems*, p.58.

Evan MacGillivray MBE, Orkney's first county librarian, has speculated[3] that 'it is the spiritual urge to act or compete heroically as part of the winter sacrificial festivities that is relevant and has most probably survived until this day'. He traces the origins of the Ba', with its 'tight swirling scrimmage – representing possibly the ancient mythological spiral of life's journey into the underworld' to the elements of Viking paganism that were subsequently embodied in kirk yard dances.

The Story of Tusker

The following delightful old tale is told about the origin of the game. Hundreds of years ago the people of Kirkwall were downtrodden by a petty tyrant called Tusker, so named on account of his large protruding front teeth. Eventually his merciless extortions and general oppressions brought revolt and forced him to flee the islands. But there was always a fear that he might return, and so a brave young fellow vowed to seek out the exiled despot, cut off his head and take it back to exhibit to the people as proof that their bondage was finally over. The youth rowed across the Pentland Firth, took horse and brought the infamous Tusker to bay near Perth. The villain was slain, his head severed, and the hero set out for the north with bloody trophy swinging loose from the pommel of his saddle. During the journey Tusker's large front teeth broke the skin of the rider's leg, and by the time he reached Kirkwall the limb had become badly poisoned and death was near. With a dying effort the champion gained the Mercat Cross and threw the gory head to the waiting people. Grieved at the young man's untimely death, and incensed and elated at the sight of the hated Tusker's head, the people fell to kicking the grisly object around the street. From this, it is alleged, stem the annual Ba' games.

There is a similarity between this story and that told in *The Orkneyinga Saga* concerning the affray between Earl Sigurd and Maelbrigte Tusk, a Scottish Earl. In order that they might 'settle their quarrel once and for all', the two leaders agreed to meet with forty combatants each. Sigurd apparently feared treachery and so doubled the permitted number of his fighting men by mounting two men on each horse. The Scottish Earl and his inferior force were overwhelmed, their heads severed and fastened to the saddlebows of the Norsemen's horses. On the return journey Sigurd spurred his horse and broke the skin of his calf on Maelbrigte's tusk. 'The sore grew into a painful swelling, so that he got his death of it. And Sigurd the Mighty is buried in a barrow on the banks of the Oykell.'

[3] Unpublished MS, 'Speculations on the origin of the Ba' game', January 1987.

FIG. 93: Christmas Day 1997.

FIG. 94: New Year's Day 1992.

The Saga does not say, but perhaps the Norse Earl's men gave vent to their anger and grief by aiming kicks at the fatal head.[4]

Old Orkney Football

We know that the Norsemen had ball games, certainly one of them requiring the use of bats or clubs (see Part 4, 'The Origin and History of Mass Football'). However, there is no history of any type of ball play in the streets of Kirkwall stretching back through the centuries, and a firm connection with the 'playing at the ball' mentioned in the tenth-century Saga of Gisli cannot be established.

The ultimate basis of the present game does certainly seem to be old style mass football. The old Orkney football on the Cathedral Green stemmed from the same root as Shrovetide football in England and Fasternse'en football in the Borders. We know that even in its Kirk Green days opposing sides were in existence, and had readily adopted the game for their purposes. As we have seen in Chapter 1, 'Up-the-Gates and Down-the-Gates', in days gone by there was a definite division in Kirkwall, viz: the Laverock or Bishop's domain, and the Burgh or King's sphere of influence. The boundary between the two parts was the present St Magnus Lane, which runs west from opposite the Market Cross. Hossack says on page 7 of *Kirkwall in the Orkneys:* 'The rivalry between the youths of Burgh and Laverock always found ready vent in the trials of strength and skill afforded by the popular sports. Thus the fierce struggle which annually takes place round the "New Year's Ba'," and which always begins at the ancient boundary, is in its origin a tug-of-war between Crown and Mitre.' This popular belief handed down from earlier times was used as the basis for George Mackay Brown's short story,[5] from which the following extract depicts a gruesome game in 1495 after the murder of Jeremiah Tulloch, chief magistrate and ill-fated owner of the Crown Tavern, where the trouble began:

> A very bright lantern hung from the lintel of the Crown Tavern. Like moths, the earl's men began to eddy and drift towards that promise of hot spiced ale. The bishop's men lifted their heads from their archery in the cold Palace yard. What was the enchantment that assailed their nostrils? Ah, it could only be coming from the new tavern – the Crown – that potent mix of malt and nutmeg and brown sugar. They flung down their bows and set out for the Crown Tavern.

[4] *The Orkneyinga Saga*, trans. A. B.Taylor, pp. 139, 140.

[5] G. Mackay Brown, 'The first football match – a story', *Scotland on Sunday*, 24 December 1995.

Outside the door, on the very threshold, earl's men and bishop's men melled with each other – clashed with each other – began to hurl abuse at each other. Soon the Kirkwall street was hideous with the yelling and shouting. Dogs barked all over the town. The quiet townsfolk hurried home and locked their doors. Under the lantern of the Crown Tavern, amid the uproar, a dagger flashed here and there.

There was a young courtier called Jamie Geddes from Leith among the earl's men. He had gotten, in his ill-starred travels, a Turkish scimitar that he was very proud of. Now he unsheathed it – it flashed in the winter darkness like a meteor.

At this point Mr Jeremiah Tulloch came out of the hostelry, with all his authority about him, to restore peace. He took two of the gentlemanly ruffians by the scruffs – a red coat and a blue coat – and clashed their heads together. The unseemly brawl might have been broken off then, but Jeremiah Tulloch slapped Jamie Geddes, the loud-mouth, very briskly on the face, first this side, then that. What proud young blood would have put up with an indignity like that? Not Jamie Geddes, son of a chandler in the port of Leith.

The scimitar flashed like a meteor at Mr Tulloch. And not only at Mr Tulloch, right through Mr Tulloch, where his head was joined to his body. The threshold of the Crown Tavern was starred with sudden splashes of blood. The young swaggerers – the blue coats and the red coats – felt the warm blood on their hands and faces. Mr Tulloch's head bounced on the street, and rolled this way and that.

The young braggarts recoiled in horror! Then after a few seconds, some kind of primitive urge compelled them to fall on the severed head; get it away; hide it somewhere, as if the burying of the head might somehow cancel the fearful crime, blot it from their memories, make them what they had been ten minutes before, young braves with the clean gale of life blowing through them.

Who knows what possesses the minds of men in such a crisis? But it seemed to the earl's men that the head should be taken by them to the far end of the town and hidden in a field there, and thence smuggled out of the islands into Scotland, a skull; until, at last, time healed the frightful wound that had been inflicted on the whole of Orkney. Simultaneously the bishop's men wanted to take the head and bury it fathoms-deep in the sea. They were descendants of Norse seafarers, who had gotten rid of many a victim that way. It was an instinct bred in them. The sea washes everything clean at last.

> Red coats and blue coats hurled themselves on Jeremiah Tulloch's sodden head, to take it to some bourne of utter oblivion. Body piled on body, a wild whirl of arms and legs. The battle swayed this way and that, up and down the street. Sometimes towards the field at the edge of the town, sometimes towards the waterfront.
>
> A steam arose, like fog, and covered the mêlée, as it shifted a few yards this way and that way, till three hours passed and the sky was sprinkled with stars.
>
> It is not recorded who won this first football match in the western world . . .
>
> . . . the game of football has come a long way since that first crude blood-splashed beginning, five hundred years ago.
>
> And yet the original game is still played twice a year in the streets of Kirkwall in Orkney, on Christmas Day and New Year's Day, a wild chaotic day-long surge and ebb and flow, not all that different from the original struggle between the earl's men and the bishop's men. But now, instead of the chief magistrate's head, the young men play with a well-stitched leather ball stuffed with cork.
>
> Students of myth will tell you that the game is much much older, of cosmic origin. It may be the struggle of Winter and Summer, Fire and Ice, for possession of the sun.

While I do not consider that the true origin of the game lies in this rivalry between local factions, nevertheless there can be no doubt that as old style Orkney football developed into Kirk Green and then street play, it provided a suitable vehicle for the expression of this age-old enmity.

The Change to Street Football

The change which took place around 1800 and which radically altered the game to one of competitive street football may have happened gradually over a few years and may have been completely independent of Ba' games played elsewhere on the streets of towns. Certainly there is no reason why this should not have been perfectly possible. On the other hand, our Ba' game has a distinct resemblance to other examples of mass football played throughout the country, and the altered game as such may even have been introduced direct from the Borders of Scotland.

The important change in style could have been brought about either by natural evolution, or possibly by the grafting on of a certain amount of outside influence. The alternative of a new style imported street football game fresh from Scotland immediately supplanting the old game or filling the void created by its earlier departure does not seem likely. Indeed, there is no evidence to this effect, and at no time in this period was there any sort of gap in the playing of old Orkney football in and around Kirkwall. Whatever produced the change, its effect was to make the Kirkwall Ba' fall roughly into line with the game as it had evolved elsewhere.

Similarities with Traditions of Mass Football Elsewhere

Naming of Sides

In substantiation of the suggestion that there was some outside influence, it should be noted that those who play mass football in Ashbourne are known as 'Up'ards' and 'Down'ards'; the contestants in the Jedburgh Ba' game are 'Uppies' and 'Doonies'; at Workington, 'Uppies' play against 'Downies'; and 'Uppies' and 'Doonies' are in opposition in the Ancrum game. At Chester-le-Street the game was played between 'Up-streeters' and 'Down-streeters'; at Witney the sides were 'Up-town' and 'Down-town'; and at Campton and Hobkirk 'Uppies' played against 'Doonies'.

Severed Heads

Moreover while it is unnecessary to consider seriously the lingering Kirkwall belief that the game was originally played between Earl's and Bishop's men with the head of some undesirable, the fact that a similar belief exists elsewhere provides a further link connecting these street games. In Jedburgh it is held that the game was originally played with the head of an Englishman slain in a Border battle before the Reformation. In Ancrum there is a legend connected with the severed heads of French prisoners. At Chester the Shrovetide game is said to have been to commemorate the barbarous kicking about of a captured Dane's head. An identical story is told to account for the origin of the game at Kingston-upon-Thames. There, it is alleged, the Danes having been defeated in battle by the townsmen at the time of their Shrovetide sports, and 'the Captain of the Danish forces having been slain, and his head kicked about by the people in derision, the custom of kicking a Foot Ball on the anniversary of that day has been observed ever since.'[6] Around 1793 this tradition was used in evidence at the trial of some men accused of riotous conduct during the annual game. The

[6] W. D. Biden, *The History and Antiquities of the Ancient and Royal Town of Kingston-upon-Thames*, 1853, pp. 58, 59, note b.

indicted were acquitted on the ground of their having only observed an immemorial custom.

In 1321 there was a real-life case of this gruesome form of football when John de Boddeworth, servant of the abbot of the monastery of the Vale Royal of Cheshire, was murdered by the brothers Oldynton at Darnhale. It is stated that after the perpetration of the crime the murderers played football with the victim's head – *ad modum pilae cum pedibus suis conculcaverunt.*[7]

Furthermore, there are several references in early literature to playing football with a human head. For example, in the fourteenth century *Sir Gawayne and the Grene Knight* there is an incident when members of Arthur's court kick at the Green Knight's severed head as it rolls along the ground towards them:

> The faire hede fro the halce • hit to the erthe
> That fele hit foined with her fete, • there hit forth roled.[8]

This is of course not actual football, but simply that the courtly company kick the head about, possibly in horror, but more probably because they believe it to be pregnant with supernatural powers.

Football Superstitions

A firmly held view was that originally football was played not solely as a recreation, but rather as a ritual designed to ensure prosperity and fertility, or generally to work some good for the community – particularly when played annually.

This promotion of prosperity and fertility could be achieved in a number of ways, for example: by the winning side securing the ball in which the good fortune for the ensuing year was supposed to be embodied, so ensuring a substantial advantage such as good crops or good fishing;[9] by playing football as a rite to influence the weather and crops or to ensure health and wellbeing; by the expulsion from the community of the ball in which the evil and misfortune were located, resulting in a betterment of conditions for the people; by holding football contests as a simple, straightforward fertility rite often between married and unmarried people; and by involving a newly married person or persons who would donate the ball, start the contest, etc.

[7] 'They kicked at it with their feet as if it were a ball.' G. Ormerod, *The History of the County Palatine and City of Chester*, revised edn, 1882, vol. 2, p. 162, col. 1, item 32.

[8] *Sir Gawayne and the Grene Knight, c.*1360, 5, 427–428. 'The fair head from the neck hit on the ground, (So) that many thrust at it with their feet where it forth rolled.' See also Magoun, 'Sir Gawain and Medieval Football', *English Studies 19*, 1937, pp. 208–209. The article gives other examples in literature of football play with a human head.

[9] J. G. Frazer, *The Golden Bough*, 1936, part 6, 'The Scapegoat; the expulsion of embodied evils', p. 184.

Harvest and Weather

Kirkwallians considered that an Up-the-Gate win brought a good harvest and splendid crops whereas bountiful fishing resulted from a Down-the-Gate victory. Details are given under 'Tatties and Herring' in 'Interesting Games and Unusual Incidents' (Ch. 11).

The winning side in the parish of Rendall claimed and kept the ball in the staunch belief that it would bring a good crop of potatoes (see page 255). In Devon, Good Friday was the great day for potato planting, and it was believed that potatoes planted that day came up better than those planted on any other day. After the planting had been completed a football was kicked around, and it seems that this ritual had a definite connection with the belief that Good Friday potatoes grew more vigorously. A local author Cecil Torr (1857–1926) states that in his early years a football was hardly ever seen in the parish of Lustleigh, a location where the custom was observed, except on Good Friday.[10]

At Whitby, Yorkshire, it was believed that if balls were not 'well played' by the country youths on Shrove Tuesday 'they will be sure to fall sick at harvest.'[11] (That is, they would be less effective at their work then.)

In Normandy, it was believed that the winning parish would have a better crop of apples that year.

Much further afield, in Morocco, games of ball were played in order to procure rain or sunshine, and it is possible that in this instance the ball represented a rain cloud. To promote sunshine, one side had to win, and for wet weather it was arranged that the other side would be victorious. The location of the goals was dependent on the direction of the prevailing wind, on which the rain came.[12] Assuming the prevailing wind was from the west, if the west side forced the ball through the east goal, rain would follow. If, however, it was desired that the drought would continue, it was arranged that the east side would win and consequently the rain was driven away.

There is a connection with the Norwegian village of Lillehammer, 130 miles north of Oslo, which touches on the aspect of good fishing and heavy crops. For over half a century Willie Groat, Longhope, has been in annual contact with Halvor Mork, a woodcarver in Lillehammer who is curious to know which side has won. He passes the information to interested friends, some of whom are farmers and others fishermen on the nearby large lake.

[10] C. Torr, *Small Talk at Wreyland,* 3rd series, Cambridge University Press, 1923, p. 102.

[11] F. K. Robinson, *Glossary of Words Used in the Neighbourhood of Whitby*, Preface, Folk-lore-Easter, p. vii. See F. P. Magoun, *Shrove Tuesday Football,* p. 37.

[12] J. G. Frazer, *The Golden Bough*, 1936, part 6, 'The Scapegoat', pp. 179, 180.

Banishing Misfortune

A Fasternse'en Ba' was played in the border village of Kirk Yetholm until about 1930, and after the ball had been made it was brightly painted and bedecked with gaily coloured ribbons. Then it was taken from door to door and the women and children gave it a token kick, at the same time handing over a small donation. It is possible that these kicks had in the dim past some connection with the ritual transfer of the guilt, evil and accumulated misfortune and ills of the people to the ball and then ejected in the material and visible vehicle from the confines of the community, to the goals.[13]

Marriage and Fertility

A record of playing football and the giving of ba' money at weddings in Orkney is dealt with in Chapter 16, 'Mass Football Playing in Orkney'.

In Sedgefield, County Durham (see page 304), it is believed that if a girl kicks the ball she will be married by the end of the year, and the fertility of a married couple is assured if they both touch it.

The game was played in the villages of Kirk Yetholm, Morebattle and Duns between married and unmarried men, as it was in Melrose until at least 1866.[14] Although the composition of the sides is now different, the Denholm game was at one time played between married men and bachelors. Similarly, in Alnwick and Wooler in Northumberland, the Shrove Tuesday game was between married men and bachelors,[15] and these were the sides in Scone, Perthshire.[16] In France, the struggle was sometimes between sides composed of married and unmarried men.[17]

The fertility aspect appears in an annual ritual still observed by the fishwomen of Inveresk at the end of the eighteenth century. An account of the ritual says of the fish-wives: 'As they do the work of men, their manners are masculine, and their strength and activity is equal to their work. Their amusements are of the masculine kind. On holidays they frequently play at golf; and on Shrove Tuesday there is a standing match at football, between the married and

[13] J. Gray, 'Fasternse'en', *Scots Magazine*, February 1964. J. G. Frazer, *The Golden Bough*, 1936, part 6, p. 184.

[14] G. Watson, 'Annual Border Ball-Games', *Hawick Archaeological Society Transactions*, 1922, pp. 5, 8.

[15] F. P. Magoun, *Shrove Tuesday Football,* pp. 24, 44.

[16] Sir John Sinclair, *The Statistical Account of Scotland,* part 18, no. 2, pp. 88, Parish of Scone. Information provided by Robert Thomas, Preacher of the Gospel.

[17] J. Lecoeur, *Esquisses du Bocage Normand*, 1883, p. 164, and J. J. Jusserand, *Les Sports et les Jeux d'Exercise dans l'ancienne France*, 1901, p. 268.

unmarried women, in which the former are always victors.'[18] That the married women always won is of significance – what was enacted had a ritual origin and was not a competitive game.

Fasternse'en ba's in several Scottish border towns and villages are donated by couples married between one Ba' day and the next, or by a couple on the occasion of their silver, golden or diamond wedding anniversary.

In 1551 at Corfe Castle, Dorset, articles of agreement of the Company of Marblers were renewed and confirmed, and one clause reads: 'Seaventhly: that any man in our Company the Shrovtewsday after his marriage shall paie unto the Wardings for the use and benefit of the Company twelve pence and the last married man to bring a foot-ball according to the Custome of our Company.'[19]

Brand's *Observations on Popular Antiquities*, published in 1841, makes three references to football money given immediately after a wedding:

> In the North of England, among the colliers, etc., it is customary for a party to watch the bridegroom's coming out of church after the ceremony, in order to demand Money for a Foot-ball, a claim that admits of no refusal.

Coles, in his *Dictionary*, speaks of another kind of ball money given by a new bride to her old playfellows:

> It is the custom in Normandy for the bride to throw a ball over the church, which bachelors and married men scramble for. They then dance together.[20]

An early fifteenth-century connection between marriage and football is contained in the medieval archives of London. This consists of a proclamation issued in 1409 in the reign of Henry IV and written in Norman French:

> And that no person shall levy money, or cause it to be levied, for the games called 'Foteball' and 'Cokthresshyng', because of marriages that have recently taken place in the said city, or the suburbs thereof; *(Ne que null' use ne face lever argent pur lez iewes appellez Foteball' et Cokthresshyng a cause des novels mariages faitz en la dice Cite ou lez Suburbes dicell')* on pain of imprisonment, and of making fine at the discretion of the Mayor and Aldermen.[21]

[18] J. Sinclair, *The Statistical Account of Scotland*, vol. 16, p. 19, Parish of Inveresk. Information provided by the Rev Dr Alex Carlyle, Minister of Inveresk.

[19] O. W. Farrer, *The Marblers of Purbeck*, papers read before the Purbeck Society (Wareham, 1859–60), pp. 191 ff. See F. P. Magoun, *Shrove Tuesday Football*, p. 15.

[20] J. Brand, *Observations on Popular Antiquities*, 1841, vol. 2, p. 98.

[21] Letter Book I, fol. 77b, trans. H. Riley and contained in *Memorials of London and London Life*. The proclamation was probably made by the mayor with the authority of the Court of Aldermen. The apostrophe indicates a mark of abbreviation.

While the connection is not entirely clear, the broad intent was certainly that at the time of marriages there should be no levy of money for these pastimes, which were doubtless a part of the general proceedings. (See the foregoing remarks by Brand.)

In the same year as the proclamation, and very possibly resulting from it, a bond was given by 'John Kelsey, William Bonauntre, Ralph Spayne, Thomas Wade, Robert Hebbe and William Bullok, tapicers, and John Port and Philip Tayllour, parishioners of St Denis Bakchirche, for their good behaviour towards the mistery of Cordwainers, and that none of them would in future collect money for a football *(pro pila pedali)* . . . under penalty of £20.'[22]

Turning to French customs associated with marriage, at La Lande-Patry the ball was supplied and thrown up by the most recently married bride. In the parish of Vieux-Pont in Normandy the man last married before the first Sunday in Lent had the honour of throwing a ball from the foot of the cross.[23] Indeed some French writers believed that the mass football game of *Soule* took its name from *solde* (pay). This was because of the money paid by those who married during the year, and which went to the men who caught the *soule*.[24] Other origins of the word are given in the Part 4, 'The Origin and History of Mass Football'.

Also in France, a more refined type of *Soule* was played at or shortly after marriage. The ball or *eteu* was smaller than the *soule* and, packed firmly with tow or bran, usually contained one or more coins.[25]

Sometimes on the day of the wedding, but normally on the Sunday following the ceremony, the new bride, dressed in wedding finery, was escorted from her pew to the cross in the cemetery. There the bridegroom threw the *eteu* as high over the cross as possible, and the lads of the parish fought for it. In several districts the bridegroom had to throw it over the church roof. It became the property of whoever got possession, extricated himself from the scrimmage and managed to cross a stream or the district boundary without the others catching him.

Some couples married within the year went to the '*soule* meadow' on the morning of Shrove Tuesday, each with their *eteu* or small *soule*. At an agreed signal

[22] *Calendar of Plea and Memoranda Rolls, 1381–1412,* p. 291, ed. A. H. Thomas, 1932. The date of the entry is 4 March 1409. St Denis or St Dionis Backchurch was a London parish, and the church, which was taken down in 1878, lay on the north side of Fenchurch Street. Tapicers were tapestry weavers. The Mistery of Cordwainers was the Company or Guild of Shoemakers, and it is likely that they would have made any leather cover for a ball.

[23] A. de Nore, *Coutumes, Mythes et Traditions des Provinces de France,* Paris et Lyons, 1846, p. 244 ff. See J. G. Frazer, *The Golden Bough*, 1936, part 6, p. 183.

[24] J. Lecoeur, *Esquisses du Bocage Normand*, 1883, p. 165.

[25] Information on throwing the *eteu* at or after weddings has been taken from J. Lecoeur, *Esquisses du Bocage Normand*, 1883, pp. 324, 325.

the balls were thrown up by the bridegrooms. About noon, when all had been won, they were taken back to the meadow and opened, the money handed to the purse bearer and the total sum used for a celebration the following Sunday.

The custom of throwing the *eteu* in which 'foot and fist often played too big a part',[26] was sometimes observed at baptisms. In 1883 the old practice still existed in one or two districts, and was so firmly rooted that couples who were unwilling to conform were snubbed, and even ill-treated until they cooperated.

These traditions are found much further afield. In connection with their festival of the new fruits, the Yuchi Indians of Oklahoma engaged in a game of ball, which, while it was not football as each player had two racquets, is nevertheless worth mentioning, as being part of ball fertility magic. Significantly the goals were located east and west of each other, and the ball game, which was a ritual rather than a recreation, was part of the rites which the Indians said were instituted by the sun. Prior to the game the men purged themselves before eating the new corn, being convinced that otherwise they would fall sick. The following night a general laxity in moral standards among the young people received no discouragement.[27]

W B. Johnson has also dealt with the possibility that football originated as a fertility rite, and he suggests that the ball of the sun has become represented by an actual ball, that bringing the ball within the confines of the parish represents capturing the sun for the people, and that burying the ball in the ground is an attempt to secure the benefit of the sun's heat for the crops.[28] The dipping of the ball in a stream or pond has always been a feature of mass football played at Shrovetide, Fasternse'en and other times of the year both in Britain and France, and this may be accounted for by the need for sun and rain to promote good crops.

While it is not entirely relevant to football playing, a ball was not always used in the magical promotion of fertility, and sometimes the sun was symbolized by a flat circular stone that would induce a vitalizing influence to the ground. This representation by a stone occurred, probably not later than the end of the eighteenth century, in the parish of Rendall, Orkney, mentioned earlier. There, when fields were ploughed, a round stone, frequently dark red or brown, was hung on the beam of the old Orkney plough and trundled in the fresh furrow as the wooden implement was pulled along, and it is particularly significant that the stone was always kept on the side nearest the sun. The stone was about the size of a soup plate or perhaps a little smaller, it was rounded by hand and was

[26] J. Lecoeur, *Esquisses du Bocage Normand*, 1883, p. 325.
[27] J. G. Frazer, *The Golden Bough*, 1936, part 5, vol. 2, p. 75, 'The Sacrament of First-fruits'.
[28] Johnson, p. 229.

thicker in the centre than at the edges. There was a small hole about an inch in diameter near one edge, and through this hole the stone was attached to the plough, usually by a rope made of horses' hair.[29]

The importance of stones generally in homoeopathic or imitative magic, including the value of particular stones according to their individual qualities of shape and colour, as well as the significance of stones in the magical control of the sun, is fully discussed by Frazer.[30]

[29] This information was given to me by Mr H. Louttit, Glenisla, Finstown, and formerly of thc farms of Lower Bigging and Hogarth, Rendall. Mr Louttit informed me that a woman was usually in attendance and it was she who turned the stone to keep it always on the side nearest the sun. In 1936 Mr Louttit found one such stone about two feet down in a peat bank near the top of the West Hill, Rendall. It was later given by him to a local antiquarian who sent it to a museum. The stone was known as a dian or darrow stane. See also E. W. Marwick *The Folklore of Orkney and Shetland*, p. 65.

[30] J. G. Frazer, *The Golden Bough*, 1936, part 1, vol. 1, pp. 161–165 and 312–314.

16

Mass Football Playing in Orkney

In common with other parts of Scotland, there is a tradition of football playing in the different islands and parishes of the Orkney Islands, and it is recorded in 1787: 'Football is the principal diversion of the common people, which they practise with great dexterity.'[1]

On various fields of play there were no sides, touchlines or goals as we understand them, and an inflated bladder of a cow, sheep or pig, encased in leather and usually fashioned by the local cobbler, was kicked about in a rough and tumble on the parish Ba' Green. Where the game was competitive it was generally speaking a survival of the fittest, and the only rule in this rumbustious pastime seems to have been that the ba' could not be lifted, only kicked. In some localities the object may have been to keep the ba' on one's own side, but this is not clear. There may also have been slight variations observed regarding style of play that were peculiar to a district or parish, and it seems that latterly in some districts 'hails' or goals were introduced. For example in Sanday the game was played with an inflated animal bladder or sometimes a large herring cork or even a bundle of tightly compressed paper, and it was considered a greater feat to kick this high over the goalkeeper's head than past his side. The lofted kick was called 'a hail' and counted as five goals or 'rows'.[2]

The game started about midday, large numbers of men of all ages took part, and aided by copious draughts of home-brewed ale play went on for hours, usually ending when the light failed.

[1] J. Fea, *Considerations on the Fisheries of the Scottish Islands to which is Prefixed a General Account Elucidating the History, Soil, Productions, Curiosities, &c., &c., of the Same, the Manners of the Inhabitants, &c.*, London, 1787.

[2] In connection with the 'hail', see the *Scottish National Dictionary*, 1956, vol. 4, part 4, p. 363. (This information on Sanday was confirmed and supplemented in 1966 by Walter Meil, Esq, of Work, St Ola.) Also on p. 363 from Orkney: 'Hail – the goal or mark itself; and in pl. hailse. Phr. and combs.: hail-ba, a variety of handball played by boys; hail-door, used fig. in phr. corman (gettan) near the hail-doors, "coming to an end of supplies of potatoes, meal, ale, etc."; hail-post, goal-post; to win a hail, to score a goal.'

While latterly the game was played primarily at the festive season on Yule Day or Old Christmas (6 January) and Old New Year's Day (13 January), and then from the 1860s and early 1870s on the new Christmas Day (25 December) and New Year's Day (1 January), the *Orkney and Shetland Miscellany* records that formerly the game also took place on other occasions: 'Football was played on Yule Day, New Year's Day, Uphelli Day, the fourth day after Old New Year's Day.' Again: 'Brose Day (Fastern's E'en) was called Milk Gruel Night in Harra, where also the baa (football) was played on Aphelliday.'[3] Another favourite time for football was after weddings.

By the early part of the nineteenth century a Ba' had become an established part of the festivities on Yule Day and New Year's Day in most, if not every parish, district and island in Orkney. In an article in the *Orkney Herald* 5 January 1876, a correspondent from Glasgow reminisces about Yule time in the Orkney of days gone by. After dinner was over 'the youngsters left to join in that public institution now unfortunately on the wane – a kick at the ba'.' A ball was made for the occasion and play continued till dark. 'Many came out of the fray with blued and broken shins and all with gutter to the eyes but that was exactly wherein the glory lay; and had it passed off without this, or an out and out fight it would have been considered a dull affair.'

This original style football was looked on much more favourably than the Kirkwall Ba', and *The Orcadian* 8 January 1876, reporting that in Kirkwall on New Year's Day the players had been covered with mud 'to the no small merriment of the onlookers' went on: 'The old Orkney game of football is a very excellent one when properly played in a suitable place, and far superior to the new one according to the Rugby rules.'

Ba' Grounds

From the Norse term *leika,* to play, have sprung place names such as Lakequoy and Leaquoy – O.N. *Leik-kví,* sports-or games-quoy, and Lyking, O.N. *vin,* pasture, *Leik-vin,* sportsfield.[4] These were thus the locations where games, very probably including ball play, occurred. Lakequoy can be found in Westray, North Faray and Tankerness; Leaquoy is present in Stronsay, Shapinsay, Birsay

[3] A. W. Johnston, *Orkney and Shetland Miscellany,* vol. 1, part 7, pp. 246, 247.

[4] *Proceedings of the Orkney Antiquarian Society*, vol. 5, 1926–27, p. 70; H. Marwick, *Antiquarian Notes on Sanday.* See also Dr Marwick, *Orkney Farm Names,* pp. 29, 40, 153. In the same book on p. 42 Marwick says that *quoy* is derived from O.N. *kví,* a cattle-fold or place where animals congregate (for the night chiefly), and that in the early rentals *quoyland* is a specific term for unskatted land, such lands not being broken out or in cultivation when *skat* (land tax) was imposed.

and South Ronaldshay; and Lyking occurs in Holm, Sandwick and Rendall.[5] In the case of South Ronaldshay the name is on record from 1329 when among other farms bought by Katherine, Countess of Orkney, was a Leikakvi. In 1492 the name of this land had changed to Leoquoy (and afterwards it is found as Lykquoy).[6]

There are many Ba' Greens or Ba' fields scattered throughout the islands, and in connection with Kirkwall, Hossack gives the following record:

> Three of the Pabdale fields have to some extent a public interest. From as far back as the middle of the seventeenth century, the Ba' Lea, as the name indicates, had been a field where men and boys played football. There were really two Ba' Leas – the upper, as far out as Warrenfield; and the lower, down where the U.P. Manse stands – both were burgh property, and both are now included in the lands of Pabdale. From the fact that golf had been played in the Ba' Lea, requiring greater space than either of the two taken separately can afford, the inference is that the upper and lower leas were the extremes of one common, and that Pabdale's first encroachment was a bite out of the middle.

The popular rights were not very well protected by the Magistrates, and in 1793 the noted historian Malcolm Laing of Pabdale granted a charter in connection with this ground, then described as the 'Ball Lay of Pabdale'.[7]

Football and the Church

The game was something of a nuisance, particularly during and after church service. In Kirkwall the following entry dated Wednesday, 28 September 1670 is contained in the Session Book of the cathedral:

> After invocation of the name of God. Ordains to admonish all parents and masters publicklie out of pulpitt that they be answerable for ther children and servants' carriage on the sabbath day, Conforme to former

[5] The locations are as follows: Lakequoy – Westray, a small croft at Point of Cott; North Faray, a small croft between Hamar and Windywall; Tankerness, a small croft below the Post Office. Leaquoy – Stronsay, a house on the west slope of Stebb Hill; Shapinsay, a quoy attached to Ness farm; Birsay, a farm in Marwick (origin doubtful in this case); South Ronaldshay, land in the Brough neighbourhood. Lyking – Holm, a farm situated north-west of Hurtiso; Sandwick, a farm in South Sandwick; Rendall, a small farm south of Tingwall.

[6] *Records of the Earldom of Orkney, 1299–1614,* 1914, Scottish History Society, 2nd series, vol. 7, p. 12. See also Marwick, *Orkney Farm Names,* p. 29.

[7] B. H. Hossack, *Kirkwall in the Orkneys*, pp. 395, 401.

> acts made theranent. Becaus it is reported that severall idle boyes playes at football in tym of and after sermon. And, ordains the eldar who visits, and the Officers with him to tak diligent notice that no such abuse be committed in tym coming, and, recommends the care thereofe to each eldar in ther severall precincts, and that the delinquents' names be given up to the Session.

At Burrik, South Ronaldshay, on Sunday 25 December 1659, we learn that 'Eftir sermone and prayer intimatioune maid by the Minister that the Elders in their respective boundes tak speciall cair that no gaming be at football or othir wantone playes and to report. And to that effect the Elders ar to conveine upon the 29 December.' Only two days later, however, there was a report from the Elders of the North Parish, and the minute reads: 'At Peterkirk 27 December 1659 being Twysday. Eftir prayer . . . The Elders of the North Parisch report their diligence inquyring if there had beene any abuse committed in their bounds by football or othir wantone gaimes and did find none.'[8] However, as we have already seen in Chapters 4 and 7, 'Acquiring and Making the Ba'' and 'The Boys' Ba'', the Cathedral Session by 1684 adopted a rather more benign approach to the game with the enactment that couples marrying should donate a football to the grammar school.

Sunday Football

Sunday was a popular day for football in the various districts, play often taking place on the open area around the kirk, including the graveyard. But any holiday or public celebration was an opportunity to indulge, and football was particularly popular after weddings which often took place on Sundays.

Writing in his book *A Peculiar People and Other Orkney Tales,* J. T. Smith Leask says: 'Not only was drinking on Sundays customary but football was not neglected.' Apparently in Stenness until the end of the eighteenth century the young people regularly played football in the churchyard after service. Mr Malcolm, the minister,[9] was horrified at seeing the ba' produced each Sabbath day and determined to have it stopped. 'He considered the matter and decided on a course of action. The following Sunday, after service, when the ball was produced he threw off his coat and joined vigorously in the game, and being a

[8] South Ronaldshay Parish Register, Baptisms and Marriages, 1657–1669, p. 35. This is really a volume of Kirk Session minutes.

[9] John Malcolm, a native of Aberdeenshire, was minister in Stenness from 1785 until his death in 1807.

fine athlete, direct from College, was a clever player. The result was fully equal to his expectations – the boys stopped play at once, shocked, horrified, scandalised at the idea of the minister playing football on Sunday, and leaping the churchyard wall, left him alone and never again was the ball produced.'[10]

Football Playing and Ba' Money at Weddings

The following is an extract from the 'Proof Led By William Gordon Esquire Of Outer Evie In The Action Of S Division Of The Commonty Of Evie Raised Before The Court Of Session At His Instance Vs. The Right Honorable Earl Of S Zetland And Others' (dated July 1842):

> William Halcro, residing at Gairngreena . . . 'I depone that there was a custom between the Parishes of Evie & Birsay whereby when a marriage took place between the people of these Parishes the Bridegroom paid or gave a foot Ball to the school of the other Parish & when they played with the Ball they stopped at the Boundary of the Parish & if the Football was not given or paid for the people of the Brides parish took of the Brides shoe.'[11]

Walter Traill Dennison (1826–94) gives us a delightful insight into the playing of football in connection with weddings:

> Before leaving the marriage-day, a custom must be noticed, once universal here. If the bride and bridegroom belonged to separate parishes, the best-man had to provide the boys of one of the parishes with a football. The old rule gave this ball to the boys residing in the parish to which the bride belonged, but, in process of time, the ball was sometimes claimed by the youths of the bridegroom's parish, and in this case the dispute generally ended in a fight. Where the parties were stingy, the best-man sometimes refused to pay the 'ba' siller', and in this case the wedding party was liable to an attack from the youths. The boys always met the wedding party as it issued from the church or manse, and loudly demanded the 'ba''. In most cases the best-man had provided himself with a ball, which he

[10] J. T. Smith Leask, *A Peculiar People and other Orkney Tales*, p. 61. It would seem likely that Mr Malcolm stopped the Sunday churchyard football in Stenness in the early part of his ministry, and that the practice did not, as suggested in the book, last until the beginning of the nineteenth century.

[11] From manuscript copy provided by Ernest W. Marwick, Kirkwall, which contains several references to Ba' playing.

> flung to the boys. But if he had a right to pay, and refused either ball or money, the wedding party was subjected to no little annoyance from the attacks of the boys.

As late as the second decade of the twentieth century, a miserly best man refused the boys their right. In returning home the wedding party unluckily had to pass the seashore. The company had been a good deal provoked by the pelting of the boys, which was no improvement to their fine clothes, and seeing the large sea-tangles lying on the beach, they seized the marine weapons and commenced an attack on the youths. The young generation followed the example of their elders; blood was shed on both sides before they parted, and one fair maid had her leg so lacerated with a marine weapon that she was unable to participate in the wedding festival.[12]

In *Reminiscences of an Orkney Parish* John Firth recalls:

> If the bridegroom chanced to be neither a native of, nor a residenter in, the parish where the wedding took place, the boys of that parish were entitled to receive from him as much money as would enable them to purchase a football from the local cobbler. So while the company partook of the refreshments, the barn door was besieged by a crowd of boys shouting for 'ba'-money'. It was useless for the bridegroom to ignore those importunate urchins for they insisted that their demands must be met before the marriage ceremony should take place, and if he deferred payment of the tax until the ceremony was over, the whole wedding company was subjected to considerable annoyance. If the bridegroom did not give a liberal donation, or if he dared to refuse altogether the youths were not slow in venting their spite upon him whenever an opportunity occurred.[13]

The custom has been tenacious in certain districts, and in Deerness as late as 1931 there was an instance of an incoming bridegroom donating a ba' to the boys of the local school.[14]

At the present time in Stromness the best man at a wedding may still throw a handful of coins to the young people waiting after the ceremony, either outside the church or where the reception is being held. Indeed it was normal for the boys (and girls) to shout 'the ba', the ba'' if the money was slow in coming, and

[12] W. Traill Dennison, *Orkney Folklore and Traditions,* pp. 90, 91.
[13] J. Firth, *Reminiscences of an Orkney Parish,* 2nd edn, p. 58.
[14] Information received from Rev. H. L. Mooney, Deerness.

in that town 'the ba'' was understood as being synonymous with the money given after a wedding. It is still called Ba' money although the younger generation may not realize the connection with the Ba' played over the streets of Stromness for several decades. When the custom was universal in Stromness the pennies were sometimes supplied by the bride's father and sometimes by the bridegroom himself. No distinction was made between local grooms and those outwith the town. On at least one occasion the best man played a trick by heating the pennies on a shovel before throwing them to the waiting children!

And so the custom of throwing ba' money after a wedding lingered on until recently, although it is perhaps not generally understood that this largesse is an echo from the past and a direct though attenuated connection with the Orkney custom of providing a ba' or ba' money at the conclusion of a wedding ceremony.

The provision of a ba' or ba' money after a wedding in the country districts and parishes was the equivalent of the Kirkwall ba' money included in the proclamation fees and collected from each couple when they gave in their marriage banns (see Ch. 4, 'Acquiring and Making the Ba'').

17

The Stromness Ba'

In Stromness 25 December 1856 and 1 January 1857 were observed as holidays, instead of the old style,[1] and shooting and football were the order of the day, particularly of New Year's Day.[2] On Christmas Day 1882 'in a field adjacent to the battery a game of football was contested which lasted for several hours and was only brought to a termination by John Mackay seizing the ball as it was being kicked into the town, and making it a prisoner.'[3] This was one of the last instances of old Orkney football to be played in the Stromness area, as shortly afterwards the Kirkwall Ba' style was introduced and became firmly established.

History of the Ba' in Stromness

The first recorded instance of ball play on the streets of Stromness was on Christmas Day 1884, between North and South. The Southenders won the game after a keen contest of over an hour, and took the ba' to the Town Hall. A report refers to 'the time honoured game of football' being played on the street in the afternoon.[4] There was a contest on New Year's Day 1886 at one o'clock between 'North' and 'South' and afterwards between 'Town' and 'Country', when the 'Town' was victorious.[5] However, the measure of public support varied from time to time, and a year later on Christmas Day 1886, when the ba' was thrown up at three o'clock very little interest was aroused.[6]

[1] By the Old or Julian Calendar (revised to the Gregorian Calendar in 1752), Old New Year's Day was 13 January and Old Christmas Day was 6 January. In some parts of Orkney the Julian Calendar was observed until well into the nineterenth century.

[2] *O*, 19 January 1857.

[3] *O*, 30 December 1882.

[4] *O*, 3 January 1885 and *OH*, 31 December 1884.

[5] *O*, 9 January 1886.

[6] *O*, 1 January 1887.

FIG. 95: Orphir v. Stenness to celebrate the Queen's Silver Jubilee, Scorradale Brae, 6 June 1977.

It is not possible to say exactly when a Ba' was first played on the streets of Stromness, and the above reference to 'time-honoured' is, I believe, to old Orkney style football as played in the parishes. Stromness men with long memories say that street play was introduced towards the end of the nineteenth century by a Kirkwall man called Flett. This would make the 1884 contest mentioned one of the first played. In support of this belief we are told that on New Year's Day 1896, 'for the last four or five years a game of football – in imitation of the Kirkwall game – has been played here in the public street.'[7] There were no sports or amusements of any kind on Christmas Day 1901 'and the young men of the town showed their good sense in abstaining from what may be termed a recent innovation – the playing of football on the streets.'[8] My view is that ball play on the streets of Stromness started in the early 1880s, probably as an importation from Kirkwall.

[7] *O*, 4 January 1896.
[8] *OH*, 1 January 1902.

By New Year's Day 1890 the Ba' had become well established in Stromness, and that day 'a game at football resulted in some unseemly rows but the police officers quickly dispersed the crowd and the ball also disappeared.'[9] On New Year's Day 1894 'a game at football was played on the street which seemed to be thoroughly enjoyed by both old and young.'[10] The annual event continued to have the support of the populace although the report of the New Year's Day contest 1897 was not entirely favourable: 'and it was a game of strength and not of play but it pleased the combatants and we have nothing to say. After a hard struggle for over an hour the ball was carried to the North end amid great rejoicings.'[11] There were two Men's Ba's on New Year's Day 1899, both in the afternoon and both won by the Southenders. The disapproving correspondent was at work again anent New Year's Day 1902: 'The streets were quiet until the ba' was thrown up, and then the usual struggle commenced, but happily it did not last long.'[12]

On New Year's Day 1904 a Boys' version was introduced and both it and the Men's Ba' were played in the afternoon.[13] On New Year's Day 1907 three games were played, Juveniles', Lads' and Men's.

By New Year's Day 1910 the tussles were taking an almost identical form to their Kirkwall counterparts. The Boys' ba' was thrown up at 10 a.m. and the Youths' Ba', which was confined to lads of under twenty years of age (a year younger than in Kirkwall), commenced at noon, and 'after a very keen contest in which it was difficult to say which side had the best of it, the encounter closed as a draw.'[14] The Men's Ba' later that day lasted about fifteen minutes. The first record of individual winners is on Christmas Day 1909 when both games were won by the Northenders: the winners being Boys' ba' – Stewart Spence, and Men's ba' – John Lee.

Over the years opposition continued, and in connection with the New Year's Day Ba' 1909 *The Orcadian* reporter stated that there was no science displayed, only brute strength to push the leather to either side, and it would be in the interest of everyone to stop 'this silly game'.[15] Around this time there was a somewhat stark assessment by an observer: 'It is really rough work at best, and where the pleasure comes in it is very difficult to imagine.' The comment is attributed to Dodo Marwick, latterly a much respected Provost of Stromness.

[9] *OH,* 8 January 1890.
[10] *OH,* 3 January 1894.
[11] *OH,* 6 January 1897.
[12] *OH,* 8 January 1902.
[13] *OH,* 6 January 1904.
[14] *OH,* 5 January 1910.
[15] *O*, 9 January 1909.

FIG. 96: Stromness Ba' in Victoria Street, *c.*1910.

The usual three games were played on New Year's Day 1912 but a stranger apparently considered that it was 'a most disgraceful scene on the public street, and the wonder is that the Town Council do not prohibit it as they undoubtedly have the power to do.'[16] On Christmas Day 1913 public opposition was mounting, and 'it seems to be the general opinion that the Town Council should take steps to put an end to football games on the streets and we hope they will see their way to do so.'[17] Stromnessians were keen on street football, and notwithstanding the outbreak of war in August 1914, three contests took place on Christmas Day. These were repeated a week later on New Year's Day 1915.[18]

The Town Council must have felt that there was a likelihood of the Ba' continuing the following year, for a Minute of its proceedings on 23 December 1915 reads: 'The meeting agreed unanimously that football should not be played on the streets either on Christmas or New Year's Day, and the Provost was instructed to see the senior Naval Officer of the Port that he may lend assistance in carrying this out.'

[16] *OH,* 3 January 1912.
[17] *OH,* 1 January 1914.
[18] *O*, 2 January 1915 and 9 January 1915.

FIG. 97: Stromness Ba' at the pier head, *c.*1910.

With the cessation of hostilities there was a request by the Town Council that Ba' playing should not be restarted. This was ignored, and on Christmas Day 1919 an enthusiast threw up the ba' at the foot of the Church Road, exclaiming that he would take all responsibility for broken windows.[19] Thereafter for a few years the annual contest took on a new lease of life culminating on Christmas Day 1923, when a large crowd took part. 'It was strenuous work, and one wonders what rate of pay men would require if they were paid for such work. A thick haze of steam rose from the perspiring "multitude."'[20]

A week later support was limited, partly due to the very wet weather and more particularly because of the incipient displeasure which was known to exist within the Town Council regarding Ba' play. The Boys' Ba' went South and was won by Master Ronald Mowat, but only a dozen took part in the Youths' game, which also went South and was awarded to J. Knight. A Ba' for men which comprised about a score of players was won by the Northenders, David Linklater obtaining the coveted trophy. These games turned out to be the last Ba's played in Stromness.[21]

[19] *O*, 1 January 1920.
[20] *O*, 27 December 1923.
[21] *O*, 3 January 1924.

The circumstance that caused the Town Council to ban the game was the installation of a large plate-glass window by Guilio Fugaccia at his Victoria Street café. The councillors felt that the possibility of replacing this costly window, as well as the danger to players, made it necessary for them to prohibit further ball play on the streets. Thus after forty years the Stromness Ba' came to an end. A revival must have been contemplated for some time, for at its December meeting every year from 1924 to 1927 the Council renewed its ban and gave instructions for bills to be posted on the stages, prohibiting street football.

Stromness Customs

Throughout its fairly short history in Stromness there is no record of the Ba' being played on any festive occasion other than Christmas Day and New Year's Day. The turn-out on 1 January was usually better and that day's game was considered the more important.

At the conclusion of the contest the ba' was awarded to one of the players, but unlike Kirkwall, the trophy was normally given to the man who had played best on that particular occasion. Another difference was that latterly the ba' used was an ordinary inflated leather football.

The time of the throw-up was not regular and this led to some confusion. The order of play could be altered and it was not unknown for a draw to be declared. In some years more than one Men's Ba' was played with the normal sides, and on other occasions the composition of the sides varied, for example Town v. Country and Stromnessians v. Trawlersmen. On New Year's Day 1898 at two o'clock a ba' was thrown up and taken South with a rush, but the Northenders contended that they had no chance as very few knew about the contest. Thereafter several ba's were thrown up, some going one way and some the other.[22] Possibly because the distances from the throw-up point to the goals were fairly short, the Ba's did not last as long as in Kirkwall, although in the Christmas Day game 1913 play surged North and South for two hours before the Northenders were reinforced, and won.

The records show that nearly all the Boys' games went South, the Youths' Ba' was shared evenly, and most of the Men's contests were won by the North end of the town. This is probably accounted for by the help given to the Northenders by fishermen in Stromness for the festive season, and by the fact that a majority of the farmers played North. Farmers from Cairston, Howe, Clouster, Quholmslie, Buan and Deepdale, provided the Northenders with some of their best players.

[22] *O*, 8 January 1898.

The ba's were purchased from the proceeds of door-to-door collections, and before the contests they were exhibited in shop windows. Any damage to property was paid out of the town's rates.

In *History of Stromness, 1900–1972*, Provost George S. Robertson JP commented that annually the Men's Ba' 'attracted a large crowd and provided a needed episode in the dark, drab days. Persons from all walks of life took part in the tussle, suitably dressed for the occasion'.[23]

The Sides and the Goals

The Stromness contestants were known as Northenders and Southenders, and the boundary was the burn flowing under and across Graham Place. Although allegiance was not determined by birth but was dependent rather on where one lived, an established player would not change colours if he moved house. I have been unable to ascertain if this division predates the Ba' or is merely one that was created when a fairly equitable distribution of the town's population was required for the purposes of the game. Certainly in the Yule Tree contest the contestants observed the same natural division, and possibly there had always been an element of rivalry between the two parts of the town so conveniently defined by the open burn.

The starting point of the contest varied from time to time, as did the Southenders' goal. Someone of note in the town usually commenced proceedings, and the ba' was originally thrown up at Jessie Leask's Corner, Graham Place. At this time the Northenders' endeavoured to take the ba' to the Warehouse building, while the Southenders had to reach the foot of Hellihole. This put the Southenders at a disadvantage due to the steep slope of Dundas Street (Porteous Brae). To equalize conditions the location of the start was changed, and for one or two years in the early 1900s play commenced at the foot of Puffer's Close,[24] when the goals were the Warehouse building and the Town Hall (the present Museum). Thereafter the start was at the foot of Church Road, when the Northenders' strove for the Warehouse building and the Southenders' destination was the foot of Dundas Street (Jessie Leask's Corner). This finally eliminated the disadvantage of the Dundas Street brae. Victory was achieved by the Northenders when they forced the ba' against the south wall of the Warehouse building.

[23] G. S. Robertson, *History of Stromness, 1900–1972*, p. 9.

[24] The close was named after a Mr James Leask, at one time town crier in Stromness. Mr Leask lived in the close, and was known locally as 'Puffer', his father having been the skipper of a small local coaster or 'puffer'.

Unlike Kirkwall, there was no water goal, but while the ba' did not *have* to go into the sea it usually did, and then a player or players would plunge into the icy waters in pursuit of the prize. Sometimes victory for the Northenders resulted in the ba' being trucked on the mast of a convenient sailing ship. The Southenders too indulged in this ceremony and after the Christmas Day game 1897 when the Southenders had won, the ba' was hoisted to the topmast of the *Maggie* amid great cheering.[25] This game was unusual in another respect as the Boys played only after the seniors had finished.

In his *History of Stromness* mentioned earlier, Provost Robertson recalled: 'A diversion occurred when the ba' emerged from the crowd at a close end, and the person in possession aimed to carry it to a point south or north of the contest. The most famous was the occasion when deaf Tommy Clouston escaped north, with the crowd in pursuit. Reaching the pier, he climbed the rigging[26] of the schooner *Minnie*, and descending, threw the ba' into the basin, and along with others dived in to recover it. On one occasion, he is credited with swimming with the ba' from the basin to his own pier below the Commercial Hotel.'[27]

As in Kirkwall the Youths' Ba' was bedevilled by the participation of players over the age limit, and on New Year's Day 1913 we read: 'At twelve o'clock the Youths' ba' was thrown up and in a few minutes quite a number of very old-fashioned youths took part in the fray.'[28]

Although the ladies gave active encouragement and support, there was never a Women's Ba' in Stromness.

Games and Incidents of Interest

A Smuggle

On New Year's Day 1896 there was some doubt as to when the game was to begin. At 2.20 p.m. the ba' was turned at Jessie Leask's Corner at the burn and gradually forced north to the New Pier. There a number of players jumped into the water and continued the contest until a boat put off and took both ba' and combatants ashore. It was agreed that there had been a misunderstanding about the throw-up time, and the ba' was taken back to the Corner and thrown up again. A desperate struggle ensued but slowly the Northenders took play over the Plainstones, past the Union Bank and the Free church. On reaching the Mason's Arms Hotel (now the Oakleigh Private Hotel and adjacent building)

[25] *O*, 1 January 1898.
[26] Perhaps this was a trucking of the ba'.
[27] G. S. Robertson, *History of Stromness, 1900–1972*, p. 9.
[28] *OH*, 8 January 1913.

the ba' was adroitly tossed over a gateway behind which the Southenders had cunningly stationed one of their number. He immediately made off with the trophy to the South goal, and certain defeat was turned into victory.

During the game the struggling mass of players 'swayed against our respected town's bellman and drove him through a thick plate glass in the door of Mr William Watt's shop',[29] 32 Victoria Street.

Through a Window

The Boys' Christmas Day game 1908 was a long tussle. After the ball had been thrown up at the foot of Church Road at 10.30 a.m., there was a determined struggle before the it was forced as far north as the Mason's Arms Hotel. There the Southenders rallied and slowly forced back the scrum. After the ba' had been down several closes it was finally carried past the burn to the South goal where one of the contestants was pushed through a plate glass window of the shop belonging to Charles Garson (half-way up Porteous Brae).

Perhaps because of the roughness of the Boys' game and the risk of injury due to broken glass, the bellman went his rounds at one o'clock that afternoon with the call: 'The Men's Ba' will be thrown up at the foot of the Church Road at 2 o'clock. Old Age Pensioners will not be allowed to play. By Order.' The bellman may have been successful regarding the exclusion of Old Age Pensioners, but there was a dispute at the end of this Ba' in connection with the time of the throw-up, so the game was replayed.[30]

The Police Intervene

The Men's New Year's Day game 1911 was unusual. Once again the Northenders were assisted by trawl fishermen and in ten minutes the Warehouse pier was reached and the ba' thrown into the sea. A Northender, William Sangster, plunged in followed by others, including a fisherman wearing clogs who jumped on top of Sangster and knocked him senseless. A boat attempted to bring the players ashore, but it was swamped and its occupants thrown into the water. The police went to the rescue and one of them was pushed into the sea, the crowd howling with laughter when he rose gasping and spluttering in slightly more than four feet of cold January water. Eventually order was restored but by this time the fisherman had got away from the hostile crowd which numbered some hundreds, and swam out underneath the pier to his vessel. The police intervened, took possession of the ba' and returned it to Sangster. Thereafter

[29] *O*, 4 January 1896.
[30] *O*, 2 January 1909.

the English fishermen offered to pay for another ba' on condition that they were allowed to play for the Northenders. This was agreed, and they won again after a very keen struggle.[31]

Dispute

On New Year's Day 1912 the Men's ba' was thrown up at the foot of Church Road at 2 p.m. and carried quickly north to the National Bank where there was a dispute regarding the boundary line. The exact goal for the Northenders having been determined, the ba' was played there when another dispute arose, this time as to who the winner would be. A parley followed, after which the ba' was returned to Church Road where it was again thrown up. This second tussle was over quickly, for as soon as the ba' touched the street 'it was picked up and with a great rush carried to the North end and handed over to the individual whom the crowd declared the winner.'[32]

The Ba' is Knifed

On New Year's Day 1910 the Youths' game was particularly strenuous and eventually someone put a knife through the ba'. This ended the contest, which was declared a draw and described as a fight rather than a game and 'savage work at best'.[33]

Trawlersmen v. Stromnessians

In addition to the Boys' and Youths' contests on Christmas Day 1910 two Men's Ba's were played in the afternoon. The first was won by the Northenders, who were greatly assisted by trawlersmen. The ba' was taken aboard a trawler, but this was very much against the wishes of the locals who did not relish the idea of the trophy being taken to Grimsby. Later on, 'scores of trawlersmen landed, a new ball was procured and the event of the day took place – Trawlersmen versus Stromnessians – the former pushing north while the latter's goal was the burn. With zest did the combatants enter the fray good humoured in the extreme, yet each side determined to win. Townspeople who probably never tried it before were only too willing to help when their side appeared in danger, which it did on several occasions, and the ball gradually went south until the Plainstones were reached when opposition was practically gone and it was hurried to the burn. Stromness had won. No damage was done and doubtless all had enjoyed the tussle.' Hearty cheers were then accorded to both winners and losers. It

[31] *O*, 7 January 1911 and *OH*, 4 January 1911.
[32] *OH*, 3 January 1912.
[33] *O*, 8 January 1910.

was during this game that a trawlersman was heard to remark as he staggered exhausted from the scrum, 'This beats rugby, Bill!'[34]

The Old Lady and the Ba'

In spite of official opposition the Stromness Ba' had a considerable number of devotees, and women were counted amongst its staunchest supporters. In the early years of this century a sprightly old lady called Mrs Brigden ran a small shop on the main street in the south end of the town, near the lifeboat slip. One year the struggle was particularly stiff, and in taking the ba' to their goal the Southenders pushed it through Mrs Brigden's only window. Some of the crowd sympathized with her, but dismissing what must have been quite a catastrophe, she declared 'Never mind, never mind, the Ba' went Sooth'.

The Game Described

The following amusing description of the Stromness Ba' is contained in *The Orcadian* of 9 January 1904:

> The game as played can scarcely be called football as we have been taught to look upon and play it. There is a ball of course but the kicks do not always light on it – unfortunately – and very frequently the exact situation of the leather is a matter for speculation. This however, does not matter so long as you keep your immediate opponent in view, and in his proper place, and steadily advance against the surging mass in front of you. You need not care also whether you know the rules of the game either from an Association or Rugby point of view, not at all; if you can kick – and this comes easy to most – shove, butt, and use your fists, then you may fairly lay claim to be the possessor of the qualifications which entitle you to be ranked with the votaries of the so-called game and to enrol yourself on one side or the other when the fun begins. It goes without saying of course that an umpire is not required, and this is a great convenience more especially as the services of a suitable person might in the circumstances be difficult to get – there being few in the neighbourhood who are known to possess the qualification of being able to render first aid.

But after saying all this the writer concluded:

> By all means let the game be kept up. It is a time-honoured custom and as we have few old customs left let us hang on tenaciously to what survives!

[34] *O*, 31 December 1910 and *OH*, 4 January 1911.

The Stromness Yule Tree

While it is not really within the scope of this book, I have thought it worthwhile to mention the Yule Tree annual contest between Northenders and Southenders which outlived the Stromness Ba' game by more than a decade. This contest took place on Christmas Eve, which is essentially the time for the Yule Log.

There have been throughout Europe a remarkable number of practices, beliefs and superstitions connected with the Yule Log – to avert fire for example, or ill-luck or death, to ward off lightning, to promote fruitfulness, to secure the vitalizing influence of the sun for the ensuing year, to cure illness, and so on. These celebrations were private or domestic festivities normally held within doors and always connected with the burning of the log, keeping and using a piece of the log, the fire or ash from the log, etc.[35] There is no record of anything in the magico-religious field attaching to the Stromness Yule Tree custom.

The only event resembling the Stromness contest was the annual tug-of-war between Up-the-Gates and Down-the-Gates over the Middle Tree or pole, which took place in Kirkwall during the Queen's Birthday celebrations on 24 May. While the two contests were held at different times of the year, and may not have been contemporary, they were nevertheless similar, did not occur elsewhere, and accordingly the possibility of a relationship cannot be discounted.

There is doubt as to when this unusual event started. The first written account I have been able to find is of a contest on Christmas Eve 1907, although the custom was observed in the early 1890s and in all probability before then. Indeed, on Christmas Day 1912 there is a reference to the 'long-established custom of a tug-of-war over the time honoured Yule Tree.'[36]

The procedure was that on Christmas Eve a tree was obtained from a local garden, invariably without the owner's consent – this being considered part of the fun – and then usually between eight and nine o'clock the prize was carried in triumph by a motley crowd of boys and young men to Jessie Leask's Corner in Graham Place. There chains, wire ropes or sometimes ordinary stout ropes were fastened to the ends, and the trial of strength or tug-of-war began – the Southenders endeavouring to pull the unwieldy prize to Ma Humph's Pier, while the Northenders strove to drag it to the New Pier. Once at the goal, with a great cheer, the tree was jettisoned in the water. Sometimes the tree was hauled on to the foreshore and burned.

In latter years the contest was started at the foot of Church Road, and this move eliminated the steep slope of Dundas Street. Victory was achieved when

[35] J. G. Frazer, *The Golden Bough*, part 7, vol. 1, *The Midwinter Fires.*

[36] *OH,* 1 January 1913.

the Yule Tree was taken north to the New Pier or south to the foot of Porteous Brae (Graham Place). As can be imagined these boundaries were only general indications of where the contests ended, and doubtless there was a further mêlée before the prize was finally disposed of.

Shop windows and doors were stoutly barricaded for this event. Lit only by flickering street lamps, a riot of bodies, broken branches and ropes erupted up and down the main street to strident shouts of 'North she goes' and 'South wae her'. The contest was rough, tough and sometimes dangerous. On Christmas Eve 1912 the tree got such cavalier treatment that it eventually disintegrated. What was left was thrown into the harbour, two young men following somewhat unwillingly![37] A youth was pulling hard on a branch on Christmas Eve 1921 when it gave way and he catapulted head first through a window in Dundas Street, and was cut about the neck.

There are many stories in connection with the Stromness Yule Tree contest, and I have been fortunate in obtaining a few from older inhabitants of the town.

One Christmas Eve while an uncompromising struggle was at its fiercest a Southender armed with a bag of pepper ran round and flung the contents in the faces of his Northend adversaries. With the opposition thus confused and in uproar the Southenders had no difficulty in clinching the contest.

Sometimes the lads selected a tree during the course of the day, and on one occasion they explored a number of gardens before coming upon something suitable. After considerable trouble they managed to saw down their choice, and everything was in readiness for the evening's fun. Their annoyance and chagrin can be imagined when, on returning to collect the prize, they discovered that the owner had foiled them by cutting it up for firewood.

On a further occasion the boys acquired their Yule Tree from the garden of Rev. James Christie. The divine had a great keeping on this tree, and suspecting that it had been earmarked, sat up alert for the marauding band. In spite of this the lads slipped past him, cut down and carried off their prize. The minister was wrathful over the loss of his precious possession, but his ill humour was blithely put down to the fact that, being childless, he did not really understand the vagaries of youth!

A Southenders' stratagem in another game was to slash the rope on their opponents' side during play, landing twenty or more sturdy Northenders on their backs, and quite powerless to stop the opposition from dragging the Yule Tree to the south goal.

[37] *O*, 28 December 1912.

About 1910 an amusing tactic was introduced at Jessie Leask's Corner when the Northenders found that, try as they might, they could budge neither opponents nor tree. It transpired that in the darkness the Southenders had secured their end of the rope to a stout iron bar fixed in the wall at their backs! This was probably the iron rail positioned at the very narrow opening to prevent passing carts damaging the wall.

There is the story of the garden boasting five trees. When they had grown to a reasonable size, envious Yule Tree eyes were cast in their direction, and one Christmas Day the owners awoke to discover four trees and one stump. The following Christmas Eve brought the ratio to three trees and two stumps, and so on until eventually only five stumps remained!

A typical game took place on Christmas Eve 1908. After the boys had amused themselves by throwing crackers at the girls there was a lull in the proceedings, but this proved the calm before the storm. About nine o'clock, scores of boys appeared on the streets dragging an old tree with stout ropes attached. 'Where the tree came from was a mystery. Somebody's garden had been plundered but nobody seemed to recognize it just at the moment. It leaked out later on, however, that it was "very like one that grew at the back o' the U P kirk." Shopkeepers in all haste brought out their shutters and put them up before any damage could be done.'[38] In this contest the tree eventually broke and each side claimed victory.

The game was so rumbustious that it was not uncommon for the tree to break. When this happened the boys usually obtained one or two old boats, which were dragged through the streets and sometimes placed across the thoroughfare. On Christmas Eve, a close watch was kept on likely trees, and small boats were made secure. But in spite of this and a disapproving Town Council, the custom maintained its hold over the young men of Stromness. On Christmas Eve 1916 the local Authorities 'belled' an order to the effect that there would not be a Yule Tree tussle that year, but this went unheeded.

The contest fell away after the First World War and its continuance was discouraged by a restriction imposed by the Town Council in 1933. At a meeting in January of that year the Council noted that for the 1931 and 1932 contests a tree had been stolen from the same garden, and apart from the damage done in cutting down the prize, the garden walls had suffered in the process. On several occasions in the past the Council had paid for such damage, and no doubt partly because of this it was decided that the custom of the Yule Tree would only be permitted if a tree was donated, and this gift confirmed in writing by the owner.

[38] *O*, 2 January 1909.

Furthermore it was decided that the following bill should be displayed on the stages before Christmas Eve 1933: 'That the cutting down of a tree or trees in any person's garden must be done only with the written consent of the owner of the garden and handed to the Police, who will have the same verified by the person or persons signing the purported note. If this notice is not adhered to prosecution of offenders will follow. By Order.'[39]

Yule trees were obtained by the prescribed method for the following five years, but the Council's decision damped enthusiasm and hampered the continued observance of the contest. At the last moment on Christmas Eve 1934 a tree was made available from the National Bank garden, and after a tussle of nearly an hour it was pulled to the pier head and dumped in the harbour. On Christmas Eve 1935 the first tree received was considered too small, and so a second and larger one had to be donated. Both trees were eventually heaved into the harbour. A year later the customary warning notices were posted, and once again these had the effect of restraining young people from plundering a garden. Nevertheless at ten o'clock a band of youths erupted down Church Road pulling a monster tree, the biggest for many years, its branches filling the street in parts. Strong ropes were attached, and the prize, which was presumably obtained with its owner's permission, was finally taken South and thrown over Ronaldson's Pier.[40]

Sadly, this was the last Yule Tree contest. A tree was legally acquired on Christmas Eve 1937 but no attempt was made to pull it through the streets.

Christmas in Stromness has never been quite so colourful since the Yule Tree contest disappeared from the streets. There were sporadic attempts to restart the contest after the Second World War, and for three or four years it seemed possible that this might come about. On Christmas Eve 1945 a severe storm kept the contestants at home, and regarding the proposed tussle two years later the *Orkney Herald* of 30 December 1947 said: 'The young people appeared willing enough but seemed to lack initiative and leadership.' The report mentioned that elder Stromnessians were scornful about the youths' failure to produce a tree, and quoted one veteran as saying (with a touch of hyperbole) that in his young days the boys of Stromness had to go as far as Binscarth for their tree, and did so willingly!

And so the excited Yule Tree blood no longer courses, the vivid pageant is dead, the difference gone, and another old custom has succumbed in a world of changing conditions and outlook.

[39] *O*, 12 January 1934.
[40] *O*, 31 December 1936.

18

Parish and Island Games

Graemsay

A Ba' was being played in Graemsay on New Year's Day 1866 when the *Albion,* a full-rigged ship of 1225 tons, was wrecked at the Point of Oxen. The island men stopped playing to help in rescue operations. Isaac Skinner was among those who ran to help, and he was drowned when a boat overturned. The game was between East and West, the ba' was thrown up at the White House and played along the Lighthouse road.

Rousay

A manuscript describing Rousay in the early 1800s has a reference to ball play on Christmas Day (presumably Old Christmas Day, 6 January) and the relevant part is as follows: 'The young men played football till dark. Then they went to a fiddler's house and danced till twelve-o-clock at night.' The manuscript records that New Year's Day was equally well kept, and doubtless football was played then as well. The game was still being played in 1868 (New Year's Day, 1 January),[1] and there is a piece of doggerel about a game ten years later:

> 'Twas on the New Year's evening of 1878,
> The boys they left the Ba' Green and went to Breckan straight
> The lasses followed aifter them as I do hear them say
> Some of them went for whiskey and some of them went to stay.
> Sittan butt and sittan ben, and luckan very dull,
> When in cam' the apostle wae his whiskey bottle full
> Sayan 'Drink and be merry boys for in it I delight
> And I have more whiskey than you will drink the night.

[1] *O*, 28 January 1868.

Breckan was where both young and old folk gathered to enjoy themselves. Succeeding verses contain remarks (not always complimentary) about the people present that night.

Birsay

The parish of Birsay was for long a stronghold of the sport, and the first record I have of what was by then a long-established custom (previously always played on Old New Year's Day, 13 January) is of a game played at the Palace on Old New Year's Day 1864: 'About noon fowling-piece pistols and lead guns began to be discharged about the old Palace and gave intimation that those who intended to join in the amusements of the day had begun to assemble.' Football play started at two o'clock by which time a considerable crowd had gathered, and it was carried on with spirit for some time. Towards evening, the tide having gone out, numbers of both sexes set out for the Brough 'where they no doubt enjoyed a very pleasant walk during which jesting, flirtation, and genuine sweet-hearting were in all probability *not* neglected'. Those who did not visit the Brough carried on playing football or engaged in other athletic exercises till the gloaming set in.[2]

The main Ba' Green was the field immediately to the north of the Palace, but sometimes the game took place on the links. The popularity of Ba' playing in Birsay can be gathered from the fact that on New Year's Day 1876 the Ba' was as usual played at the Old Palace when there were a large number of spectators. That same day football occurred in other districts of the parish. The neighbouring parishes of Sandwick and Harray celebrated the Ba' that year, but at the Palace 'the game was entered into with more vigour, determination, and skill, than at either of the former places'.[3]

On New Year's Day 1877, in spite of occasional snow showers a large party was engaged at football, and 'a well-kicked battle raged for some time'.[4] The spectators included a number of ladies and their presence no doubt encouraged the young gallants among the players to give of their best. On New Year's Day 1888 play was again reported as taking place in different parts of the parish, although on a small scale.[5]

In the early part of the 1890s old style football became less popular, although on New Year's Day 1898 about eighty men took part in a game on the south links.[6] At this time the ba' was made by Thomas Moar, a cobbler living at

[2] *O*, 19 January 1864.
[3] *O*, 8 January 1876.
[4] *O*, 6 January 1877 and *OH*, 10 January 1877.
[5] *O*, 7 January 1888.
[6] *O*, 8 January 1898.

Barnhouse, but as in other districts, when a leather ba' was not available, an animal's scrotum stuffed with grass, cork or horsehair was used.

Thereafter the pastime fell into decline, but in *The Orcadian* of 23 December 1911 there was intimation that football would be held on New Year's Day on the Ba' Green at the Old Palace. The ba' was the joint gift of Messrs W. D. Comloquoy and J. Spence, and was to be given to the Oxtro School when the event was concluded. Before play commenced the donors were accorded 'three lusty cheers and three times three' by the players and the school children who were to be the ultimate recipients of the ba'. Among the crowd of some 200 there were champions of fifty years earlier, and to begin with they looked on disparagingly. Interrupted only by a tug-of-war the contest continued until dusk, and by that stage the veterans had reviewed their criticism and opined that the standard was well up to that of former years.

It might have been one of these once sturdy champions who was involved in the following tale. A barefoot Birsay man returning from Stromness came upon a crowd of Sandwick men playing at the Ba'. The story goes:

> Four and Twenty Asie pearls
> Playing at the Ba',
> By came a Birsay man
> And took it frae them a'

and kicked it for miles, being hotly pursued until he came near the Auld Palace, and it is said the last kick he gave split his muckle toe.[7]

The First World War put an end to the revival, and although on New Year's Day 1923 some play took place on the links,[8] and two years later a number of lads gathered at the Old Palace for the purpose of Ba' playing,[9] this was merely the flickering embers of what had been for over a century a great traditional New Year's Day custom in Birsay.

Harray

On Old New Year's Day 1856, around mid-day a party of young men and women assembled at the house of Messrs Smith and Corrigall to get themselves weighed for amusement (see section on Stenness), and the men then proceeded to a location called Fedger where they played football. There was a stout contest and afterwards the party broke up to drink out of a three-horned cog and eat

[7] *O*, 6 January 1912. 'Asie pearls' is a corruption of the local, derogatory, name for Sandwick men, viz. 'Ash Patties.' See also 'assie pattle' – a useless or lazy person.

[8] *O*, 4 January 1923.

[9] *O*, 8 January 1925.

some sowan scones. The young people in those days were certainly energetic, for about seven o'clock that evening 'both sexes again assembled at the barns of Tofta and Gartha and the upper room of Dykeside, where dancing and leaping were kept up with great spirit till twelve o'clock.'[10] Not only young men but also those more advanced in years heartily joined in football on 1 January 1888.[11] On New Year's Day 1902 the only outdoor amusement was ball playing.[12] In Harray the pastime lasted for a few years after this, but in its heyday players came from as far afield as Germiston.

The established location of play was a field called Jobel opposite the Harray Post Office, bounded on the south by the Netherbrough burn and on the west by the main road. Matthew Spence, a cobbler who lived at the Post Office, made the ba' for some years and he stuffed it with hay or withered grass. About sixty years ago goals had become established and, as in Shetland, these were known as hails.

As in other locations, at times tempers became frayed, and once during the course of a real set-to, a player was summarily up-ended in the adjacent burn. A quaint story is told of a game at the Post Office when a wag substituted an iron ball for the leather one. The first man to kick it broke his leg, and what gave added spice to those sufficiently stimulated to appreciate the rough joke was that the injured unfortunate was a strict abstainer from strong drink. No doubt his wife had very serious doubts about his sobriety when he was carried home that New Year's Day!

Rendall

On Yule Day 1864 (6 January), at an early hour youths congregated at the Gorseness Ba' Green (this was probably at Hogarth), 'having no objections to a breathing before breakfast'. About noon, young, middle-aged and even old men began to assemble and from one o'clock till dusk a stirring encounter took place. The following is a description of the scene:

> Old and young seem equally interested and animated. The energy and activity of the young are only equalled by the animation and excitement of the old Daddy Baldhead with his striped mittens and 'lugged shoon', and Grandfather Greybeard with his smooth round-headed staff and bright-buttoned bottle-green coat, feeling 'their auld hearts grow young

[10] *O*, 19 January 1856.
[11] *O*, 7 January 1888.
[12] *OH*, 8 January 1902.

> again', as they witness the nimble agility and sturdy shouldering of their young days reproduced by the active young scions of their respective races. Hear them how they chuckle and crow as they see those hearty young fellows perspiring at every pore as 'shouther to shouther the braw lads *kick.'* It does one's heart good to see those ancient worthies encouraging by word and deed those feats they so much enjoyed some fifty or sixty or seventy years ago. And see yon plucky old grand-daddy not a bit afraid to encounter the stout, strong, stalwart young fellow – twice his bulk and three times his weight – and take the ba' from him too. Of course he did! But did you observe how carefully and tenderly the young man – glorying in his strength – met the old with cannie care? He wouldn't hurt him for worlds, nor take the ball from him for the life interest of the best farm in the mainland 'No no, lets *humour* as well as *honour* the aged', says he, retiring willingly discomfited from the 'meet.' And now as the sun sinks down beyond the west hills the strife grows fast and furious 'Off coats and till it again my lads,' is the shout; and a loud 'Hurra' by way of response makes the Rendall hills to ring again. The very best of good humour prevails from first to last; not a shade of ill-feeling; not a 'cross word' or 'an ugly look' can be discerned. Although a fellow gets a tumble, he falls on the green sward and feels nothing, but a slight regret that he can't kick away, on his beam ends without losing time by getting on his *pins* again. What a hearty genial affair the Yule day 'game at the ba'' is in the country, the occasion is a great jubilee when all previous injuries are forgiven, and all former animosities forgotten.[13]

Old New Year's Day 1868 had fine weather and some boys gathered for football that, while it lasted, was kept up with glee.[14] The sport was observed on Christmas Day 1890 but not celebrated a week later.

That the men of Rendall were addicted to football is confirmed by the following story. Until about 150 years ago, mourners from Halkland, Isbister and the North side of Rendall met Gorseness men at a point on the Gorseness Hill between Hogarth and Aviedale, and from there proceeded to the old cemetery near South Ettit on the Bay of Hinderayre. The assembly point, which was marked by six or so large stones in the rough shape of a cross, was known as the 'Wheeling Cross'.[15] It was there that the coffin was placed, while the bearers

[13] *O*, 12 January 1864.
[14] *O*, 21 January 1868.
[15] H. Marwick, *The Orkney Norn*, p. 209: a spot where (traditionally) funeral companies rested on their way to a kirkyard; *wheel:* to set down or rest. He cites two places with similar names in Stronsay and Sanday.

took a final rest before proceeding to the interment. When this traditional staging post was reached it was customary for the men, who had been stimulated with quantities of drink, to take part in competitions such as lifting and throwing the stones sited there. The main part of the proceedings was Orkney football. About the beginning of the nineteenth century, after the coffin had been laid down, a spirited game was commenced. As was normal no rules were observed, fouls were frequent, tempers rose and play became violent – no doubt aided by further libations of the home-brewed ale that was then a feature of Orkney funerals and which had doubtless been procured from the nearby, long-established alehouse at Hogarth. After a time matters got completely out of control and developed into a real brawl or *heckèd teullyo*[16] – while corpse and coffin lay quite forgotten! Eventually darkness put an end to the proceedings, the mêlée perforce broke up, and the story goes that it was the next day before the erstwhile football players reassembled and the subdued cortège wound its way to the shore-side cemetery. Although the surrounding ground has now been ploughed out, the scene of the strife can still be identified, and in 1966 I was shown those stones which remain, and which had long ago been silent witnesses at this bizarre football brawl.

At one time men from Evie came to Rendall to take part, and there was fierce rivalry between the parishes. Apart from a prohibition on lifting the ball, the tussle was unimpeded by rules. Play started at noon and continued until darkness set in, when the side which had acquitted itself best claimed the ba'. Until at least the middle of the nineteenth century it was believed that to keep possession of the trophy would bring a bumper crop of potatoes. The event normally took place in a field immediately to the south of the farm house of Hogarth, and convenient indeed for the popular ale house there, known as Tammy Halcro's.[17] Spectators were numerous and they travelled from far and near to witness the stiff tussle. The ba', usually an animal's bladder, was sometimes inflated and at other times was stuffed with horse or cow hair. When the supply of bladders was exhausted a herring cork was used. Casualties from the contest and John Barleycorn were numerous, and sore, incapacitated players and spectators were assisted out of the cold winter's day and given shelter in the barn at Hogarth where they were left overnight to recover.

The annual event in Rendall died out at the end of the nineteenth century and one of the last games was on New Year's Day 1896, when once again the scene of the struggle was the old Ba' Green at Hogarth.

[16] J. Firth, *Reminiscences of an Orkney Parish,* p. 87, which gives: Ork. *heck,* to grab, Scot. *tuilyie,* a quarrel – a hand-to-hand fight.

[17] J. Firth, *Reminiscences of an Orkney Parish,* p. 87.

Evie

On 1 January 1861 there was trouble at the game. A party of young men from a nearby parish (probably Rendall) had arrived rather the worse of liquor. They had come to see what was going on and 'behaved in a foolish manner. They wished to fight with some of the Evie young men at the ball-playing and they broke some bottles and glasses in the public house and used very improper language because they were not allowed to enter, and get more drink.'[18]

Bad weather did little to dampen enthusiasm and on Christmas Day 1864 and New Year's Day 1865 (Old Style) football took place in spite of very stormy wet weather, the game being played briskly till darkness set in.[19] In 1868 there was again play on both Christmas and New Year's Day (Old Style).[20] Sometimes the sport took place after the volunteers had disbanded following drill and carbine practice.

On New Year's Day 1878 acrimony crept in. First of all there was a muster of volunteers and this was followed by a game: 'There was like to have been a little foul play at the football, but the game happily ended without any serious consequences.'[21]

The following year the ill-humour boiled over into a real fracas when, as a correspondent told *The Orcadian:*

> youths and middle-aged men met as usual for the purpose of having a friendly 'rap' at the football; but we are sorry to say that however friendly they met, some of them at least did not part in such good terms. In your last issue you told us that you had no regular stand-up fights at this game in your good town. You may congratulate us, for we had a lot. It would be difficult for one to say whether the fights were stand-up ones or not, as some of the combatants seemed to be oftener down than they were up. The game was kept up with great spirit all day long, but towards evening some of the 'south-enders' would every now and then give some of the 'north-enders' a 'friendly' kick, which of course caused a little grumbling. This state of matters could not be tolerated long, and shortly there were twos and threes belabouring each other most heartily, as a proof of which it told with considerable effect on the proboscis. The 'game' over, each and all sought their way home to satisfy the inner-man.[22]

[18] *OH*, 22 January 1861.
[19] O, 24 January 1865.
[20] O, 21 January 1868.
[21] *O*, 12 January 1878.
[22] *O*, 11 January 1879.

The Orcadian of 7 January 1932 had this to say about the tussle in Evie: 'Time was when Evie had its New Year Ba' we are told, and it was "some" game – if one was able to tackle the opposing player "sorrow-odds" aboot the ba'!'

Firth

The game was played in the village street, and on Old New Year's Day 1869, about eleven o'clock in the morning 'the young people from the surrounding districts began to assemble at Finstown for the purpose of having the usual game at football, which was stoutly contested during the day.'[23]

There was violence on Old New Year's Day 1878 and the *Orkney Herald* of 23 January 1878 gave an account 'of an event which one would have looked for in a half-civilized community in the backwoods of the New World, or among the shillelagh-whirling ruffians at a West of Ireland fair, but which is not to be dreamed of as having happened under the shadow of the Christian Churches of Finstown.' The report continued:

> On Monday the 14th inst., about eleven o'clock in accordance with the old custom, numbers of men, lads and boys assembled in Finstown and began to kick at football on the road or street leading up through the village. Play was kept up in the usual rough style for some time till all were mud-bespattered from head to foot, the heated and thirsty frequently resorting to the 'Pomona Pump' to damp their ardour. Quarrelling began with two or three parties, and soon –
>
> Drink in the man
> Sense in the can
>
> – there was a general melee in which blows and kicks fell like winter shower, and blood flowed freely. Some were carried bleeding and senseless into the neighbouring houses, where their wounds were sewed and bandaged. The contingent of fighting men was augmented by reinforcements from Kirkwall and Harray; traffic was stopped for a time; and the screaming of women and swearing of men rose above the general uproar. This is not an overdrawn picture. We do not believe the like has ever been witnessed in Orkney before; – certainly not in this parish even in the previous palmy days of the public house. Query – Will the next meeting of Quarter Sessions send us a policeman as hurriedly as the last inflicted on us a licensed house?

[23] *O*, 19 January 1869.

Subsequently, a letter appeared in *The Orcadian,* 26 January 1878, in which the *Herald's* report blaming the Pomona Inn for the trouble was emphatically refuted. After stating that the inn had only a licence to sell beer and that trade had seldom been quieter, the writer went on to say that there had been 'more *spirit* than beer in the affray', and suggested that the *Herald's* correspondent might find out where this 'spirit' came from. (Finstown was at one time famous for at least one illicit still.) There was no denial of the rough and violent scenes so graphically described.

The sequel to the affray occurred on Tuesday 24 January 1878 when at the Sheriff Court, Kirkwall, William Corrigall and James Stevenson were charged before Sheriff Mellis with disorderly conduct and a breach of the peace. Corrigall, who had apparently been previously convicted of a breach of the peace, was fined 25*s.* or six days' imprisonment, and Stevenson was fined 15*s.* with the alternative of six days' imprisonment. *The Orcadian* of 26 January 1878, stated that the damage sustained by persons and property was actually less than when there had been no licensed premises in the village. The other games must have been very fierce!

On New Year's Day 1883 football was played between 'north side' and 'south side' boys, each doing his best to keep the ba' to his own side, and in the true tradition, players were permitted only to use their legs and feet. Lifting the ba' was not allowed. Participants were often knocked down, and since conditions were very wet they were soon covered with mud. *The Orcadian* reported 'for a while the game was continued, and when they were tired of the contest a few assembled in the local inn to establish or renew friendship with each other over a glass of foaming ale.'[24]

Interest waned in the 1890s, and on New Year's Day 1898 only a score of schoolboys took part.

Holm

This was another locality where the pastime was popular. Play took place on New Year's Day after the volunteers had completed their drill and carbine practice, when spectators who had been watching joined in. On New Year's Day 1882 a lad had his shoulder bone broken,[25] and on New Year's Day 1889 football was played all day, both at the East end and at St Mary's.[26]

An interesting connection between old style Orkney football and the Ba' played for a few years on New Year's Day along the main street of St Mary's

[24] *O*, 20 January 1883.
[25] *O*, 7 January 1882.
[26] *O*, 5 January 1889.

occurred on New Year's Day 1910 when 'football was engaged in the Ayre park during part of New Year's Day and as the day advanced they came to the village and the East and West-Gates of the village had a contest. Who were the successful parties it is hard to say.'[27] The sides were the East and West ends of the village and the throw-up took place at the Post Office, the Youths' Ba' starting at noon, and the Men's Ba' two hours later. The goals were St Mary's Loch at the West end and the old Grain Store at the East end. The West side thus had to travel a distance of approximately 350 yards and the East side slightly more. That there should be a water goal was in the true tradition of the game.

The contests were rough and punishing, and in 1960 one of my informants, who had been present nearly sixty years before, said 'they tore the very claes aff yer back.' There were one or two exciting tussles, particularly the occasion when a local worthy, 'Sodger Bob' Wylie, had a real set-to with an adversary called Langskaill waist-deep in the waters of St Mary's Loch.

This street game was observed for four or five years around 1910, and was stopped because of the danger from the steep sea banks on the south side of the road.

Long before that, in 1778, old style football was played in Holm. The following entries come from the Account books of Patrick Graeme of Graemeshall.

> 1778, January 5 – By the prize played at the Foot Ball on New Year's Day. Piper 1/- – 8/-.
>
> 1781, December 26 – By given for a prize to be played for at the Foot Ball on Christmas Day – 15/-.
>
> 1782, December 25 – By given the People to play at the Ball on Christmas this day 15/-, the Boys 2/6 – 17/6.
>
> 1784, December 27 – By Given to the Tennants to be played for at the Foot Ball of this date £1 1/-, to the Boys 2/6 – £1 3/6.
>
> 1785, December 26 – By Given of this date Monday to be played at the foot Ball the Men £1 1/-, the Boys 3/- – £1 4/-.

There are several interesting features about these five entries concerning the playing of mass or old style football in Holm more than two centuries ago. In two instances, 5 January 1778 and 26 December 1781, the word 'prize' is used. In January 1778 the prize was 7*s*. and in December 1781 the amount had increased to 15*s*. On the earlier occasion a piper was paid 1*s*., presumably to entertain

[27] *O*, 8 January 1910.

participants and spectators. On 25 December 1782 'the People' were given money 'to play at the Ball on Christmas this day,' 15*s.* to the men and 2*s.* 6*d.* to the boys. So there was a difference made between boys' and men's play. Undoubtedly they had separate games. By 27 December 1784 the money had increased to £1 1*s.* 'to the Tennants' and 2*s.* 6*d.* to the boys, while on 26 December 1785 'the men' received £1 1*s.* and the boys 3*s.*

In 1795 the annual rent of the farm of Graemeshall was £21 and in December 1777 a tradesman was paid 1*s.* for a day's work. Thus the money involved was considerable whether paid as a prize or as a donation for refreshments.

These payments by the laird were made not primarily as an encouragement to Holm men and boys to take part in the game, but rather they were the customary annual recognition of a well-established parish pursuit.

Orphir

The contestants were East and West and allegiance was determined by the side of the throw-up point on which one lived. The contest, which was in existence in the 1890s, was not played during the First World War and on being recommenced afterwards, survived until the mid-1920s. The last tussle was on New Year's Day 1926 when West won, and amid much cheering and good humoured banter the ba' was handed over to G. Kemp, Lingoe.

The ba', which was made by Billy Gunn, shoemaker at Kirbister, was stuffed with sawdust or cork. Although latterly it was awarded to the man who held it longest on the day, in the 1890s it was gifted either to the boys at Kirbister School or to those at Orphir School, depending on which side had been successful.

Play took place only on New Year's Day and the throw-up, at two o'clock, was at the bridge over the Swanbister burn, a few yards from the War Memorial. The goals were for the West side the burn at Donaldsons, and for the East side the Lerquoy burn. Thus in order to win, the East side had to carry the ba' roughly 650 yards, while the West side had to travel a little further.

There was also a Youth's Ba' at noon which was introduced in the first few years of this century. For this the maximum permitted age was twenty.

It is noteworthy that the throw-up should be at a bridge and that there were water goals. The Ba' was stiffly contested, sometimes lasting for two hours, and was played along the public road. Normally some thirty men were in contest. Until 1914, although old Orkney football had ceased to have any real significance in Orphir and did not exist as a separate contest, the Ba' played along the public road was always preceded by a general kick about in a field near the throw-up point, i.e. where the War Memorial is situated. This provides an interesting connection with the old style pastime.

The Orphir Ba' died out about 1927. However, 50 years later a special contest took place at Scorradale on 6 June, to commemorate the Queen's Silver Jubilee (see FIG. 95). This was between Orphir and Stenness, and involved at least 60 participants, including some enthusiastic women. Two referees had been nominated: William Muir, Stenness, and John Hay, Orphir. Their main functions were to ensure that no outsiders took part, and to signal the end of the tussle after an hour.

Just before 8 p.m. James Swannie, Stenness, addressed the waiting players and said that the organizers hoped the event would be enjoyed by all, played cleanly and with no bad feeling. He continued that only Orphir and Stenness people would be permitted to play and that no one under the age of fifteen could take part. Furthermore the ba' was not to be awarded to any person but had to be handed back at the end of the event.

Amid much excitement Mrs Meg Harvey, Stenness, who had provided the ba' threw it up from a platform specially constructed on the top of Scorradale brae. This men's ba' had been won by Robert Gunn, a Doonie, on Christmas Day 1929.

At the outset a scrum formed, and uncompromising, hard play took participants north and then south from the road, over heath and heather and sometimes into ditches, which fortunately were dry. Stenness men initially held the advantage but eventually the ba' was forced back to Orphir ground, where dogged defence and fierce tackling kept it until the whistle went at 9 p.m., and the contest came to an end. Amid much jubilation Orphir was declared to have won.

The game was tough and of much interest to the many spectators. The rugged struggle inevitably brought some cuts and bruises, but was played in a very sporting manner. Certainly there were bone-shaking tackles when the ba' ran free.

It was indeed a memorable and exciting hour for players and spectators, and demonstrated that Orphir and Stenness men know very well how to play and enjoy the Ba'.

Sandwick

In the early part of the nineteenth century, football was the chief amusement on both Yule Day and Old New Year's Day.[28] On New Year's Day 1876 there was play on the links at Skaill 'without goals or touchline; every man thoroughly convinced that he has done his duty manfully if he manages to trip the feet from a few of his opponents.'[29]

[28] *O*, 5 January 1889.
[29] *O*, 8 January 1876.

The event became increasingly neglected in the mid-1890s, and gradually petered out in the first few years of the twentieth century. The ba' was stuffed with cork and for some years it was made by Tammy Merriman, a cobbler who lived at Leigh.

Stenness

Play took place beside the Hall of Ireland which was made available by Mr J. R. Irvine. Until approximately 1885 the contest was held on Old New Year's Day, and thereafter on 1 January. The field is hard by the ruins of an old church and churchyard, and perhaps the location was due to the fact that play had originally taken place there after service on Sundays. While, as elsewhere, there were no rules, there does seem to have been some distinction between the players from Ireland and those from Clouston. There was no general agreement regarding playing together as a team, but rather an understanding that one did not tackle the player with the ba' if he happened to be from the same district. Sometimes the ba' was a ram's scrotum packed with grass or horse hair. After the game the pundler was taken from the mill and everyone was weighed. This custom was an innocent amusement to see how much weight had been gained or lost over the year.

South Ronaldshay

On Christmas Day 1863 the principal outdoor amusement was football. A report in *The Orcadian* of 12 January 1864 said that the game 'has been of long standing – beyond the memory of any living man'. The description then continues in an amusing vein:

> In one district the bachelors and married men were pitted against the young men, and, strange to say, although the latter had all the support which their sweethearts could furnish, both by word and deed, they were completely beat off, leaving the field, many of them, with a sore head, and more of them with a sorer heart. Some of the young lads about Grimness will not soon forget the bad luck which attended them on this occasion; neither will the wooers about Hoxa and Herston venture to show off, or cut any more Christmas capers before their dears for some months to come. A couple of brisk young lads, as proud as turkeys and as chokeful of conceit as peacocks, lost the good graces of their ladies; and another, not three miles from Herston, lost his sweetheart altogether by their unmanly conduct that day!

Football was also played on New Year's Day 1864 (1 January) and the South Parish is mentioned as the location.

In the latter part of 1911 the boys at Tomison's School in the South Parish collected for a football and they met with success. Unfortunately the ba' did not arrive in time for Christmas and there was a postponement until New Year's Day when 'about thirty or forty old and young met in the park opposite the school where flags were flying. The game was commenced at noon and was carried on with great zest and good humour for two or three hours.'[30] The following year there was a similar event in a field at Flaws.[31]

Burray

The Orcadian's local correspondent wrote in January 1891 that they were 'all alive and been *kicking*. On Christmas Day and New Year's Day we kicked the football on the Links till we were tired, and on the evening of the last mentioned day, our brawest lads and bonniest lasses kicked up their heels in the Good Templar Hall from 7 p.m. till 5 next morning, to the stirring strains of Messrs Swannies' fiddles.'[32] There was a good turnout for the match on the Westermill links on Christmas Day 1899, and although there had been signs of the game losing favour for some years a keen interest was taken in the contest – 'to judge by the number of combatants who went home with a decided limp in their gait and the dilapidated condition of their holiday garments.'[33]

St Andrews

There was New Year's Day play in this parish until approximately 1890, usually in a field on the farm of Sebay.

Deerness

A favourite location for play was Brandyquoy and although the contest was usually held on New Year's Day, it also occurred at ploughing matches between Deerness and Holm. There was much rivalry between the two parishes and when they met, doubtless stimulated by drink readily available from a nearby alehouse owned by John Esson, the ba' was kicked and play was furious with fisticuffs sometimes in evidence. Football was also enjoyed on the links of Netherstove and of Skaill.

[30] *O*, 6 January 1912.
[31] *O*, 11 January 1913.
[32] *O*, 10 January 1891.
[33] *O*, 6 January 1900.

Flotta

On New Year's Day 1889, 'according to long established custom, the Ba' was hotly engaged in for many hours in the Bow parks, the players including not only youths and those in the prime of life, but veteran footballers over whose heads so many New Year's Days had passed that their grand-children mingled with them in the friendly tussle. Bravo! the sturdy heart that never grows old – the eye retaining its youthful fire that beams from under locks long since grown grey.'[34] There was play also on Christmas Day but the game did not last long into the twentieth century.

Hoy

Between 11 a.m. and 3 p.m. on New Year's Day 1871 the young men of North Walls were engaged at the Ba'. The contest took place in a park tenanted by Thomas Sutherland and 'abundant refreshments were on the ground, which added spirit to the match'. At the close there were three hearty cheers for the royal family and another three for Mr Heddle who was the proprietor of the ground.[35] This game was held at North Seatter (locally known as Greenquoy).

On Christmas Day 1878 'a good many of the young however managed to spend a few hours in that exercise which was no doubt beneficial for keeping the feet warm and the blood in circulation.'[36] The Ba' took place on the links of Mo'ness, north Hoy, on Christmas Day 1901.

There was an established Rackwick game played at the Ba' Green, Greenhill. The Rackwick tussle was obviously of some importance as Hoy men (from the east side of the Ward Hill) travelled to Greenhill to participate.

The ba' was an inflated sheep's bladder covered with leather, and in the latter part of the nineteenth century the ba's were fashioned by James Thomson, a local cobbler who lived in Rackwick.

North Isles

As one would imagine, the custom tended to be observed for longer in the North Isles, and every island had its Ba'.

Shapinsay

Play took place at Balfour village.

34 *O*, 5 January 1889.
35 *OH*, 11 January 1871.
36 *OH*, 1 January 1879.

Westray

The game was played on the links north of Pierowall, and the contest was between the north and south ends of the island. The custom was in existence up to the start of the First World War.

Papa Westray

Football was still played after the First World War. On New Year's Day 1920 there was a hard frost, 'and in the forenoon ball playing in a field was indulged in and taken part in with great zest by men of all ages.'[37] In the *Proceedings of the Orkney Antiquarian Society* there is an article on Papa Westray games in which football at Christmas is mentioned. The article was written for the session 1922–1923 and referred to the writer's boyhood days:

> We were wont each to contribute so much towards the buying of a football. This football was made by an islander who filled it with corks, etc., so you will know it was pretty hard. Then it went its rounds as one boy would take it home one evening another, another. Of course we were very proud when we got the ball for the night.[38]

A former resident of Papa Westray, Bill Irvine, who lived at Links until 1998, believes that the Ba' green was on the lands of Whitelooms towards the north end of the island, the sides being the North-yard and the South-yard. The cork-filled ba's were made by David Groat of Quoys who died in 1931. Play took place on Christmas Day and New Year's Day, and there is a suggestion that the champion was whoever could dribble the ball for the longest period. Afterwards the ba' was given to the schoolchildren who 'kicked it to pieces'. Soccer, Papa Westray v. Westray, took place in the 1920s during the summer months.

North Faray

There was a game on Christmas Day and New Year's Day, and the custom was observed until about 1914.

Stronsay

On Old New Year's Day 1864 'a number of young men got up a match at the foot ball, and for several hours, notwithstanding well kicked shins, contended for victory with a zeal, energy and activity worthy of a matter of greater importance.'[39] This celebration died out after the First World War.

[37] *OH*, 7 January 1920.

[38] *Proceedings of the Orkney Antiquarian Society*, vol. 1, 1922–1923. The article was by Mr John Drever. *OH*, 26 January 1864.

[39] *OH*, 26 January 1864.

EDAY

Up till the mid-1890s and possibly a little later, football was played, and favourite locations were Greentoft, Breck and Stenaquoy. The game was celebrated on an inter-district basis, e.g. Southend and Westside v. Northend (comprising Cuisbay, Guith, Millbounds and Calfsound) and play was usually only on New Year's Day. Play started at midday and lasted for about two hours, between twenty and thirty youths and young men taking part. The ba' was an inflated pig's bladder, covered in leather, the casing being made by a cobbler, Tom Gullion, who lived at Gateside and latterly Schoolplace. The players defrayed the cost of 5*s*. Sometimes a home-made ball was used, and this consisted of a mixture of cows' hair and soap, moulded together and left to dry and harden. The side which forced the ba' over their opponents' goal line the most times took it home as a trophy, but there does not seem to have been any belief that the winning party would have better crops. As in other districts there was no referee, and although the ba' could not be lifted there were no other recognized rules, play being robust.

SANDAY

There is a tradition that the islanders assembled at Queensbrig to play at the Ba' on Yule Day.[40] We know that at an unknown location on Christmas Day 1865, after the volunteer corps was dismissed, 'a hearty game at football as a finale was carried on a short time.'[41] The game was played into the first few years of this century, and the ba' was an inflated sheep's or pig's bladder stuffed with hay. Sometimes a herring cork was used. In the early part of the nineteenth century it was played on the plain of Fidge, in the centre of the island between Leavisgarth and Newark.

There is a shoal called the Ba' Green of Rinnabreck some four miles north of Sanday, and a legend concerning this rock says that in the dim past it was well clear of the sea and the surface was covered with grass. It is alleged that at Yule as part of the festivities people went there to play at the Ba'.[42] However, the following explanation of the name is given in Dr Hugh Marwick's county book *Orkney:* 'The "Green" is probably a corruption of the Old Norse word for a shoal, *grunnr,* which in Orkney has become "grunie" or "grunyie" (e.g. Eday Grunyie), and "ba" or "bo" is the Orkney term for a breaking wave on such a shoal (O.N. *bcòi,* a breaker: literally a foreboder or warner).'[43]

[40] *Proceedings of the Orkney Antiquarian Society,* vol. 1, 1922, *Antiquarian Notes on Sanday* H. Marwick.

[41] *O*, 9 January 1866.

[42] *Proceedings of the Orkney Antiquarian Society,* vol. 1, 1922, p. 28.

[43] H. Marwick, *Orkney*, p. 236.

North Ronaldshay

In this island a Ba' was held on New Year's Day and was a regular occurrence until the first few years of the last century. About midday men and youths gathered at the Standing Stone in the south end of the island, and kicked an improvised ball which consisted of an animal's bladder, and which was stuffed hard with straw. Boots were not common, most people being clad in rivlins,[44] and the football had a reasonable length of life. The proceedings were stimulated by generous libations of home-brewed ale, and after an hour or two the gathering proceeded to the lighthouse and some of the more energetic youths climbed to its top. Thereafter, if the weather was suitable, an open-air dance was held in the lighthouse courtyard.

[44] A type of shoe made of raw hide.

19

The Game in Shetland

In nineteenth century rural Shetland, life was devoid of much incident and the Baa' was an event of great moment, a medium of expression and a celebration in itself – mainly on Yule Day (6 January) which was one of *the* days of the year. Except in isolated instances the game did not survive into the twentieth century, its importance diminishing as fresh interests were created, and new amusements became possible in a more affluent society. The Yule celebrations went on for several days and the Baa' took place on more than one day.

Before the great day the bladder of a cow or pig was inflated and hung up to dry. Leather, quartered and sewn together, was fashioned into an outside cover. The finished article was fairly rough and seldom entirely round, but it was nevertheless strong and serviceable and usually manufactured by the young people in the community.

Before daylight on Yule morning, families were awakened by fiddlers going the rounds playing an ancient Scandinavian air called 'The Day Dawn'.[1] No work which could possibly be avoided was undertaken on Yule Day, and 'Playin' da Baa'' began as soon as breakfast was over, males of all ages taking part. The participants normally broke off in time for the midday meal, and often restarted in the afternoon, continuing while the light lasted.

The baa' was produced at little cost, but any small expense or the price of a baa' from the local cobbler was defrayed from the money that the bridegroom traditionally handed over after a wedding. The following is an extract from *Shetland Traditional Lore* by Jessie M. E. Saxby: 'The newly-wed couple came first arm-in-arm, he proud, she smiling. Following them came the "married folk" together . . . Soon the boys of their district came to cheer and kick a football along the way. They expected and got the price of a new Yule "Baa'" from the bridegroom.'

[1] 'The Day Dawn' was set to music by a Miss Kemp of Edinburgh about 1875.

As in Orkney the baa' could not be lifted and there were no other rules, the emphasis being on individual endeavour. The following vivid description of the game is taken from *Life and Customs in the Shetland Isles* by E. W. Hardy: 'There are no goal-posts, no scientific play, no attempt at combination by the players, each plays for himself, and tries to score with a long, terrific drive.' It is not entirely clear what is meant by 'tries to score with a long terrific drive', and this may signify making one's mark or achieving distinction by a lengthy kick, or by kicking the baa' a significant height. There was no studied play, and what is described is probably an exhibition of individual prowess in propelling the baa' horizontally or vertically.

The Yule Baa' was played throughout Shetland, and the following details of district games have been obtained either from the personal reminiscences of Shetlanders present at the Baa' game, or from memories handed down to them.

Brae

The game was continued until the early 1900s. The owner of the barn in which the Yule night dance following the Baa' was held was recompensed beforehand, by some evening assistance in the threshing of his corn.

Aith

A game was played as late as 1920.

Whalsay

On a typical Yule morning activities started early, probably around 4.30 a.m. when the younger male element summoned those still asleep with vigorous blasts on a luder-horn,[2] used in Shetland haaf fishing boats for all signalling purposes. While it was still dark, everyone gathered at the bonfire, which usually consisted of a tar barrel, and this was sometimes made mobile by being mounted on two wooden beams. When the blaze had died down, houses in the locality were visited and drams exchanged.

After breakfast came the principal event of the daylight hours – the Baa' – and this was participated in by males of all ages. A separate part of the football proceedings in Whalsay consisted of taking especial note of the player who could kick the baa' highest, and this was called 'a pookie a' air'. The old lady who passed on this information said admiringly: 'I aye mind, Magnie Simpson could kick the baa' higher as onybody else.' Champion Magnie and my informant were

[2] Pronounced 'looder' (in one district 'ludder'), O.N. *Ludr*, a trumpet. Apparently some people on land could identify individual boats by the note of the luder-horn.

alive and well when I made contact in early 1960, some sixty-five years after the event. In all Baa' playing districts in this island there were goals, called 'doors',[3] at each end of the pitch, and these were marked by stones placed on the ground. It was permissible to propel the baa' with feet and fists, and while each side had a goalkeeper, there was no referee. The only rule observed was an embargo on tripping, and, as in modern soccer this was a foul, a free kick being awarded against the offending side. The player taking the kick was allowed 'hailin' room', i.e. the opposition had to stand back and not impede him. 'Hailin'', or hauling room is a fishing expression still in use in Shetland and refers to the unrestricted space round him that a fisherman requires when pulling in his nets. While this could be the origin of the term, more probably the derivation lies in the word 'hail' meaning to drive (the ball) through or over a goal or boundary.[4] This seems to be borne out by the fact that certain players in Whalsay were termed 'good hailers', that is, they possessed strong shots.[5]

Thus the Whalsay game had evolved into something semi-competitive, and starting with an undetermined number of players, any new blood which reached the field was allocated to keep the sides as even as possible. As in other parts of Shetland the game terminated in time for the midday meal, but it was not unknown for play to be resumed in the afternoon. The game died out after the First World War.

Yell

The goals were known as 'doors'.

Walls

In 1960 a participant recalled taking part in a Yule Day game on flat meadow-land near Finnigarth, Mid Walls, probably around 1910.

Levenwick

There was a village Baa' game at Yule, which allegedly dated from the depths of folk memory. The name Levenwick may well be a corruption of O.N. *leika* – to play, *vín* – a pasture or field, and *vík* – a bay, i.e. the bay of the sports field. Latterly the ball was an inflated bladder covered with canvas.

[3] Perhaps 'Hail-doors'- see note 4 below.

[4] *Scottish National Dictionary,* 1956, vol. 4, part 4, p. 363. Also on p. 363, in connection with Orkney, *hail-doo,* used fig. in phr. *coman (gettan) near the hail-doors,* 'coming to an end of supplies of potatoes ale meal etc'.

[5] This information was obtained in 1966 from Mr John Irvine, Symbister, Whalsay.

Foula

There was a Baa' game on Yule Day.

Dunrossness

The Vadal Green was the location for a rousing Yule Day game, which lingered on until 1920. The Baa' was also played on the links of Quendale.

Fair Isle

The game was played mainly on old Yule Day (6 January), and latterly on Christmas Day and New Year's Day, and there is a field in Fair Isle called the Baa' Green – at Meoness in the south-east corner of the island. Baa' playing in its old style did not survive into the twentieth century.

Alec Doloughan BEM MA, at one time the schoolmaster and preacher on the island, commented that in the 1930s there was no real counterpart to the Kirkwall Ba' but that 'on rare and special occasions the Island divided itself into "Uppies and Doonies" and engaged in a contest which though designated as football bore little resemblance to that game.' He continued that there was a natural division in the island created by the two lighthouses at the extreme ends of the island, each with three families resident in their enclaves. When a game was arranged, the crofts north of the Post Office (formerly the croft of Shirva) sided with the North Light. These were Shirva, Midway, Hool, Schoolton, Upper Stoneybrake, Lower Stoneybrake, Schoolhouse, Field and Wassetter, and provided the Doonies with their players. The Uppies arranged themselves with the South Light and came from the crofts of Leough, Low Leough, Taft, Rock Cottage, Haa, Busta, Springfield and Melville Cottage. Youngsters (for some reason usually in fancy dress) joined the adults, numbers were not restricted, the event had very few rules and some handling was allowed. In 1935 Alec remembered the Silver Jubilee celebrations game being halted and the contestants scattered by the arrival of a Tiger Moth piloted by the pioneering Captain E. E. Fresson, prospecting for an emergency landing place between Orkney and Shetland.

* * * *

The Baa' over, Yule celebrations were incomplete without a dance at which all in the district congregated. Raw shins and bruised shoulders were forgotten as tired bodies responded eagerly to the traditional reels provided by a willing team of local fiddlers.

Finally, the following is part of a poem representing the thoughts of a long-exiled Shetlander, and found in *Shetland Fireside Tales*,[6] first published in 1877. It includes a description of Yule Day activities on the Baa' Green, and the setting is the parish of Dunrossness, Shetland, the links being the Links of Sumburgh or the Links of Quendale:

Da Guid Auld Times

A merry day wis Auld Yüle Day,
An' up we aye got early,
To try wir New Yüle suits o' claes,
An' see dey fitted fairly.

* * *

Da brakwist ower – wi' baa' an' gun
Aff ta da links we run fast,
An' gled to fin' whin we cam dere
Dere wis nane o' da fun past.

Dere scores o' boys wi' bang an' noise,
Da wind baa's keeps careerin';
While shots fae guns wi' big touch holes
Gae some poor gunners sair een.

A' dey lang, bang gengs da baas,
Sic fechtin', faain', an' racin',
Dat new claes maks us sairly dread
At hame ta shaw wir face in.

Wi' legs weel tired at close o' day
We slept da nicht sae soondly;
Bit still in dream da licht wind baa'
Kept iver dancin' roondly.

Auld sober sense, an' prime soor dook
Micht ca' da day a fúle day,
Bit ta da hert o' sprichtly youth
A glorious day wis Yüle Day.

[6] G. Stewart, *Shetland Fireside Tales,* 2nd edition, 1892, pp. 99, 100.

After referring to the 'pleasures gay' of the city, the poet concludes:

> Yet I can see dey've pleased me no;
> An' aft ta cure my chagrin,
> I've wissed ance mair for *Auld Yüle Day*
> *My leaden guns and baa' green.*

Part IV

Origin and History of Mass Football

20

Prehistory and History of Mass Football

In tracing the origin of the Kirkwall Ba' the history of similar games played elsewhere is of importance. Although this chapter is not intended to be an exhaustive study of Shrove Tuesday or Fasternse'en street football in Britain, a short history of mass football may throw some light on the beginnings of our street contest. It is not an easy story to tell. Games tend to alter over the years and to assume an independent form, and local conditions and circumstances play a significant part in determining along which lines development will take place. Views and opinions clash, but the available material has been assimilated into what I believe is a fair statement.

Since prehistoric times the ball has held a unique place as a source of recreation and exercise for both old and young alike. Homer refers to the playing of handball at the time of the destruction of Troy, roughly 1194 BC, describing in *The Odyssey* how the Princess Nausicaa, the daughter of Alcinous, King of Phaeacia, and her handmaids 'fell to playing at ball' in Scheria (Corfu). Later at the King's palace Odysseus is entertained with minstrelsy and public games, and Laodamas and Halious toss 'a gaudy bright-coloured ball' to each other, accompanying this with a dance.

Harpastum

The Romans played a game called *Harpastum*, the name being derived from the Greek word αρπαζειν (Harpazein), to seize. A small hard ball (or *harpastum*) stuffed with sand[1] was used, and the players were divided into two opposing sides, the object being to force the ball beyond a line drawn behind one's opponents. The ball was thrown up in the air in mid-field, and an energetic game then ensued in which the players pushed and struggled backwards and forwards. It

[1] J. Carcopino, *Daily Life in Ancient Rome*, 1941, trans. E. O. Lorimer, p. 283.

appears that each player had a position in the field, and while there is not a great deal of reliable information available, it does seem that *Harpastum* was a team game with opportunities for combination, both in attack and defence. Certainly it was vigorous, calling for agility and strength, and the form of play was that the ball was passed or thrown from player to player but not kicked, charging and tackling being permitted.[2] It was thus more studied than early mass football, which by contrast was violent and undisciplined with no sanctions regarding the method of play.

There can be little doubt that *Harpastum* was played in Britain during the 400 years of Roman occupation, and it so happens that in several cities and towns of Roman origin there are records of early mass street football, for example in London, Chester and Chester-le-Street. It can be argued that in these locations the street game stemmed from *Harpastum*, but there is an absence of any real supporting evidence, and it is very doubtful if any link can be established with the old Roman game. Indeed, the local tradition at Chester that the first ball used was the head of a Dane may mean that the event was a local method of celebrating victory over one's enemies. We can, I think, discount *Harpastum* as a possible origin of mass football in this country.

Ball Games of the Norsemen

Ball games are mentioned in a number of the sagas, and in the narrative they provide an opportunity for the hero to exhibit his strength, skill and manliness.

There were two kinds of ball play, *Sopleg* which was similar to mass football as played in France from at least the twelfth century, and almost certainly taken to England by the Normans, and *Knattleikr* in which a hard ball and bats or clubs were used. It is possible that both these games originated in the British Isles, although some authorities have held that *Knattleikr* originated in Norway.[3] *Knattleikr* was also played in Iceland, colonization of which took place from Norway around 870. Shortly afterwards there was a considerable immigration from the British Isles, and a number of the settlers were Irish thralls. The Irish immigrants colonized the west-north-west and a part of the north side of Iceland, and it is in precisely these regions that *Knattleikr* is mentioned in the sagas. This supports the theory of a British origin for the game.[4]

In the *Karlamagnus Saga* there is a description of a contest that has been identified as *Sopleg*, and the following is an extract:

[2] R. T. Bridge and E. D. C. Lake, *Select Epigrams of Martial*, 1908, notes IV, XIX, pp. 73, 74.
[3] Knudsen, *Træk Af Boldspillets Historie*, pp. 116, 118.
[4] Knudsen, *Træk Af Boldspillets Historie*, pp. 116, 118.

> I will tell you a piece of news. Tomorrow a game will be held outside your father's castle. There many young men will assemble. They will have a ball with which they will play, and he who three times in succession can secure this ball, without anyone catching hold of it in the meantime, he will be praised and honoured above all. And there shall you, Landres, show how stout your heart is, and your valour.
>
> Landres then set forth until he came to a piece of level ground where a crowd of young men played with a large ball.
>
> Then he went over to the game, pushing his way in among the people to where the crowd was most dense around the ball. And Landres did not stop in his mission before he succeeded in getting at the ball and carrying it out from among them. And when he had done this, he threw it the second time into the scrum, and threw himself in after it; and there he managed to get hold of it a second time. Then said Landres: 'If I had only brought the ball out the first time I got hold of it, you could have said that by injustice I conquered in this game, for I am unknown to most of you. But now I have won the game twice. Therefore will I yet once more throw the ball in among you all; and if I succeed for the third time in bringing it out from among you, you will all know that I have won the game by fairplay and not by cunning.' Thereupon for the third time Landres threw the ball into the midst of them, where the crowd was most dense, and in a short time he succeeded in getting hold of the ball and bringing it out from among them, and he was very happy.[5]

In the saga *The Story of Gisli the Outlaw* we find the following account:

> So now the sports were set afoot as though nothing had happened. Those brothers-in-law, Thorgrim and Gisli, were very often matched against each other, and men could not make up their minds which was the stronger, but most thought Gisli had most strength. They were playing at the ball on the tarn called Sedgetarn. On it there was ever a crowd. It fell one day when there was a great gathering that Gisli bade them share the sides as evenly as they could for a game . . . Now they began the game, and Thorgrim could not hold his own. Gisli threw him and bore away the ball. Again Gisli wished to catch the ball, but Thorgrim runs and holds him and will not let him get near it. Then Gisli turned and threw Thorgrim such a fall on the slippery ice that he could scarce rise. The

[5] Knudsen, *Træk Af Boldspillets Historie*, pp. 115, 116, quoting the *Karlamagnus Saga,* Unger's, 1860, cap 2, 11–12.

> skin came off his knuckles, and the flesh off his knees, and blood gushed from his nostrils.[6]

This game too was almost certainly *Sopleg.*

Knattleikr was a savage, bloody struggle and was played with a hard ball, usually wooden, and bats. People took part in pairs or in large numbers, and the play was of a particularly violent character whereby it sometimes gave rise to bodily injuries that could result in death. Spectators came from far and near.[7] Later in the saga of Gisli, another ball contest is mentioned in which bats are used, and this second game appears to be *Knattleikr*:

> They are partners in the game at ball, Gisli and Thorstein, and against them were matched Bork and Thorkel. One day a host of men came to see the game, for many were eager to behold the sport, and all wanted to know who was the strongest man and the best player. But here, as elsewhere, it happened that the players played with greater spirit when there were many lookers-on. It is said that Bork could not stand against Thorstein that day, and at last Bork got wroth, and broke asunder Thorstein's bat; but Thorstein gave him a fall, and sent him spinning along the slippery ice. But when Gisli sees that he says: 'Thorstein shall go on playing with Bork with all his might. I will change bats with thee.'[8]

From this it seems that *Knattleikr* was more of a contest than a sport, and certainly physical strength was an important factor.

Similar Games – Hurling, Knappan and Camp-ball

In passing it is interesting to note other mass games which existed from early times and which may have been descended from *Harpastum*. These are *hurling,* played primarily in the western English counties of Devon and Cornwall; and *camp-ball* (from Anglo-Saxon *camp,* a combat), popular in the eastern English counties of Norfolk, Suffolk and Essex. Neither of these events was specifically 'football' (which was termed 'kicking camp', or 'savage camp' if played with shoes on) as the ball was thrown or *hurled,* rather than kicked, but in many respects they closely resembled mass football with which they developed side by

[6] *The Story of Gisli the Outlaw,* trans. from the Icelandic by G. W. Dasent, chapter 8, pp. 47, 48.

[7] Knudsen, *Træk Af Boldspillets Historie*, pp. 116, 117.

[8] *The Story of Gisli the Outlaw,* trans. G. W. Dasent, chapter 10, p. 57.

side, and with which no doubt they intermingled – one could term them first cousins, or at the very least allied to one another.[9]

As we will shortly see, in the French mass ball game of *Soule* the ball was propelled sometimes by hand but more usually with feet, and in one location at least it was called *savate* for this reason (a word meaning a worn-out or old shoe: footwear eminently suited to the sport!). One wonders if perhaps the type of camp-ball mentioned above was originally 'savate camp', and if so this would establish a definite connection between camp-ball and *Soule*.

There were two types of hurling in Cornwall, hurling to goals in the east part of the county, and hurling to the country in the west. The following information is taken from an early seventeenth-century report.

> In hurling to goals a number of rules were observed, and some skill was necessary. It was often played at weddings, 'where commonly the guests undertake to encounter all comers'. There were approximately fifteen to thirty players on each side, 'who strip themselves into their slightest apparel, and then join hands in rank one against another. Out of these ranks they match themselves by pairs . . . they pitch two bushes in the ground, some eight or ten feet asunder; and directly against them, ten or twelve score off, other twain in like distance, which they term their goals . . . some indifferent person throweth up a ball, the which whosoever can catch, and carry through his adversary's goal, hath won the game . . . he that is once possessed of the ball, hath his contrary mate waiting at inches, and assaying to lay hold upon him. The other thrusteth him in the breast, with his closed fist, to keep him off; which they call butting, and place in well doing the same no small point of manhood.'[10]

Play in hurling to the country was very different:

> Some two or more gentlemen do commonly make this match, appointing that on such a holiday they will bring to such an indifferent place, two, three, or more parishes of the east or south quarter, to hurl against so many other of the west or north. Their goals are either those gentlemen's houses, or some towns or villages three or four miles asunder, of which either side maketh choice, after the nearness to their dwellings. When they meet, there is neither comparing of numbers, nor matching of men;

[9] J. Strutt, *The Sports and Pastimes of the People of England*, 1801, enlarged and revised by J. C. Cox, 1903, pp. 91, 92, 93.

[10] R. Carew, *Survey of Cornwall*, 1602, Tonkins, 1811, pp. 195–199.

> but a silver ball is cast up, and that company which can catch and carry it, by force or sleight, to their place assigned, gaineth the ball and victory . . . Such as see where the ball is played, give notice thereof to their mates, crying, Wear east, Wear west, &c. as the same is carried.
>
> The hurlers take their next way over hills, dales, hedges, ditches; yea, and through bushes, briars, mires, plashes, and rivers whatsoever; so as you shall sometimes see twenty or thirty lie tugging together in the water, scrambling and scratching for the ball . . .
>
> There are horsemen placed also on either party (as it were in ambush, and ready to ride away with the ball, if they can catch it at advantage . . .). Sometimes the whole company runneth with the ball seven or eight miles out of the direct way which they should keep. Sometimes a footman getting it by stealth, the better to escape unespied, will carry the same quite backwards, and so at last get to the goal by a windlass which once known to be won, all that side flock thither with great jollity; and if the same be a gentleman's house, they give him the ball for a trophy, and the drinking out of his beer to boot.
>
> The ball in this play may be compared to an infernal spirit; by whosoever catcheth it, fareth straigtways like a mad man, struggling and fighting with those that go about to hold him . . . when the hurling is ended, you shall see them retiring home, as from a pitched battle, with bloody pates, bones broken, and out of joint, and such bruises as serve to shorten their days; yet all is good play, and never attorney nor coroner troubled for the matter.[11]

The Welsh game of knappan closely resembled hurling to the country, and a full account of the game is given in *The Description of Pembrokshire* written by George Owen in 1603.[12] According to Owen, knappan was played either on certain set days, known as *standing knappans;* or a match would be arranged between two gentlemen. The standing knappans were five in number in Pembrokeshire, and one of these days was *shroft tewsdaie.* As will be shown later in this chapter Shrove Tuesday was for centuries one of the great days for mass football play in England.

Knappan arranged between two gentlemen occurred 'at such holedaye or sondaie as pleased them to appointe the tyme and place, which most comonlye fall out to be the greatest plaies, for in these matches the gentlemen would

[11] R. Carew, *Survey of Cornwall*, 1602, Tonkins, 1811, pp. 195–199.

[12] George Owen of Henllys (1552–1613), *The Description of Pembrokshire.* ed. H. Owen, 1892, vol. 1, pp. 270-277.

devide the parishes, hundreds, or sheres, betweene them, and then would eche laboure to bringe the greatest nomber, and would therein intreate all his frindes and kinsmen in everye parishe to come and bringe his parishe wholelye with him by which meanes greate nomber would most usuallye meete.'[13]

The sides usually came together about one o'clock in the afternoon when they stripped for action, being clad only in a light pair of breeches. The clothing was laid together in great heaps under the charge of keepers.

The ball used was of a size 'so as a man may hold it in his hands and no more. This ball is of some massy wood, as box, yew, crab, or holly tree, and should be boiled in tallow, for to make it slippery, and hard to be held.'

The game commenced when the ball was thrown in the air, and then each side endeavoured to throw or force it towards their own parish or district. If the knappan came into the hands of a hurler, he threw it as far as possible towards his own country. If it came into the hands of a good runner he detached himself from the main body and made off, followed by the others who gave chase as soon as the breakaway was discovered. A tactic used by the weaker side was to stop play and surround the knappan with their own players 'so that you shall see a hundred or six score thus clustered together as bees, when they swarm . . . which the other party seeketh to open or undo by hauling and pulling.' During the play 'you shall in an open field see two thousand naked [i.e. stripped for action] people follow this ball backward and forward, east, west, north, and south, so that a stranger that casually should see such a multitude so ranging naked, would think them distracted; it is strange to behold with what eagerness this play is followed, for in the fury of the chase they respect neither hedge, ditch, pale, or wall, hill, dale, bushes, river or rock, or any other passable impediment.'

Horsemen took part and they wielded cudgels three and a half feet long with which they gave chase to horsemen on the other side who made off with the ball, or knappan. These cudgels were used to belabour opponents if the ball was not given up on demand.

It is noteworthy that there were no set goals, and play did not stop until the knappan was carried so far that there was no hope of taking it back that night.

The game was violent, and Owen's description goes on: 'you shall see two brothers the one beating the other, the man the master, and friend against friend, they now also will not hesitate to take up stones and there with in their fists beat their fellows . . . the horseman chooseth the greatest cudgel he can get . . . he will also assault anyone for private grudge.'

[13] This and the following quotations on knappan are all taken from Owen.

At the closure the participants returned 'with broken heads, black faces, bruised bodies, and lame legs, yet laughing and merrily jesting at their harms, telling their adversaries how he brake his head, to an other that he strake him on the face, and how he repaid the same to him again, and all this in good mirth, without grudge or hatred. And if any be in arrerages to the other they score it up till the next play, and in the meantime will continue loving friends, whereas if the least of these blows be offered out of this play, it presently breedeth unquenchable quarrels.'

There are several references to hurling in early Irish tales, and we may be tempted to establish a connection between it, and Welsh knappan and Cornish hurling. While these three games may have had a common root in Ireland, knappan and Cornish hurling – particularly hurling to the country – developed separately and parallel with each other. It is noteworthy that no sticks or clubs were used in Cornish hurling, and in knappan only the horsemen had cudgels, these being used for belabouring the opposition and not for striking the ball. On the other hand in Irish hurling every player seems to have had a stick or a bat with which the ball was hit.

In an account of the Irish hero Cuchullin's deeds as a boy, we are told that when he reached Emania (Emain Macha, then the chief town of Ulster) he found 150 of the boy-corps hurling on the green:

> The lad dived right in among them and took a hand in the game. He got the ball between his legs and held it there, not suffering it to travel whether higher up than his knees or lower down than his ankle-joints, and so making it impossible for them to get a stroke or in any other way to touch it. In this plight he brought it along and sent it home over the goal. In utter amazement the whole corps look on; but Follamain mac Conachar cries: 'Good now, boys, all together respond to this youngster . . . and kill him . . . ' The whole of them assail Cuchullin, and simultaneously send their hurlies at his head; he however parries all the hundred-and-fifty and is scathless. The same with the balls, which he fends off with fists, fore-arms and palms alone.[14]

Camp-ball was similar to hurling to goals, and had achieved widespread popularity in the eastern counties in the seventeenth and eighteenth centuries. It was described thus in 1823:

[14] *The Cuchullin Saga in Irish Literature.* The Cattle-spoil of Cooley (Táin Bó Cuailgne). Comp. and ed. by E. Hull, 1898, pp. 136, 137. The story of Cuchullin is very ancient, and the translation coincides in the main with the version in a mid-twelfth century MS, The Book of Leinster. The Táin is of course much older.

> Goals were pitched 150 to 200 yards apart, formed of the thrown-off clothes of the competitors. Each party has two goals, 10 or 15 yards apart. The parties, 10 to 15 a side, stand in a line, facing their own goals and each other, at 10 yards distance, midway between the goals and nearest that of their adversaries. An indifferent spectator throws up the ball – the size of a cricket ball – midway between the confronted players, whose object is to seize and convey it between their own goals. The shock of the first onset to catch the falling ball is very great, and the player who seizes it speeds home, pursued by his opponents, through whom he has to make his way, aided by the jostlings of his own side. If caught and held, or in imminent danger of it, he *throws* the ball – but must in no case *give* it – to a comrade who, if it be not arrested in its course, or be jostled away by his eager foes, catches it and hurries home, winning the *notch* or *snotch* if he contrives to *carry* – not *throw* – it between the goals. A holder of the ball caught with it in his possession loses a *snotch.* At the loss of each of these the game recommences, after a breathing time. Seven or nine snotches are the game, and these it will sometimes take two or three hours to win.

The game was violent and became less popular on account of the numerous and sometimes fatal accidents to players: 'Two men were killed at a grand match at Easton, Suffolk, about the close of last century' (i.e. the end of the eighteenth century).[15]

Origin of Football in Britain

There is very little doubt that mass football was taken to England by the Normans and was part of the carnival festivities they introduced. The later prevalence of football in Scotland may have been due to direct French influence, or alternatively the game may have spread in a natural way from England.

J. J. Jusserand, an authority on the history of both medieval France and medieval England, in his book *Les Sports et Jeux d'Exercice dans l'ancienne France*[16] supports the theory of a French origin, and says that almost everything to do with games,

[15] J. Strutt, *The Sports and Pastimes of the People of England,* 1801, revised edn 1903, p. 93. The 1823 description was by a Major Moor, and both quotations, which were cited in 1892, are taken from *Notes and Queries,* 8/2, pp. 213, 214.

[16] All information in this and the succeeding paragraphs on *Soule* and the prohibition of *Soule* have been taken from (1) *Les Sports et Jeux d'Exercice dans l'ancienne France* by J. J. Jusserand, Paris, 1901, pp. 265–283, and (2) *Esquisses du Bocage Normand* by J. Lecoeur, Condé-sur-Noireau, 1883, pp. 13, 153–165.

entertainment or relaxation in medieval England originated in Normandy or Anjou. He instances early French records which predate the establishment of mass football in England, and even a casual reader of his description of *Soule* cannot fail to be struck by the number of common factors between the two games, for example the absence of rules; the violence of play; the wild enthusiasm of players; the blockage of town and village streets; the prohibition by Royal authority; the propulsion of the ball by both hand and foot; the frequency of injuries, some of which were fatal; the fact that district played against district or sometimes married men against bachelors; that although the goals varied in different areas, once established they normally remained the same; that these goals were often ponds in which the ball had to be 'drowned'; that the most common day for play was Shrove Tuesday; and finally that football does seem on occasion to have played a significant part in fertility proceedings.

La Soule

In view of its position as by far the most likely ancestor of mass football in Britain, some information on the French game may be of general interest. As we have already seen in Chapter 15, 'Origins of the Kirkwall Ba'', mass football was primarily played on Shrove Tuesday, although it was also, as in Britain, on occasion played at weddings and on the day of the patron saint of the parish, on Easter Day, Christmas Day and sometimes Boxing Day.

While the origin and meaning of the game are lost in the mists of time, more than one French writer saw in it a vestige of sun worship (Celtic *heaul*, sun). According to others the word *soule* stems from the fact that the ball was kicked with the sole of the boot (*solea*).

Jusserand has recorded that *La Soule* was played in the time of St Louis (Louis IX, 1226–1270), and even in the time of Louis le Jeune (Louis VII, 1137–1180). In 1147 a lord ratifying a deed of gift in favour of a church, specified among various benefits to his own account the payment of a sum of money and the delivery of 'seven balls of the largest size'.

Variously called *Soule*, *Choule* or *Cholle*, the noun *choule* had a corresponding verb *choler*, to kick the ball. Although hands were sometimes used, the ball was normally propelled with the feet, and indeed at Valognes it was called *savate* (shoe) for this reason.

The ball itself was generally called a '*soule*' and it could be solid or hollow and made of either wood or leather. In the latter case it was filled with hay, bran, horsehair or moss, or alternatively pumped with air. At Bellou-en-Houlme, where contestants numbered between 700 and 800 and there were about 6000 specta-

FIG. 98: The battle of the *Soule*. The *soule* is about to be thrown up between the two sides in front of the church door. This reproduction is of an 1835 steel engraving by Réveille, and was originally published in *La Galerie Bretonne* by O. Perrin.

tors, the *soule* was three feet round and weighed between eleven and thirteen lb. The covering was of thick leather, containing hard packed bran and straw. In this particular contest, it seems the losing side frequently cut the *soule* with their knives, and to prevent this happening the ball was sheathed in tin from 1841.

Usually it was the local squire, the village mayor, or some other leading man who threw up the ball, and after the struggle there was drinking and dancing in the evening, players and spectators entering into the general merrymaking. Both contest and celebration were eagerly anticipated, and they provided a welcome relief from the tedium of everyday life and work in feudal times.

In spite of the subsequent festivities there is no doubt that violence was prevalent, and there are records of letters of remission in the fourteenth century which granted a pardon to players who had mistakenly split open a head instead of kicking the ball!

Soule was universally popular, particularly among what Jusserand calls 'the common people', but that it was played by all classes can be gathered from the fact that Philippe de Chabot, Admiral of France, in the reign of François I (1515–1517) took his badge and motto from the game. Moreover it is known that the succeeding King, Henri II, was a keen player, usually in company with the poet Ronsard. Doubtless play by them and attendant nobles was reasonably refined.

During the Renaissance country gentlemen often took part in *Soule* accompanied by their servants and village peasants. The diary of the Norman Gilles Picot, Lord of Gouberville and Mesnil-au-Val, written in the mid-sixteenth century, mentions contests in which he took part.[17] This was entirely different from Britain where mass football was really only popular among the common people.

In certain towns even the clergy played. At Auxerre each new canon was obliged to give his colleagues a ball, and what took place there on Easter Day was a most odd mixture of religion and sport. Proceedings commenced with a prose chant '*Victimae Pascalis laudes*',[18] and ended with all the canons together performing a round dance. The custom was very old and the rules were codified in a regulation dated 18 April 1396: '*Ordinatio de Pila facienda*'.[19] The *pila* or ball was of considerable size and, since every new canon prided himself on outdoing his predecessors, in 1412 a limit was put on the size of the ball. At the same time, however, it was laid down that it was not to be so small that it could be held with one hand. This custom did not disappear until 1538.

The same squire of Gouberville mentioned above also refers to the local priest taking part: 'On the 24th July (1556) the priest of Tourlaville departed from this house in the morning (it was a Sunday), went and said Mass at Tourlaville, and then came back at Vespers. He played hard at *choule* the whole of the rest of the day.'

These games of *Soule* often gave expression to fierce interparish rivalry, and in 1883, in *Esquisses du Bocage Normand,* Lecoeur writes that in days gone by, and still in certain parishes, carnival time had a strange complement to its celebrations, 'that is, a traditional game of brutal savagery: the *Soule.* It was a furious scrimmage, in which blows rained as thick as hail. They used to take their pleasure in this game during the afternoon and evening of Shrove Tuesday.'

There were sometimes more than two contesting groups. The protagonists were men from the surrounding parishes and villages, each side mustering its boldest players – tough peasants firmly resolved to uphold the honour of their parish with fist and foot! An opportunity was taken of settling old scores and there were many injuries. The ball on occasion was bedecked with ribbons,

[17] E. de Robillard de Beaurepaire, *Le Journal du sire de Gouberville*, Caen, 1892. See J. J. Jusserand, *Les Sports et Jeux d'Exercice dans l'ancienne France*, p. 272.

[18] 'The praises of the Paschal victim', i.e. Christ.

[19] The rule for making the ball.

just as it is today in parts of the Borders of Scotland, and after the throw-up which usually took place in the centre of a village, battle was joined. Hardly had the ball touched the ground when the contestants rushed upon it, bumping, pushing, wrestling, jostling and hitting each other, each side striving to secure the ball: 'It was an indescribable brawl from which arose furious shouts, curses and yells of rage, mingled with the groans of those who were being squashed and kicked.' The object was to force the *soule* to their own parish goal (often a pond), and immerse it in the water, the old belief being that the winning parish or village would be favoured with a more abundant apple harvest.

During the struggle property was in no way respected, and the human avalanche milled around, crashing through hedges, and trampling over gardens and seeded fields. At one time when the victors arrived home they took the *soule* to the house of a person of importance, and he in turn exhibited it in a place of prominence. Thereafter the men who thus had upheld 'the honour of the parish', together with the escorting company, entered into uninhibited junketing during which the event was discussed and analysed, incidents recounted and wounds proudly displayed.

Brittany

Soule was particularly popular in this part of France, and in the eighteenth century there is a record of men fanatically pursuing the ball into the sea and, in the confusion, drowning. In another district it is alleged that there was a prohibition after forty men were drowned in the Pont-l'Abbé pond when in a frenzy they rushed headlong after the ball. The contest was prized in Brittany as helping to sustain strength and courage, and, while it was also recognized as being dangerous, as late as the nineteenth century it was still considered one of the national sports. The following account is a graphic description of a contest played by Bretons about 1835:[20]

> The *soule* has been thrown up. The two armies now form only one, mingling, wrestling, smothering. On the surface of this impenetrable chaos can be seen thousands of heads moving like waves on an angry sea, and inarticulate savage cries are released . . . Thanks to his strength or skill, one of the champions has managed to make his way through this compact mass, and flees, carrying the *soule*. He is not noticed at first, as the frenzied combatants are so wild with the intoxication of the struggle!

[20] Perrin and Aouet, *Breize-Izel, or, The Life of the Bretons of Armorica*, Paris, 2nd edn, 1844, vol. 3, p. 21. See J. J. Jusserand, *Les Sports et Jeux d'Exercice dans l'ancienne France*, p. 282.

> But when those who remain rather calmer than the others see that they are wearing themselves out with vain efforts . . . the huge mass of bodies breaks up of one accord, and divides and scatters. Each man flies off suddenly to the new field of battle. As they run, they insult or attack each other and trip each other up, and a score of individual fights take place on the outskirts of the main action.

Another vivid description dates from 1855 and is of a contest between married men and bachelors which took place at Royallieu near Compiègne. The game described closely resembles that still played annually on Christmas and New Year's Day on the streets of Kirkwall, Orkney, between Up-the-Gates and Down-the-Gates. Indeed the passage might well have been taken from a Kirkwall newspaper of the 1880s, a period when as many as 500 men took part:

> At this moment, the spectator can see no more than a confused mass of individuals who appear to be making every endeavour to squash each other; the ones who are outside the circle attempt to seize hold of those who are in the centre . . . These individual efforts, constantly renewed, impart a most peculiar motion to the mass: sometimes it moves towards the right, sometimes it goes towards the left; more usually it turns slowly round upon itself; it looks, one might say, like a fantastic animal with thousands of heads and thousands of feet. From time to time, one of these heads collapses and disappears: this is a player who has fallen; the struggle goes on over his body, and, when the eddy has passed, he arises again pale, and sometimes even bruised and bleeding.

Prohibition of Soule

The game was banned from time to time, and in 1319 a regulation of Philippe V, the Tall, prohibited '*ludos soularum*'. In 1369 Charles V forbade all games of '*solles*', and a decree of the Parliament of 1781 renewed Philippe V's prohibition and forbade 'all persons to throw any leather balls on Christmas Day or any other day; to assemble to chase the ball under any pretext, under penalty of a fine of fifty *livres*'.

At La Lande-Patry the priest of the parish, Maître Jacques Saillard, had the game forbidden by a decree of the Law Court at Rouen dated 27 January 1694. Maître Saillard explained in his petition that '*Soulle*' took place between peasants of his parish and the neighbouring parishes on Shrove Tuesday, that the '*Soulle*' or leather ball was thrown up by the most recently married woman, and that

600 or 700 hundred persons took part, 'several of whom are choked and others torn or get their arms and legs maimed in this scrimmage, into which a whole lot of drunkards often slip, and they belabour their enemies with a stick, when they recognize them in the press, or even people that have done nothing to them whom they do not even know.' Apparently when the petitioner had sought to lodge complaints with the local magistrates mentioning particularly those poor folk who had suffered broken arms, the magistrates answered that these were misfortunes that happened on Shrove Tuesday, as if this fact authorized such violence and turmoil!

When *Soule* was forbidden in a particular parish frequently it was started in a neighbouring location. Seemingly after the game was banned at La Lande-Patry it was transferred to St Pierre d'Entremont.

Soule was still very popular in the nineteenth century although there was periodic prohibition because of violence. Injuries were common and deaths not unknown, and probably because of this the contest did not find favour with the authorities. In 1852, after several unsuccessful attempts, the struggle between the neighbouring parishes was suppressed at St Pierre d'Entremont (between Condé and Tinchebray), one of its strongholds, but only with the help of four or five brigades of police!

But by the first decade of the twentieth century *Soule* had everywhere become extinct.

At the present time a game called *Choule* is played in the department of Oise in France. The ball is much smaller than that used in the *Choule* of days gone by, the current ball being only six inches in diameter. It consists of sending the ball through a circle of stretched paper hanging on a mast approximately thirty feet high, each side having its own circle. Played during the Easter period[21] the sides are generally bachelors against married men, and the circles often bear the letters H (*hommes*) and G (*garçons*).

England

In William Fitz Stephen's *Descriptio Noblissimae Civitatis Londinae* there is mention of a ball game, and this is found in the section dealing with sports of the city. The *Description* was part of a biography of St Thomas à Becket (1118–1170), and was written shortly before 1183, probably in 1175:

> Moreover, each year upon the day called Carnival – to begin with the sports of boys (for we were all boys once) – boys from the schools bring

[21] Information obtained from Musée des Arts et Traditions Populaires, Paris.

> fighting-cocks to their master, and the whole forenoon is given up to boyish sport; for they have a holiday in the schools that they may watch their cocks do battle. After dinner all the youth of the City goes out into the fields to a much frequented game of ball. The scholars of each school have their own ball, and almost all the workers of each trade have theirs also in their hands. Elder men and fathers and rich citizens come on horse-back to watch the contests of their juniors, and after their fashion are young again with the young; and it seems that the motion of their natural heat is kindled by the contemplation of such violent motion and by their partaking in the joys of untrammelled youth.[22]

The 'Carnival' referred to was Shrove Tuesday, on which day it was customary for revels to be held immediately prior to Lent.

The youth of the City going 'to a much-frequented game of ball' *(ad ludum pilae celebrem)* may well have been attending football. Morris Marples has given several good reasons why he believes it was football and, as he says, this is important in that if accepted as such the passage both establishes football as a Norman sport in this country and also firmly connects the game with twelfth-century Shrovetide activities.[23] Shrovetide football is dealt with separately, later in this chapter.

Violence and Prohibition

By the beginning of the fourteenth century the sport appears to have become rough and violent, and to have lost the respectability described above. In 1314 as a consequence of the departure of Edward II to war against the Scots, Nicholas de Farndone, Mayor of London, issued a proclamation forbidding among other things the game of football:

> Whereas our Lord the King is going towards the parts of Scotland, in his war against his enemies, and has especially commanded us strictly to keep his peace . . . And whereas there is great uproar in the City, through certain tumults arising from the striking of great footballs *(rageries de grosses pelotes de pee ferir)* in the fields of the public, from which many evils perchance may arise, which may God forbid, we do command and do forbid, on the King's behalf, upon pain of imprisonment, that such game shall be practised from henceforth within the City.

[22] Translated by Professor H. E. Butler, and published in Historical Association leaflets, nos. 93 and 94. Fitz Stephen was a monk of Canterbury.

[23] M. Marples, *A History of Football*, pp. 20, 21.

The proclamation was made pursuant to the writ of the King directed to the mayor and sheriffs enjoining observation of the Statute of Winchester, the arrest of malefactors and the keeping of the peace within the City, and would presumably have been issued shortly after receipt of the writ. This writ is dated 13 April 1314.[24]

Football was also forbidden by Edward III (1363 and 1365), Richard II (1388 and 1401), Henry IV (1409), Henry V (1414), Edward IV (1477), and in the sixteenth century by both Henry VIII and Queen Elizabeth. What Edward III did was to address a writ to the sheriffs of all counties throughout England, in which it was stated that archery practice had seriously declined owing to popular indulgence in 'useless and unseemly games' such as handball, football and staffball. The sheriffs were then directed to make proclamation that all able-bodied men should in future desist from such games on pain of imprisonment, and instead devote their leisure to archery.[25] The 1365 injunction was in similar terms. The 1388 Enactment of Richard II was to the effect that servants and labourers should use bows and arrows on Sundays and holydays and desist from ball play: 'the pleyes at the balle nother hand nor foote' *(les jeues as pelotes sibn a meyn come a piee)* and the sheriffs, mayors, bailiffs and constables were empowered to arrest transgressors.[26] The 1409 Statute really recited that of 1388, and these same 'Servants and Labourers of Husbandry, and Labourers and Servants of Artificers, and of Victuallers', were again enjoined to acquire bows and arrows, to use them on Sundays and other festival days 'and utterly leave playing at the Balls as well Hand-ball as Foot-ball . . . and other such unthrifty games.'[27] Additionally there was a provision that offenders should be punished by six days' imprisonment, and also included were penalties that the sheriffs, mayors, etc. had to pay to the King for neglect in execution of the Statute.

These repressive measures arose both because of the violence with which the game was played and more particularly because it tended to distract men from the practice of archery on which the nation's safety much depended. In this latter connection Henry V's enactment is of peculiar significance coming as it did a year before Agincourt.

[24] *Munimenta Gildhallae Londoniensis III Liber Albus,* ed. H. T. Riley, appendix 2, p. 440. For the writ see *Munimenta Gildhallae Londoniensis,* appendix 2, pp. 437–439. Nicholas de Farndone was Mayor of London (the term Lord Mayor did not come into use until the fifteenth century) from 28 October 1313 to 28 October 1314. He was also Mayor 1308–1309, 1320–1321 and 1323.

[25] Thomas Rymer, *Foedera,* 1708, vol. 6, p. 417. For the 1365 Enactment see p. 468.

[26] *Statutes of the Realm II,* 1816, p. 57. See variant note 5, citing MS TR2. This footnote is taken from Harleian MS 4999 in the British Museum, and is a fifteenth-century translation.

[27] *Statutes of the Realm II,* 1816, p. 163.

In Walsall in 1422 football was among the games classed as unlawful and banned, except at Christmas time:

> Also it is ordeyned and stablyshed, that if eny man, man's son, servnt, prntyse within the Towne, dwellynge be founden at eny alehouse, or at eny prevey place, plaiyng at eny unlawefull games, except in Cristemas, as dyce, tables, cardes, cloke, tenys, foteball, or eny other lyke contrairie to the statute of this lande and ordnaunce of the same towne, then they that so be founden in defaute, to be taken and put in pryson, and paye vid for his fyne to the Box, for his defaute-makyng, that to be leuyed by the Bayly, and hee to have of them for his office-doyng iiiid . . . [28]

Henry VIII made it an offence for landowners to allow football to be played on their ground, but this proved ineffective, and football continued to be very popular.

Sir Thomas Elyot, writing in 1531 in his book *The Boke Named the Governour*, said of football that it 'is nothyng but beastely fury and extreme violence, whereof procedeth hurte, and consequently rancour and malice do remayne with thym that be wounded, wherfore it is to be put in perpetuall silence.'[29]

Certainly the pastime was not refined, and sixteenth-century official records give details of serious and fatal results from football. The picture is one of broken limbs and of men being deliberately hurled onto the cobblestones of village streets. Indeed there were many deaths at play.[30]

An entry in an Essex Assize record of 1567 contains a detailed account of a death during football at Hatfield, Broadoak. At the inquest it was stated that the deceased, Henry Ynggold, aged twenty-four, and a Thomas Paviott 'were together with many and divers other persons . . . merely by way of recreation playing together at pila pedalis, in English called the Footeball'. Ynggold and Paviott clashed and 'the said Henry Ynggold suddenly and deliberately threw to the ground the said Thomas Paviott in the course of the game, and while they were getting in each others way over the said ball.' The two players rose together and Paviott, apparently fearing that Ynggold would throw him to the ground

[28] The quotation is taken from 'Ordinances for the government of the Mayor, and Burgesses, and the Masters of the Guilds of our Lady and of S. John Baptist' (see 'The Calendar of the Deeds and Documents belonging to Walsall Corporation in the Town Chest', 1882, p. 16, Roll no. 46) and is contained in *The History of the Borough and Foreign of Walsall* by E. L. Glew, 1855, p. 103. The probable date of the original document is given as 1422 in F. W. Willmore's *History of Walsall*, 1887, p. 166.

[29] T. Elyot, *The Boke Named the Governour*, 1546, p. 32b. See J. Strutt, *The Sports and Pastimes of the English People*, 1903, p. 96.

[30] N. Wymer, *Sport in England*, p. 74.

again and keep him from the ball, 'intending no harm towards the said Henry, but intending then and there to run from the said Henry after the said ball, he gently then and there thrust the said Henry away from him with his hands, without any malice or other felonious intent and left the said Henry lying on the ground.' The evidence goes on that a few hours later Ynggold 'exhausted by excessive toil and labour running after the said ball and by running beyond his powers . . . turned faint', and a few hours later, 'breathed out his soul.'[31] One wonders if Paviott was quite as gentle as the evidence states, or whether perhaps he had retaliated under provocation and a brawl had developed.

At this time for their football the rustics used an inflated animal bladder without a protective covering, 'putting peas and horse beans withinside, which occasioned a rattling as it was kicked about.'[32] This practice is mentioned in Barclay's fifth eclogue, written about the year 1514, in which there is a refreshing picture of football as a rural winter sport. The poet says: 'Eche tyme and season hath his delyte and joyes', and goes on to describe football play, first of 'lytell boyes', and then plowmen:

And now in wynter, for all the grevous colde
All rent and ragyd a man maye them beholde,
They have great pleasure, supposynge well to dyne
Whan men ben busyed, in kyllynge of fat swyne.
They get the bladder, and blowe it grete and thyn,
With many beanes or peasen bounde within;
It ratleth, soundeth, and shyneth clere and fayre,
Whyle it is throwen and cast up in the ayre;
Echeone contendeth and hath a grete delyte
With fote or with hande the bladder for to smyte.
Yf it fall to grounde they lyfte it up againe,
This wyse to labour they count it for no payne,
Rennynge and lepynge they dryve awaye the colde.
The sturdy plowmen, lusty, stronge, and bolde,
Overcometh the wynter with dryvynge the fote ball,
Forgetynge labour and many a grevous fall.[33]

In 1577 there was a reference in the Repertory of the Court of Aldermen to the banning of football within the Royal Exchange, London: 'Item, it was

[31] Information obtained from Public Record Office, London, reference Assizes/35/9/2/29.
[32] J. Strutt, *The Sports and Pastimes of the English People*, 1903, p. 94.
[33] *The Fyfte Eglog of Alexandre Barclay of the Cytezen and Uplondyshman*, reprinted from the original for the Percy Society, 1848, vol. 22, ed. F. W. Fairholt.

orderyd that Sir John Rivers Knighte and Mr Dixie Alderman shall from tyme to tyme take order that there be no more football pleye or other dysorderly exercyse used within the Royall exchange at any tyme hereafter.'[34]

That James I did not think much of football is shown by the advice he gave in 1603 to his son Prince Henry: 'From this court I debarre all rough and violent exercises, as the foot-ball, meeter for lameing than making able the users thereof.' The King then commended to his son, 'running, leaping, wrastling, fencing, dauncing, playing at the caitche or teenise, archery and pallemaille.'[35]

Play in towns was one of the chief objections to football in the early part of the seventeenth century, and in William Hone's *Table Book* the following slightly ironic passage is cited from Sir William Davenant's description of London in 1634:

> I would now make a safe retreat, but that methinks I am stopped by one of your heroic games called foot-ball; which I conceive (under your favour) not very conveniently civil in the streets, especially in such irregular and narrow roads as Crooked-lane. Yet it argues your courage, much like your military pastime of throwing at cocks; but your metal would be much magnified (since you have long allowed those two valiant exercises in the streets) were you to draw your archers from Finsbury, and, during high market, let them shoot at butts in Cheapside.[36]

In a poem on London life called 'Trivia', by John Gay, published in 1716 there is a vivid description of eighteenth-century street football, dangerous to property and pedestrian alike. The scene is Covent Garden, and a throng of young lads and sturdy apprentices crowd to join in the hurly-burly as it erupts through the dirty animated streets:

> Here oft' my Course I bend, when lo! from far,
> I spy the Furies of the Foot-ball War:
> The 'Prentice quits his Shop, to join the Crew,
> Encreasing Crouds the flying Game pursue.
> Thus, as you roll the Ball o'er snowy Ground.
> The gath'ring Globe augments with ev'ry Round;
> But whither shall I run? the Throng draws nigh,
> The Ball now Skims the Street, now soars on high;

[34] Repertory of the Court of Aldermen, no. 19, f. 150, 11 December 1577.

[35] *Basilicon Doron, Book III, or, His Majesties Instructions to his Dearest Sonne, Henry the Prince*, 1603, p. 120.

[36] W. Hone, *The Table Book*, 1878, p. 85.

> The dext'rous Glazier strong returns the Bound,
> And gingling Sashes on the Pent-house sound.[37]

An intriguing possibility exists that the game now so firmly established throughout England may have been introduced as far afield as Greenland by English whalers, who from the early seventeenth century were sailing in northern waters. The following is a description of football as played by the local Inuit inhabitants, and is contained in an account of Greenland dated 1741:

> The second method of playing ball is that they position two goals three to four hundred paces apart where they then divide themselves equally into two parts; but assemble or meet midway between these two goals, where they then throw the ball down and kick it with the foot, each to his goal. The person who is now the fastest runner, and who can take the ball with him, will come soonest to the goal and will have won. It is also in this manner, they say, that the souls of the dead play ball in the heavens with a walrus head, when the northern lights appear, which they consider to be the souls of the departed.[38]

English settlers took mass football to Virginia, and as in England, the game was rough and unsophisticated. This is brought out by a 1609 description of the pastimes of the North American Indians which also makes brief reference to the turbulent game favoured by the colonists: 'They use beside football play, which wemen and young boyes doe much play at. The men never. They make ther Gooles as ours only they never fight nor pull one another doune.'[39] In a description of a St Andrew's Day festival in Hanover county, Virginia, written in the early part of the nineteenth century, is found another reference to American mass football: 'With divers other considerable Prizes, for Dancing, Singing, Foot-ball play, Jumping, Wrestling, &c.'[40]

Gradually street football came under increasing municipal disapproval, by-laws were enforced and during the latter part of the eighteenth and first half of the nineteenth century the game was generally suppressed. In the locations

[37] J. Gay, *Trivia, or, The Act of Walking the Streets of London,* introduction and notes by W. H. Williams, London, 1922, p. 23.

[38] Knudsen, *Træk Af Boldspillets Historie*, p. 120, quoting Hands Egede's *Description of Greenland*, 1741.

[39] H. Spelman, *Relation of Virginia,* London, 1872, p. 19. The book was originally written in 1609. Spelman lived among the Native Americans for many years, and was killed or lost among them somewhere along the Potomac in 1623.

[40] *Virginia Historical Register*, vol. 6, 1853, p. 30. The statement was written on 26 November 1836.

where street play did survive it was in the main a Shrovetide event, but as the nineteenth century progressed these survivals found it increasingly difficult to come to terms with the advance of utilitarianism, and the twentieth century welcomed only a mere handful of Shrovetide contests. Nevertheless, in these remaining bastions play was in no way watered down but continued in a vigorous and fiery vein.

Some football was, however, still played on village greens, usually on Sundays. Writing in 1801, Joseph Strutt indicated that a semblance of order had by then come into the rural game. He tells us that the goals, which were situated some eighty to 100 yards from each other, consisted of two sticks driven into the ground about two or three feet apart. The ball, an inflated bladder encased in leather, had to be driven through the opponents' goal 'which being achieved the game is won . . . When the exercise becomes exceeding violent, the players kick each other's shins without the least ceremony, and some of them are overthrown at the hazard of their limbs.'[41] Rules were unknown, the well-being of other players was completely ignored, and the object was simply to force the ball through the opposing goal, by fair means or foul. At this time the game was often played on an inter-village or inter-parish basis. Strutt however also commented that of late years it had 'fallen into disrepute and is but little practised'.[42]

Football and the Church in England

In that part of *The Anatomie of Abuses* (1583), by the Puritan Philip Stubbes, which deals with 'prophanation of the Saboth', football playing is described as a 'devilish pastime . . . a bloody and murthering practise . . . sometimes their necks are broken, sometimes their backs, sometime their legs, sometime their armes . . . and hereof groweth envie, malice, rancour, cholor, hatred, displeasure, enmitie, and what not els: and sometimes fighting, brawling, contention, quarrel picking, murther, homicide, and great effusion of blood, as experience dayly teacheth. Is this murthering play, now, an exercise for the Sabaoth day: is this a christian dealing, for one brother to mayme and hurt another . . . ?' The diatribe concludes with the exhortation: 'God make us more careful over the bodyes of our Bretheren!'[43]

As is apparent from Stubbes' attack, Sunday play was common, although presumably not always so violent! Indeed in the Middle Ages, when gravestones were mostly laid flat, the open area in and around churchyards was a favourite location for play, and it was not unknown for the clergy to take part.

[41] J. Strutt, *The Sports and Pastimes of the English People*, revised edn, 1903, p. 94.
[42] J. Strutt, *The Sports and Pastimes of the English People*, revised edn, 1903, p. 93.
[43] P. Stubbes, *The Anatomie of Abuses*, 1583, pp. 137, 184.

In 1425 at Ambrosden, Oxfordshire, payments made by the prior included the sum of fourpence 'to divers players at football on the feast of St Katherine, virgin and martyr.'[44] This payment could have been to help the players purchase a football, or perhaps to reward them for providing an entertaining spectacle on this special day.

As a result of a 1472 church visitation to the province of York it was decreed 'in agreement with the parishioners, that henceforth no one is to indulge in shameful and forbidden sports in the graveyard, such as, for example, football or handball, or wrestling, on penalty of paying 2*d.*' This referred to a church at Salton, and during the same visitation the penalty attaching to the misdemeanour of graveyard football at Wyghton was set at 12*d.*[45]

In 1518 in connection with the diocese of Ossory, south-west Leinster, there was a regulation that 'henceforth clergy playing football must pay whenever they do so 40*d.* to the ordinary and 40*d.* for the repair of the church where such a game is played.'[46] Payment to the ordinary, who was an ecclesiastical official and dealt with misdemeanours, was by way of fine. Damage to the church would have been to the windows and the outside fabric of the building.

A visitation in the diocese of Lincoln in 1519 noted as a black mark against Richard, the curate at Hawbridge, that he 'habitually plays football in his surplice' (*est communis lusor ad pilam pedalem in camisia sua*). The curate also regularly played at dice, and because of these discreditable pastimes and the neglect of his duties the bishop suspended him.[47]

In Chester in 1589 Hugh Case and William Shurlock were fined 2*s.* 'for playing football in St Werburgh's Cemetery during divine service', or rather 'sermon-time' (*tempore divine predicationis*). Incidentally in the same year at Chester, the Dee was frozen hard and 'the people played foteball on it'.[48]

The second volume of William Hone's *Every Day Book,* first published in 1827, records under March 14 an interesting letter to the editor concerning Sunday football, in this case by Irishmen. Play took place every Sunday afternoon in fields near Islington, commencing at three o'clock and lasting until dusk. During the game 'some fine specimens of wrestling are occasionally exhibited, in order to delay the two men who are rivals in the pursuit of the ball;

[44] W. Kennett, *Parochial Antiquities Attempted in the History of Ambrosden, Burcester, in the Counties of Oxford and Bucks*, new edn 1818, vol. 2, p. 259.

[45] *The Fabric Rolls of York Minster*, ed. J. Raine, Surtees Society, vol. 35, 1858, pp. 255, 257.

[46] *The Contents of the Red Book of the Diocese of Ossory*, Historical Manuscripts Commission, Tenth Report, Appendix, part 5, 1885, p. 223 and note 3.

[47] *Visitations in the Diocese of Lincoln, 1517–1531,* ed. A. Hamilton Thompson, vol. 1, Lincoln Record Society, vol. 33, 1940, p. 44.

[48] R. H. Morris, *Chester in the Plantagenet and Tudor Reigns,* pp. 331, 332.

meantime the parties' friends have time to pursue the combat, and the quick arrival of the ball to the goal is generally the consequence, and a lusty shout is given by the victors.' The letter writer then continued: 'When a boy, football was commonly played on a Sunday morning, before church time, in a village in the west of England, and the churchpiece was the ground chosen for it.'[49]

As it spread all over England and Scotland, football had often taken the form of a local contest rather than a sport, and as we shall see, where it survived remained so.

School Games

Although mass football in streets and rural districts gradually lost its widespread hold, it doubtless continued to be played by schoolboys. Indeed by the mid-eighteenth century it had reappeared at some English public schools, and these developed independently according to particular ground conditions, with each having its own set of rules, for example the Eton Wall Game, the Eton Field Game, Winchester and Charterhouse football. Later, the old game blossomed forth, this time in two streams; and England became in the mid-nineteenth century the birthplace of modern soccer and rugby.

The Wall Game at Eton has taken a singular form. It was probably first played on College Field in the eighteenth century by collegers who were kicking a ball against the wall that runs from Eton to Slough. While other football type games are played in a wide pitch with no physical boundaries other than lines, the Wall Game is unique in that the width of the pitch, known as the Furrow, is no more than fifteen yards wide.

The game is played by two teams of ten, comprising seven players in the bully, the equivalent of the scrum, two outsides, who play in the same positions as the half-backs in rugby, and a long, who stands about thirty yards to the back of the bully, acting rather like a full-back.

The ball is shaped as a pumpkin and the player in control of the ball has it under his shins. The rest of the bully form around him and attempt to drive him with the ball up the wall towards the scoring zone, which is marked at either end of the Furrow. Players may pass the ball to each other in the bully, but it may not travel backwards, and they may not use their hands. No player may have any part of his body on the ground other than hands and feet. Players are also not allowed to bind onto the opposition, nor strike them: movement in the bully is made by driving forwards.

[49] W. Hone, *The Every Day Book*, 1878, vol. 2, p. 187.

FIG. 99: The Eton Wall Game.

The ball can be moved forward more quickly by passing it out to one of the outsides who kicks it out of the Furrow and forwards. The next bully takes place opposite the place where the ball stops – not at the point where it crosses the line marking the Furrow.

To score, a player can kick it onto the goal (for five points): a door in a garden wall at one end and a tree at the other end. Or a bully can be forced within the scoring area at either end of the Furrow, known as Calx. In this zone the ball can be moved backwards deliberately and if the attacking team can lift the ball off the ground and touch it with a hand, the umpire may allow them a shy (a throw) at either goal: if it hits the goal ten points are scored. If it misses – and it usually does, or the defending team intercept the throw – a point is still scored for the attempt.

Thus it can be seen how football, now the most universal and popular of outdoor games with an active history of more than 2000 years, was through the centuries a feature of British life. Certainly with the development of highly organized forms of play the game had come a long way from the time when motley crowds of men furiously and with complete abandon kicked a round object such as an inflated bladder, either aimlessly or to some goal.

Shrove Tuesday Football

No history of mass football in this country, however brief, would be complete without a special mention of Shrove Tuesday football in England and the Fasternse'en Ba' in Scotland. The latter is dealt with at the end of this chapter.

The final carnival before the austerities of Lent was held on Shrove Tuesday, when pancakes and fritters were eaten and typical boisterous amusements consisted of bell-ringing, rope-pulling, stone-throwing, hen-thrashing, cock-fighting, cock-throwing, dog-tossing, bull-baiting and most important of all a game of football.[50]

While popular mass football was never restricted to one day in the year, as a Shrovetide sport it does not seem to have a recorded history before the sixteenth century: the single possible exception is the game described by Fitz Stephen and given at the beginning of this chapter.

The earliest record of football on Shrove Tuesday comes from Chester where in 1533 an unsuccessful attempt was made to suppress the game. However, in 1540 the custom whereby the Company of Shoemakers provided for the Drapers' Company 'yerleye upon Teuesday commonly caulyd Shroft Teuesday otherwyse Goteddesday at afternoune of the same unto the drapars afore the mayre of the citie at the Cros upon the Rood Dee one ball of lether caulyd a fout baule' to the value of 3*s.* 4*d.*, which was then played from the Cross on the Rood Dee to the Common Hall and which had been observed 'tyme out of manns remembrance', was put down because of 'evill disposed persons wherfore hath ryssyn grete inconvenynce'. A foot race was substituted.[51]

The Shrove Tuesday game survived longer than mass football played in towns and villages and sometimes across country, but it had largely died out by the latter part of the nineteenth century.

Derby

Because of its rough and dangerous nature the game was banned in 1846, 'but it required two troops of dragoons, a large levy of special constables and the reading of the Riot Act to secure the desired result.'[52] The contest was between the parishes of All Saints' and St Peter's, and the ball was thrown from the Town Hall into the Market Place. While the struggle was nominally a football match, latterly it became nothing less than a fight between the two parts of the town.

[50] F. P. Magoun, *Shrove Tuesday Football*, pp. 10, 17.

[51] F. P. Magoun, *Shrove Tuesday Football*, pp. 11, 12, 13, quoting *The Vale-Royall of England*, London, 1656, p. 194, and Morris, pp. 342, 343.

[52] A. W. Davison, *Derby, its Rise and Progress*, p. 210 ff. See F. P. Magoun, *Shrove Tuesday Football*, p. 28.

Afterwards, the parish bells of the winning side pealed out the joyful news of their men's victory.[53]

Kingston-upon-Thames

As a result of chaotic scenes over the years, when hooliganism and rowdyism ran riot, the street game was banned by the Town Council after the Shrove Tuesday 1866 contest, and the police were given 'strict orders to carry this into effect.'[54] Street doors and windows in Kingston were barricaded with stout timber, and the contest was started at eleven o'clock by the mayor kicking off the ball from the balcony of the Town Hall. The two goals were the Clattern Bridge and the Kingston Bridge.

Dorking

The two sides, unlimited in numbers, represented the East and West parts of the town, and two bridges over the Pipp Brook were the goals. Before the contest there was 'a perambulation of the streets by the football retinue composed of grotesquely dressed persons'.[55] The town crier kicked off the first ball at two o'clock and he stopped play at six o'clock. Started at the church gates, the game thereafter 'rioted up and down the main street'.[56] It ceased to be played about 1897 as certain local tradesmen objected, and it was officially stopped under Section 72 of the Highways Act, 1835.

Chester-le-Street

The game was contested until 1932 between Upstreeters and Downstreeters, play starting at 1 p.m. and finishing at 6 p.m. The centre of the main street (which was also at that time the A1 road) was the dividing line, and on whichever side the ball was at 6 p.m. that side won. The ball was thrown out from the Queen's Head Hotel in the centre of the town and it was known for more than 400 players to take part.[57] The game was stopped when a number of players were fined under the Highways Acts for obstructing the highways and causing an annoyance to pedestrians.

Shrove Tuesday football is still played in the following places: Sedgefield, County Durham, between countrymen and tradesmen; Alnwick, Northumberland,

[53] A. B. Gomme and G. L. Gomme, *The Traditional Games of England, Scotland and Ireland*, vol. 1, p. 13;. quoting Dyer's *Popular Customs*, p. 75.

[54] F. P. Magoun, *Shrove Tuesday Football*, p. 22.

[55] A. B. Gomme and G. L. Gomme, *The Traditional Games of England, Scotland and Ireland*, vol. 1, p. 135.

[56] Hugh Thomson, *Highways and Byways of Surrey*, 1908.

[57] A. B. Gomme and G. L. Gomme, *The Traditional Games of England, Scotland and Ireland*, vol. 1, p. 135.

between the parishes of St Michael's and St Paul's; Atherstone, Warwickshire, where there are no goals or sides, the ball is 'thrown out' at 3 p.m. and the object is to keep it in play till five o'clock when the player then in possession endeavours to acquire the trophy by smuggling it away; and Ashbourne, Derbyshire.

Sedgefield

It is alleged that the first incident associated with the game, at one time played between countrymen and tradesmen, dates from 1235. At 1 p.m. a hand-stitched small leather ball is passed thrice through a bull ring on the village green by a local person of prominence, an honour accorded by a committee, the membership of which is a closely guarded secret. There are no organizers – the game just 'happens'. After the ceremony the ball is thrown to some 300 players who kick it around, reaching the goal, a stream or beck at the foot of Spring Lane, after some hours of fluid play. Another goal, a pond near the north end, was filled some years ago and a house built on the site.

In days gone bye the ball was inscribed with the following rhyme, now sometimes added by the winner:

When with pancakes ye are sated
Come to the ring and ye'll be mated
For there this ball will be upcast
And may the game be better than the last.

Prior to the game the ball is taken to public houses where donations are exchanged for a touch of the trophy. This is considered to bring luck. The money so collected pays for the cost of the ball and damage to windows, fences and gardens. During the afternoon play is put on temporary hold from time to time when the ball is taken into a public house by the man in possession, who is rewarded with a pint of beer before he assays forth and the match continues. It is a rough and ready tussle with random movement much enjoyed by the participants. Shops and property generally are boarded up. After the ball has been immersed (alleyed) in the stream, men and youths may dispute the selection of the winner until he claims the ball as his own by passing it thrice through the bull ring. The concluding part of the game takes place shortly before 5 p.m. It is believed that if a girl kicks the ball she will be married by the end of the year, and the fertility of a married couple is assured if they touch it.

Ashbourne

The game is played every Shrove Tuesday and Ash Wednesday, and contested by Up'ards and Down'ards, depending on which side of the Henmore River a player is born – although many participants now recognize family loyalty irrespective of the accident of birth. It is organized by a committee comprising between ten and twelve men from all walks of life aided by a very efficient secretary and his indefatigable wife, both of whom commit many unpaid hours to the organization of these memorable contests. A players' committee was formed in 2002 consisting of equal numbers of Up'ards and Down'ards and it has been a resounding success in raising funds, repairing damage and facilitating contact between players and the older committee.

For some years boys up to and including the age of fourteen held a game. It was last played in 1918, when the ball was goaled by a lad Jack Robinson. Known as Sludge Robinson, he came from the nearby village of Yeaveley.

The goals are three miles apart and were represented originally by the Clifton and Sturston Mills. These have now been demolished and replaced by two six-foot pieces of locally hewn stone set on plinths, the stones representing the original mill wheels. The contest is at an end when the ball is hit three times against the goal.

It is a signal honour to be invited to 'turn up' a ball. On Shrove Tuesday the choice is a well-known personage frequently from outwith the town, and the following day a local man of distinction is accorded the honour. Ash Wednesday is perhaps the more popular day with Ashbournians, principally because fewer outsiders take part. On both days the guest is entertained at the Green Man Hotel, where 400 people sit down for lunch. There he makes a short speech, is presented with a beautiful inscribed glass chalice, and the Shrovetide Song[58] is sung, after which there is also a rendition of 'Land of Hope and Glory'. Two of the stanzas from The Shrovetide Song are as follows:

> There's a town still plays this glorious game,
> Tho' 'tis but a little spot,
> And year by year the contest's fought,
> From the field that's called Shaw Croft;
> Then friend meets friend in friendly strife,
> The leather for to gain,
> And they play the game right manfully,
> In snow, sunshine, or rain
> 'Tis a glorious game, deny it who can,
> And no weather daunts an Englishman!

[58] Composed in 1891 by Mr George Porter for the concert in aid of funds to pay the fines for playing in the streets, and put to fresh music by Daly Atkinson in 1956. He was the organist at St Oswald's Church.

For loyal the Game shall ever be,
No matter when or where
And to treat the Game as ought but the free,
Is more than the boldest dare;
Through the ups and downs of its chequered life
May the ball still ever roll,
Until by fair and gallant strife,
We've reached the treasur'd goal.
It's a good old Game, deny it who can,
That tries the pluck of an Englishman!

In earlier times the game was celebrated in the 'Ashbourne Foot-ball Song'[59] written by Mr H. Fawcett and sung in the Ashbourne Theatre on 26 February 1821. Three stanzas of this delightful ditty are as follows:

I'll sing you a song of a neat little place,
Top full of good humour and beauty and grace
Where coaches are rolling by day and by night,
And in playing at Foot-Ball the people delight.
Where health and good humour does always abound,
And hospitality's cup flows freely around,
Where friendship and harmony are to be found,
In the neat little town of Ashbourne.

Shrove Tuesday, you know, is always the day,
When pancake's the prelude and Foot-Ball's the play,
Where upwards and downwards men ready for fun,
Like the French at the Battle of Waterloo run.
And well may they run like the devil to pay,
'Tis always the case as I have heard say,
If a Derbyshire Foot-ball man comes in the way,
In the neat little town of Ashbourne.

If they get to the Park the upwards men shout
And think all the downwards men put to the rout,
But a right about face they will soon have to learn,
And the upwards men about the huzza in their turn.
Then into Shaw Croft where the bold and the brave
Get a ducking in trying the Foot-Ball to save;
For 'tis well known they fear not a watery grave,
In defence of the Foot-Ball at Ashbourne.

[59] T. Moult, *Derbyshire in Prose and Verse*, 1929, pp. 50–52.

FIG. 100: Ashbourne Royal Shrovetide Football. The sides are Up'ards and Down'ards. The goals are three miles apart and the stone plinth in this photograph is one of two that replaced Clifton and Sturston Mills, now demolished, which were the original goals.

Until and including 1862 the ball was turned up from the bull-ring in Market Place. The game now commences at 2 o'clock[60] at Shaw Croft, whither the guest is chaired shoulder high. People like to touch the ball – particularly in Dig Street – as it passes through the streets. The tradition is that this brings good luck. A special dais is used for the turn-up which has replaced an earlier one built in 1974 in the centre of the car park and funded by public subscription. The present dais is a splendid brick built structure with marble plaques and engraved with the words of the 'Royal Shrovetide Song'. Constructed in 1999 by the players themselves, it was built from material gifted by a local quarry and contractors. Over the years the principal guests have been HRH the Prince of Wales on 21 February 1928 and HRH Prince Charles on 4 March 2003. Since 1922 the game has been known as Ashbourne Royal Shrovetide Football.

Before the 'turn-up' a spirited 'Auld Lang Syne' is sung by spectators and players, numbering some 3000. This is followed by a fine rendition of the national anthem. During the course of a long game the hug or scrum comprises a core of 100 hardened Shrovetide players who will take part from beginning to end. Probably another 400 or 500 will participate at various times, sometimes only briefly. Shrovetide attracts a significant number of visitors and up to 5000 people will view the game, especially on the Tuesday, although not all will attend the start.

The ball is hand made using stout leather, stuffed with cork shavings. It weighs about 4 lb and is painted with scenes reflecting the life and profession of the person who starts the game. Also included, *inter alia*, are his name, the date, the wording 'Ashbourne Royal Shrovetide Football', sometimes the town crest of three cockerels, a sovereign's crown and the Union flag. Since 1907 only four men have made the balls: Trevor Yeomans, Percy Chadwick, his son Arthur Chadwick BEM – the latter remarkably between 1954 and 2002 – and since then John Harrison.

Once the ball has dried out, which can take some months, it is repainted. For more than seventy years the balls were painted by John Barker. He was followed for a few years by his nephew Jack Roberts, who was succeeded in turn by Arthur Chadwick's daughter Sandra, and more recently, for over a decade, by Stuart Avery and Tim Baker.

After some open play on Shaw Croft the 'hug' or scrum may proceed onto the barricaded streets of the town, over adjacent fields or into the Henmore River, where it is frequently played, often in freezing conditions, before a sudden debouchment to uninhibited mass action over neighbouring land. Open play

[60] In 1942 the committee delayed the turn-up on both days until 4 p.m. to enable the participation of 300 Irishmen working on the construction of Ashbourne aerodrome.

is favoured and is pleasing to watch. Celebrated whatever the weather, only in 1968 and 2001 were the contests cancelled due to foot and mouth disease, although in 1968 there was a small unofficial game in the town's playing fields.

The game can be rough and fluid and is not for the faint-hearted. Cuts, sprains and bruises are to be expected and broken bones are not unknown. There is only one recorded fatality when sadly, on Ash Wednesday 1878, nineteen-year-old James William Barker was drowned at Clifton Mill. He was the brother of the ball painter John Barker.

If a goal is scored before 5 p.m.[61] play continues with another ball or balls. Technically there is no limit on the number of balls, but since records began only three have been used in one day. The limitation is how many goals have been scored before 5 p.m. Play must stop at 10 p.m. and if the contest is not concluded the ball is handed back to the committee to be awarded to the man who has started the game. The committee was not always so generous in its disposal of an ungoaled ball. In the mid-1930s if the game had not been concluded by the then time limit of 7 p.m. (later increased variously to 10 p.m. and even midnight), the ball was returned to the committee and subsequently auctioned amongst its members. In 1934 it was purchased by the secretary for 10*s*. There are many customary understandings but few rules: for example, if the ball has been hidden and not played for more than an hour the game is declared void, and there is a similar outcome if transport is used to convey the ball.

To goal a ball is an achievement much prized. Before the climax there can be debate by the winning side as to whom the trophy should be awarded. If so, somewhat arbitrarily but effectively, drawing straws or draughts (e.g. five white and one black for the goaler) may be used to determine the winner from amongst the claimants. Commitment by others was also recognized. In the early part of the twentieth century there was a custom for well-to-do Ashbournians – doubtless including members of the Ball Committee – to reward outstanding players on both sides with vouchers for a pint of beer, which could be redeemed at a local public house. The names of the scorers and those who have turned up the ball are recorded on attractive wooden Roll of Honour panels sited in the Green Man Hotel.

With its origins in much earlier times, since at least the early nineteenth century in its present form, Royal Shrovetide Football in Ashbourne has been very much a part of life in that fine old town, although over the years there have been a number of serious attempts at abolition. Famously in 1860 it took the efforts of a determined lady to frustrate the police, when she threw the ball from

[61] In 1947 the committee determined that if the ball was goaled before 4.30 p.m. another ball or balls were to be used.

a window in Market Place having arrived there with the orb secreted under her skirts. Thereafter, from time to time, fines were imposed on participants which happily were satisfied by a public collection. On other occasions, rather than pay a fine, some players chose to go to jail. Mrs Elizabeth Woolley is the only member of the distaff side to have started a game and she holds a special place in the history of Ashbourne. Ladies are invariably keen supporters and not barred from participation, normally in a supporting role. Two women have goaled the ball, both in 1943.

Apart from the remarkable involvement of Mrs Woolley, as I have said a woman has never turned up the ball. However, in 1934 the committee did offer the honour to the celebrated entertainer Gracie Fields, and some years later to the popular singer Vera Lynn. Both of them declined.

An internationally famous name was approached in 1946 – Winston Churchill. He could not accept due to 'other calls on him'.

The game was celebrated throughout both World Wars, servicemen specifically requesting its continuation. During the First World War in 1918 a ball was sent to the Ashbourne contingent of the Sherwood Foresters, then in Flanders. Remarkably, on its receipt a game was played by these soldier Ashbournians at the village of Sous St Leger. It is pleasant to record that this special ball was safeguarded and after the war taken back to Ashbourne. Similarly in the Second World War, Shrovetide was celebrated in traditional style with ball play by Ashbourne men then serving in the Derbyshire Yeomanry near Grimsby.[62]

It is clear beyond peradventure to anyone visiting Ashbourne at Shrovetide that Ashbourne Royal Shrovetide Football is held in unshakably high esteem, and commands widespread support throughout the lovely old town and its environs.

In his comprehensive article written in 1932 Francis P. Magoun Jr lists forty-two towns or regions where he found Shrove Tuesday football recorded.

Christmas and Easter Mass Football

Although latterly football became primarily a Shrovetide sport it was not exclusive to that time of the year, and there was a game held in South Cardiganshire at Christmas, of which G. L. Gomme says:

> The following graphic account of Welsh customs was printed in the *Oswestry Observer* of March 2, 1887: 'In South Cardiganshire it seems that about eighty years ago the population, rich and poor, male and female,

[62] J. P. Gadsby, *The Ancient Custom of Shrovetide Football in Ashbourne*, 1986, and L. Porter, *Shrovetide Football and the Ashbourne Game*, 2002.

> of opposing parishes, turned out on Christmas Day and indulged in the game of "Football" with such vigour that it became little short of a serious fight. The parishioners of Cellan and Pencarreg were particularly bitter in their conflicts; men threw off their coats and waistcoats and women their gowns and sometimes their petticoats.'[63]

Also on Christmas Day at Llanwenog, a parish near Lampeter, the people engaged in a rough football contest. The sides were the *Bro* who occupied the high ground of the parish, and the *Blaenau* who occupied the lowlands. Gomme provides a fascinating description of play between the two sides. Apparently the more devout players joined in the service at the parish church on Christmas morning and thereafter met the other participants about midday. Then rich and poor, male and female, assembled on the turnpike road, which was the dividing line between the highlands and the lowlands. The ball was thrown in the air,

> Bros and Blaenaus scrambled for its possession, and a quarter of an hour frequently elapsed before the ball was got out from among the struggling heap of human beings. Then if the Bros, by hook or by crook, could succeed in taking the ball up the mountain to their hamlet of Rhyddlan they won the day; while the Blaenaus were successful if they got the ball to their end of the parish at New Court. The whole parish was the field of operations, and sometimes it would be dark before either party scored a victory. In the meantime many kicks would be given and taken, so that on the following day some of the competitors would be unable to walk, and sometimes a kick on the shins would lead the two men concerned to abandon the game until they had decided which was the better pugilist. There do not appear to have been any rules for the regulation of the game; and the art of football playing in the olden time seems to have been to reach the goal. When once the goal was reached, the victory was celebrated by loud hurrahs and the firing of guns, and was not disturbed until the following Christmas Day. Victory on Christmas Day, added the old man, was so highly esteemed by the whole countryside, that a Bro or Blaenau would as soon lose a cow from his cow-house as the football from his portion of the parish.[64]

[63] A. B. Gomme and G. L. Gomme, *The Traditional Games of England, Scotland and Ireland*, vol. 1, pp. 135, 136.

[64] A. B. Gomme and G. L. Gomme, *The Traditional Games of England, Scotland and Ireland*, vol. 1, pp. 136, 137, quoting the *Oswestry Observer* of 2 March 1887. The description was given by a man of over eighty, an inmate of Lampeter workhouse.

Gomme also says that in North Wales the ball was called the *Bêl Troed* and consisted of a bladder covered with a *Cwd Tarw*. In South Wales the ball was called *Bél Ddu* and was usually made by the parish shoemaker who himself took it to the ground on Christmas Day. (The Welsh words in their normal form are as follows: *Bro*, *Blaenau*, *Pêl Droed*, *Cwd Tarw*, *Pêl Ddu*. At Llanwenog the terms '*Bro*' and '*Blaenau*' mean roughly 'Hillfolk' and 'Valley-folk'; *Pêl droed* = foot-ball, *Cwd* = bag or scrotum, *Tarw* = bull, *Y Bêl Ddu* = the black ball.)

Football was also played in the streets of Kirkham, Lancashire, on Christmas Day. As soon as the midday dinner was over a general closing of the outside shutters then in use was effected and the match began.[65]

Workington

Street football is played on Good Friday, Easter Tuesday and the following Saturday. The premier event is on Easter Tuesday and it was not until the mid-nineteenth century that the other two contests were introduced. This game is very old and the *Cumberland Pacquet* of 20 April 1775 reported: 'Tuesday afternoon was determined at Workington, a long-contended annual match at Foot-Ball, which has been played there for many years, between Sailors and Colliers. The play was the severest that ever was seen there, and perhaps there never was a contest better supported on both sides, in any part of this Kingdom. The game was, however, at last won by the Colliers. Upwards of 2,000 people were present, and it is supposed, more than 1,500 of them played, and sometimes 30 or 40 of them were all in the river Derwent together; the whole afforded great entertainment to the spectators.'

The sides are Uppies and Downies, although over the years other descriptions have been used including Dockers and Sailors (Downies) and Miners and Colliers (Uppies). There is no delineation between Uppie territory and Downie territory, but it seems that previously those born above the Cloffocks were Uppies and below that area, Downies. At present the allegiance of contestants is determined by where they live or merely by following family allegiance.

The ball is constructed by stitching together four pieces of cow hide, the work taking thirty hours. Stuffed with wool flock (previously horse hair) and stamped with the date, over the years the trophy has varied in size. In 1939 it weighed 7 lb and in 1963 2¼ lb. Present day balls weigh 2½ lb. The most famous of the ball makers was Jimmy Elwood who plied his skill for over seventy years. The trophy is thrown up at 6.30 p.m. from a small bridge which crosses the Cloffocks Beck.

[65] H. Fishwick, *History* of *Kirkham*. Chetham Society, 1874, p. 206, quoted in A. R Wright and J. E. Lones, *British Calendar Customs, England*, vol. 3.

FIG. 101: Uppies and Doonies on Easter Tuesday at Workington. The photograph is pre-1920.

The Uppie goal has been long established at Workington Hall at the top end of the town and the ball is goaled by hailing it at the main archway of the derelict building, under which it is thrown three times in the air.

The Downies have to take the ball to where an old capstan once stood on the present stone jetty located at the union of the river Derwent and the harbour mouth. There, matters are concluded when it is thrown up three times.

There is no organizing committee, sponsors meet the cost of the balls and the contests are best described as 'happenings'.[66] The main field of play is the town's open ground known as the Cloffocks, reduced somewhat in size by encroachment over the years and now sadly under further threat following a proposed land sale by the Borough Council to a supermarket. This is being vigorously contested. In bygone years several thousand people witnessed the games, which boasted hundreds of players. Indeed, in the 1870s the crowd was estimated at

[66] A most commendable association with the contests is that the players and those associated with the game organize an annual 'Uppies and Downies charity'. In 2003 the remarkable sum of £8000 was raised.

10,000 and on Easter Tuesday 1930 it was said that 20,000 people were present. Interest has waned in recent years, and now at any one time fifty or sixty players will form the scrum and about 200 will take part during the contest. Play may last for a short time or for several hours, but in practice the contest continues for as long as it takes to hail the ball (one each day).

The present day games cannot compare to the mighty struggles of the past. Nevertheless the contests are still well supported and celebrated, and 1000 spectators watch the tussles. Workington remains proud of its mass street football.

Particularly in past times violence was frequent, with cuts, fingers and shins broken and eyes blackened. Fractured arms and legs have not been unknown. Over the years four players have been drowned in the River Derwent, the most recent tragedy occurring on Easter Tuesday 1983.

Nowadays the games are played in good spirit and little or no damage is inflicted on shops and houses. This is in contrast to the happenings on Easter Tuesday 1899 when a witness wrote:

> For grotesqueness and whimsicality, for fragrant odours and filthy defilement, football at Workington, as I saw it on Easter Tuesday just licks all creation . . . Something like seven or eight thousand people of all ages and conditions in life are seen trampling, and shoving, and squeezing to look at the players up to their knees in the horrible filth of a beck not more than a dozen feet wide, and the whole of them rammed, and jammed, and twisted into one inextricable knot . . . Look at the smoke and steam ascending to heaven from this living human cauldron. Look at them, panting, struggling, twisting, tumbling and striving. Too hoarse to shout, they can only eject their bare arms from that living mass, and wave them either to the east or the west to show in which direction they want the ball to go . . . One fellow has lost the biggest part of his trousers and the whole of his shirt with the exception of one sleeve . . . Not one out of twenty has a whole garment about him.'[67]

Scotland

By the early fifteenth century the game had become well established in Scotland either as an import from England or perhaps direct from France, which had fairly close ties with Scotland at this time. Indeed so great was its popularity that, as happened in England, the progress of archery was being impeded.

[67] K. Wallace, *The Barbarians of Workington, Uppies & Downies*, 1991, quoting a Sergeant C. Hall; J. Godwin, *Mass Football in Cumberland and Elsewhere*, 1986.

Accordingly in 1424 during the reign of James I, there was an Enactment forbidding football under pain of a fine: 'ITEM, it is statut and the king forbiddes that na man play at the fut ball under the payne of iiijd.'[68] In 1458, during the reign of James II, there was a further Enactment decrying the playing of football:

> It is decreed and ordained that wapinschaws be held by the lords and barons spiritual and temporal four times in the year, and that football and golf be utterly cried down and not used and that bow marks be made at each parish church, a pair of butts, and shooting be used each Sunday and that each man shoot six shots at least under the pain to be levied upon them that come not, at least twopence, to be given to them that come to the bow marks, as drinking-money . . . [69]

Further Acts were passed in 1471 during the reign of James III, and in 1491 during the reign of James IV. In spite of the royal prohibitions James IV, or perhaps his family, appears to have indulged in the game, and the following is an interesting entry in the 1497 accounts of the Lord High Treasurer of Scotland: 'Item, (the xxij day of Aprile), giffin to Jame Dog to by fut ballis, to the King . . . ij S.'[70]

Throughout Scotland the game maintained its widespread popularity up to and including the eighteenth century. In connection with play at this time the Rev. Charles Rogers, in *Scotland, Social and Domestic, Memorials of Life and Manners in Northern Britain*, writes (p. 187):

> Nearly every district had its annual ba' playin'. The able-bodied men of one district challenged those of another, or two parties were chosen from the assemblage. If the contending parties were few, the exercises were toilsome. Forty on each side implied much individual exertion. Certain rules of the game may be mentioned. It was not allowable to touch the ball with the hand after it had been cast upon the field. An opponent might be tripped when near the ball, and more especially when about to hit it with the foot, but a competitor could not be laid hold of, or otherwise interfered with, when at a distance from the ball. The party who, out of three rounds, hailed the ball twice, was proclaimed victor.

Thereafter mass football died out as a national pastime, eventually being replaced by more sophisticated forms of ball play.

[68] *Acts of Parliament of Scotland*, vol. 2, p. 5b, chapter 18.

[69] *Acts of Parliament of Scotland*, vol. 2, p. 48, chapter 6.

[70] *Compota Thessurariorum Regum Scotorum: Accounts of the Lord High Treasurer of Scotland*, ed. Thomas Dickson, vol. 1., A.D. 1473–1498, p. 330.

As we have already seen, in outlying districts such as Orkney and Shetland, the old form of ball play lingered on for more than 100 years. Indeed in some of the more remote islands it was still being enjoyed as an annual New Year's Day event during the first decade of the twentieth century. The game has also continued as Fasternse'en Handba' in the Borders and of course the Kirkwall New Year's Day and Christmas Day Ba'.

A comprehensive history of mass football in Scotland is not being attempted here, but the following details are perhaps of some general interest.

Glasgow

Football was a popular amusement, and Glasgow Green appears to have been the location.[71] The magistrates certainly gave assistance by providing the balls, and the Burgh Records show that in February each year between 1573/4 and 1578/9 the sum of 12*s*. Scots was paid to John Andro, cordiner, for six footballs. A typical entry was that of 23 February 1573/4: 'Gevin to Johne Andro for futt ballis . . . xii s', and apparently six balls were supplied for this sum.[72] It is also recorded that on 31 January 1589 or 1590, John Neill, cordiner, was made burgess and freeman, and his freedom fine remitted in consideration of his furnishing yearly during his life time on Fasternse'en, six good and sufficient footballs or else 20*s*. as the price thereof.

In later years Orcadian exiles did not disregard the pastime played in boyhood days. On 1 January 1866, in spite of the bad weather a number of men assembled on Glasgow Green to enjoy the rough and tumble sport:

> Then the 'hurrah' was given as a true Orcadian – upon whose brow time has set his 'frosty seal' – stepped between the two 'sides' and threw up the ball. Paterfamilias seemed to renew his youth and was as nimble as when at school, while the young men vied with each other in agility. The old home associations seemed to kindle in every bosom, and the fun and frolic was kept up for upwards of three hours, when they returned to the city, highly gratified with the proceedings.[73]

Scone

Up until about 1785 Scone had a famous football or rather handball game (no one being allowed to kick the ball) played annually on Shrove Tuesday. It was held between bachelors and married men, the ball was thrown up at the Cross

[71] A. MacGeorge, *Old Glasgow*, p. 262, Public Amusements.
[72] F. P. Magoun, *Shrove Tuesday Football*, p. 16.
[73] *O*, 16 January 1866.

at two o'clock and the struggle was continued till sunset. The married men had to 'hang' it, and this consisted of putting the ba' three times in a small hole in the moor, whereas the bachelors had to 'drown' it, which amounted to dipping it three times into a deep place in the river. Whichever side took the ba' to their goal most times was victorious, and in the event of a draw it was cut into two at sunset. Every man in the parish, including the gentry, had to turn out and support his side, and those who did not were fined.[74] There was usually a deal of violence between the opposing sides and the limits of fair play were often transgressed, hence the proverb 'A's fair at the Ba' o' Scone'.

Another version of the origin of this proverb is contained in *Historical Sketches of Scone* by J. D. Urquhart and was thus given to the author by an old lady:

> When I was a girl I used to hear them tell a story about the proverb 'A's fair at the ba' o' Scoon'. It's a very funny one, but I believe it's true. It's said that long, long ago, the Lord Stormont and his lady came out to the park to look at the game as it was played. Some of the players on both sides resolved to have a ploy, and what do you think they did? They made it up that they would kick the ball to Lord Stormont's feet, and then, on the sudden, play him a trick as if it was an accident. Away the ball went right to his lordship's feet, and at once the two or more opponents were at it, when in the wild and hasty scramble, one took hold of one of his lordship's coat tails, and another the other, and by a sudden jerk, as if in the hurry and by accident, rived his coat right up the back to his neck. Losh! wasn't that awfu'? My lady was very angry; highly indignant was she, and asked his lordship to report them at once to the authorities to get them punished for their impudence. But his lordship's mild answer was – 'Tuts, tuts! na, na! my lady; dinna' ye ken a's fair at the ba' o' Scoon?'[75]

It is interesting to note that the Scone custom of passing the ba' three times in a hole in the moor or dipping it three times in the river, the Sedgefield custom of putting the ball three times through a bull ring, the Workington custom of hailing the ball by throwing it three times in the air, and the Ashbourne custom of banging the ball three times on a mill wheel are similar to an old Doonie custom in Kirkwall. During the course of trucking the ba' the Doonies used to run it three times up and down the mast before finally fixing it to the truck.

[74] J. Sinclair, *Statistical Account of Scotland*, part 18, no. 2, Parish of Scone.
[75] J. D. Urquhart, *Historical Sketches of Scone*, Perth, 1883, chapter 12. See also note 67.

Blairgowrie

In 1865 it was stated that while football in Blairgowrie had been very popular in earlier times, it had recently fallen into comparative disuse. Apparently one of the reasons was the uncertainty as to the correct method of play, interpretation of the rules varying, and to clarify the matter, football as played on village greens was simply described thus:

> Any number of players are divided into two parties, who stand between two goals marked out in a field. The object of each side is to defend their own goal, and to KICK the football through the goal on the opposite side. The goals are placed eighty or a hundred yards apart, and the side which succeeds in winning two out of three goals wins the game.

This was only a general guide, and the following were then listed as laws: the maximum permitted length of the ground was 200 yards, and the maximum breadth 100 yards. The goal space was defined by two upright posts eight yards apart, without any tape or bar across. Running with the ball was permitted but any player so doing could be charged, held, tripped or hacked, or the ball wrestled from him. However, it was decreed that no player should be held and hacked at the same time! For the record, hacking was defined as 'kicking an adversary on the front of the leg below the knee', while tripping was 'throwing an adversary by the use of the legs without the hands, and without hacking or charging. A player making a fair catch could claim a free kick by making a mark with his heel – an interesting connection with rugby. Finally, it was affirmed that the best ball to use was a leather covered inflated ox-bladder.[76]

Kirkmichael

At the end of the eighteenth century it was recorded in connection with the game held in the parish of Kirkmichael, in the county of Perth: 'Foot ball is a common amusement with the school boys, who also preserve the custom of cock-fighting on Shrove Tuesday.'[77] Thus although football was obviously played at other times, one gets the impression that the writer is linking it with cock-fighting as a Shrove Tuesday schoolboy revel.

Banffshire

In *The Annals of Banff* by William Cramond there is an interesting Court Book entry between 21 October and 17 November 1629, to the effect that Alexander

[76] *A Hand-Book to Blairgowrie, Rattray and Neighbourhood*, Blairgowrie, 1865, pp. 25, 26, 27.

[77] J. Sinclair, *Statistical Account of Scotland*, part 15, no. 24, Parish of Kirkmichael, p. 520. Information provided by the Rev. Allan Stewart.

Cook came into the lands and tenements held by his grandfather Johne Ryot. Apparently some part of these were 'held of the provost bailyies and counsell in few ferme and heretage for yeirlie payment of tua footballs as few dewtie for the said tenement and yaird at the feast of Chrystismes and auchtene pennyes Scottish moe as few dewtie for the said peace land yeirlie at the termes of Witsonday and Mertimes.'[78] It seems that football was a popular sport in Banff at Christmas, and the authorities accepted these two footballs in lieu of feu duty, and provided them for the amusement of the public. In the same book it is recorded that the minutes of the Banff Town Council contain an entry dated 1 May 1682: 'Players of football on the streets to be fined 40*s*.'[79]

Until at least 1880 'the old custom of a game at Foot-Ball' was observed at Fumack Fair. This took place in February and the location was the Parish of Botriphnie (formerly called Fumack Kirk).[80]

Elgin

In the church records there are several references to the banning of football through the town. On 21 December 1599, however, an exception was made for football in the kirkyard:

> Anent the Chanonrie kirk – All prophane pastyme inhibited to be usitt be any persones ather within the burgh or college and speciallie futballing through the toun, snaw balling, singing of carrellis or uther prophane sangis, guysing, pyping, violing, and dansing and speciallie all thie aboue specifeit forbidden in the Chanonrie kirk or kirk yaird thairoff (except futball) . . .

The game was prohibited at different times throughout the year, but from the following entry it seems to have been particularly popular at Yule:

> December 18th 1618 – Insolenceis. – It is ordenit that the superstitious obseruation of auld reitis and cermoneis expresly forbidden during the tyme callit Yooll that they be altogidder awodit and escheqit, siz. that na persoun within burgh or landward within this parosche pas in gwysing, dansing, singing carallis, play at the fut ball, throch the toun nor about the Chanonrie kirk and kirkyeard . . . [81]

[78] W. Cramond, *The Annals of Banff,* 1891, vol. 1, p. 63.

[79] W. Cramond, *The Annals of Banff,* 1891, vol. 1, p. 161.

[80] Mentioned by F. P. Magoun on p. 37 of *Shrove Tuesday Football:* Magoun refers to *Book of the Chronicles of Keith* by J. F. S. Gordon, Glasgow, 1880, p. 443. The quotation is taken from Gordon.

[81] *The Records of Elgin, 1234–1800,* comp. W. Cramond, vol. 2, ed. S. Ree.

Aberdeenshire

Probably the first football poem is *The Monymusk Christmas Ba'ing* written in 1738 by the Rev. John Skinner when he was seventeen years old. The following are some of the interesting editorial comments:

> It may be proper, at the same time, to state, that at that period, and from time immemorial, it had been the practice in most of the country parishes in Aberdeenshire for parties of young men to assemble, about the Christmas season, to try their strength and agility at the athletic exercise of *foot-ball.* The contest generally took place in the kirk-yard of the parish.

The following stanzas give a fine impression of the rough fluid nature of the play:

Has ne'er in a' this countra been,
Sic shoudering and sic fa'ing,
As happen'd but few ouks sinsyne,
Here at the Christmas Ba'ing.
At evening syne the fallows keen
Drank till the niest day's dawing,
Sae snell, that some tint baith their een,
And could na pay their lawing,
Till the niest day.

Like bumbees bizzing frae a byke,
Whan hirds their riggins tirr;
The swankies lap thro' mire and syke,
Wow as their heads did birr!
They yowff'd the ba' frae dyke to dyke
Wi' unco speed and virr;
Some baith their shou'ders up did fyke,
For blythness some did flirr
Their teeth that day.

* * *

The hurry-burry now began,
Was right weel worth the seeing,
Wi' routs and raps frae man to man,
Some getting, and some gieing;
And a' the tricks of fit and hand,
That ever was in being

> Sometimes the ba' a yirdlins ran,
> Sometimes in air was fleeing,
> Fu' heigh that day.
>
> Has ne'er in Monymuss been seen
> Sae mony weel-beft skins:
> Of a' the bawmen there was nane
> But had twa bleedy shins.
> Wi' strenzied shouders mony ane
> Dree'd penance for their sins;
> And what was warst, scoup'd hame at ee'n,
> May be to hungry inns,
> And cauld that day.[82]

Football and the Church in Scotland

As we have seen, English clergy in the Middle Ages were no strangers to football, and the location of play was often the flat area near a church, sometimes even the churchyard. In Scotland too, the game was a failing of the clergy, and Sir David Lyndsay, poet and satirist of the old church in Scotland, mentions a football-playing cleric. In *Ane Pleasant Satyre of the Thrie Estaitis in Commendatioun of Vertew and Vituperatioun of Vyce*, written about 1535. Lyndsay's parson, while admitting neglect in spiritual matters, claims as a defence his zeal in temporal pursuits:

> Thocht I preich not, I can play at the caiche;
> I wait thair is nocht ane amang yow all,
> Mair ferilie can play at the fut-ball;
> And for the carts, the tabils, and the dyse,
> Above all persouns, I may beir the pryse.[83]

In the same tradition is an incident involving Archbishop James Law (at one time Bishop of Orkney) who in 1585, while minister of Kirkliston, was rebuked by the Synod of Lothian and Tweeddale for playing football on the Lord's day.[84]

[82] *Amusements of Leisure Hours, or, Poetical Pieces chiefly in the Scottish Dialect*, 1809, p. 41 ff. See F. P. Magoun Jr, 'Scottish Popular Football, 1424–1815', pp. 8, 9, published in *The American Historical Review*, vol. 37, October 1931.

[83] T. F. Henderson, *Scottish Vernacular Literature*, p. 229, *caiche* – hand-ball; *wait* – wot; *ferilie* – cleverly; *carts* – cards; *persouns* – parsons.

[84] See F. P. Magoun Jr, 'Scottish Popular Football, 1424–1815', p. 4, quoting *Fasti Ecclesiae Scoticanae*, H. Scott, Edinburgh, 1915, vol. 1, p. 212.

Mass football on Sunday, often in the kirkyard, became widespread, and on 9 June 1607 the youth of Aberdeen were charged with conducting themselves 'prophanelie on the Sabboathes in drinking, playing at futte-ball, danceing, and passing fra paroche to paroche'.[85]

In 1648 'diverse of the parishioners of Raine and Culsalmond' were guilty of 'scandalous behaviour in convening themselves upon the Lord's day to a public footballing'.[86]

On 17 September 1656, the Scottish Parliament passed an Act for the better observation of the Lord's day, and by this, boisterous games were prohibited.[87] However, the Sabbath being one of the few occasions when the populace had leisure time, Sunday football was not to be suppressed that easily.

The *Folk-Lore Review 1897* (vol. 8, p. 74) states that at the hamlet of Tullich near Ballater there was a ruined church standing in a circular graveyard, and St Nathalan, said to have been born in the district, was the patron saint of this church. His day fell in January and was kept as a holiday in the parish until around 1870, football being the favourite amusement. 'The churchyard, which had then no wall round it, was the place selected for the game, and the ball was kicked about over the tombs, often amid snow.'

In the early part of the eighteenth century the Rev. Michael Potter hit on a novel method of discouraging his Kippen parishioners from playing the Sunday game:

> It had been the practice with some of the parishioners for years to play *football* on Sunday afternoons . . . Mr Potter disapproved of this, and he therefore one Sunday afternoon embraced the opportunity of going down when the people were engaged in the sport, and begged to be permitted to take part in the game. The players were somewhat astonished, but made no reply, neither complied nor refused. Mr Potter said it was proper that all their employments should begin with prayer, and he thereupon pulled off his hat and began to pray. By the time he had concluded, the most of the players had skulked away, and the practice was in future discontinued.[88]

[85] J. G. Dalyell, *The Darker Superstitions of Scotland*, 1834, who quotes from *Presbyterie Buik of Aberdein*. See F. P. Magoun Jr, 'Scottish Popular Football, 1424–1815', p. 6.

[86] J. Davidson, *Inverurie and the Earldom of the Garioch*, p. 302. See F. P. Magoun Jr, 'Scottish Popular Football, 1424–1815', p. 7.

[87] *Acts of the Parliaments of Scotland and the Government during the Commonwealth*, 1873, vol. 6, part 2, pp. 865b, 867a. See F. P. Magoun Jr, 'Scottish Popular Football, 1424–1815', p. 7.

[88] W. Chrystal, *The Kingdom of Kippen, its History and Traditions*, pp. 121, 123. See F. P. Magoun Jr, 'Scottish Popular Football, 1424–1815', p. 8.

There is an amusing story told in connection with Sunday football in Blairgowrie. The Rev. John Ross was parish minister at the beginning of the seventeenth century, and he had for long 'taught, warned, beseeched, threatened and denounced' the Sunday sports and pastimes of his congregation, who were particularly addicted to ba' playing. As his pulpit exhortations produced no appreciable improvement, Mr Ross resolved on a firmer course of action, and one Sunday after service he changed into old clothes, and staff in hand strode purposefully to the ba' green. At his appearance the less resolute of the assembled players fled, but a small band stood defiant. Thrusting his staff into the ground and throwing his coat over it, he addressed the personification thus: 'Stand ye there, ye Minister o' Blair, till I John Ross, get a kick at the Ba'.' Thereupon he took his place on the field and seizing every opportunity of *missing* the ba' he mercilessly kicked the shins of the unfortunate players. Observing absolutely no rules, and kicking out fiercely, Mr Ross soon completed a signal victory by chasing all the Sabbath-breakers from the scene, having 'houghed them hip and thigh'![89] This resembles the story told about the participation in Sunday football of Mr Malcolm the minister in Stenness, Orkney, at the end of the eighteenth century (see Ch. 16, 'Mass Football Playing in Orkney').

The Fasternse'en Ba'

The old game survived as Fasternse'en football in the Borders, and the Fasternse'en Ba' is the equivalent of Shrove Tuesday football, the date being given by the rhyme:

First comes Candlemas
Syne the new mune;
And the first Tuesday after
is Fastern's E'en

But Fasternse'en and Shrove Tuesday do not always fall on the same day, and if there is a new moon on Shrove Tuesday, then Fasternse'en would be the following Tuesday.

Jedburgh

The Border game (now handball) is at the present time played only in Roxburghshire. Jedburgh is the main centre, and there is a tradition that the contest dates from a battle against the English at Ferniehirst Castle. When Ker,

[89] *A Hand-Book to Blairgowrie, Rattray and Neighbourhood,* Blairgowrie, 1865, pp. 22, 23, 24. John Ross was parish minister from about 1603 to about 1631.

FIG 102: An early photograph of the Jedburgh (Jethart) Handba' at Fasternse'en.

its owner, assisted by French forces, regained the castle from the English, it is alleged that the heads of the English garrison were cut off and thrown from hand to hand in a game of ball. There is also a tradition that a disguised James V once came from Melrose to take part, but George Watson, in *Annual Border Ball-Games*, comments that if this happened the King more likely came to see the local laird's fair daughter![90]

Like the other Border contests the 'Jethart Ba' is of Shrove Tuesday origin, having spread to Scotland from England or possibly direct from France. Played on the first Thursday after Fasternse'en, the Callants Ba' (for boys still in school education) commences at twelve noon from the Mercat Cross and the men's game follows at 2 p.m. The Callants contest continues until all the ba's have been played, irrespective of whether the men's game is then in progress. The sides are 'Uppies' and 'Doonies', being those born above or below the Mercat Cross. Play takes place on the streets (and sometimes in the River Jed); there are no rules, the game being self-regulating; each side plays to its own 'hail' or goal; and numbers are unrestricted. In the case of the Uppies, a ba' is hailed[91] by throwing it over the castle railings. The Doonies achieve a hail by rolling the ba'

[90] G. Watson, *Hawick Archaeological Society Transactions,* 1922, p. 5.
[91] *Scottish National Dictionary*, 1956, vol. 4, part 4: *Hail,* to drive (the ball) through or over the goal or boundary, to score a goal.

over the course of an underground stream, Skiprinnin burn, at the Townfoot. It may well be that in days gone by the Doonies' goal was the open burn itself. There is no limit to the number of ba's an individual may hail and retain.

In recent years men have been prohibited from playing in the Callants ba' and as a result numbers have increased substantially with over 100 boys taking part. There are a similar number of participants in the senior event.

The Callants play fluidly over the length and breadth of the town, the ba' being thrown, with runners prominent, there being few scrums or 'strows'. Smuggling is rare. In the men's game 'strows' are frequent and smuggling is a feature of play.

The ba' is almost always kept by the hailer as a treasured trophy, but he has the option of returning it to the donor who may have arranged a reward of money or some other benefit against its safe return. The ba' is somewhat larger than a cricket ball and is made with four leather panels and packed with chopped hay. Upwards of a dozen may be contested during a day's play. From 1920 to 1969 the ba's were made by a local man, Andrew Gray. They are now produced by a saddler in Hawick. In 2004 six Callants ba's were hailed, and the men contested eight trophies, play finishing at 7 p.m. The ba's are donated by local firms, organizations, the Community Council, etc., although as in other Border towns where handball is played, a married couple may donate a ba' for their silver, golden or even diamond wedding anniversary. All the ba's are gaily decorated with variously coloured ribbons, pieces of which are greatly prized as souvenirs.

As early as 1704 there was an attempt to abolish the traditional game. The Town Council, 'having duly considered that the tossing and throwing up of the football at Fasternse'en within the streets of the burgh has many times tended to the great prejudice of the inhabitants, calls now at once for a discharge thereof, there having been sometymes both old and young near lost their lives thereby. Therefore, they, with all unanimous advice and consent, do discharge the gayme now and in all time coming.' Nevertheless this order by the Council was of no avail and the game continued.

It appears likely that about the beginning of the nineteenth century handball was substituted for football, but in 1849 the Council again tried to abolish the game, this time because of the prevalence of cholera. A number of players were arrested and fined 10*s*. each at Jedburgh's Burgh court. On appeal the High Court in Edinburgh ruled that the game had a right to be observed, being a traditional custom.'[92] Taken from *Cases before the High Court and Circuit Courts of Justiciary, June* 2 1849, *Veitch and others* v. *Reid*, the words of the Lord Justice-Clerk were: 'I,

[92] G. Watson, *Hawick Archaeological Society Transactions*, 1922, p. 5.

for one, should hesitate to encourage the abolition of an old and customary game, which from time immemorial had been enjoyed by the community.' The rest of the court concurred.

Jethart men celebrated Shrovetide at Gallipoli in 1915 when men of the King's Own Scottish Borderers threw up a ba' behind the lines. Similarly in the Second World War Jethart men played the Ba' while training in the Western Isles for D-Day. Hand ba' was played in the town throughout both World Wars.

At one time there was a King and a Queen of the grammar school who were crowned as a result of giving the largest donation to the headmaster. The King had the privilege of throwing up the first ba' at the Callants Candlesmas game on 2 February. The last person to be crowned was Thomas Colledge-Halliburton in 1884 and he threw up the first ba' at every Callants game until his death in 1941. Ba's were played at Candlemas every year apart from 1901 when it was cancelled due to the burial that day of Queen Victoria. Nowadays the sports captain of the grammar school throws up the first Callants ba'.

The last Queen of the Candlesmas Ba' was the sister of Thomas Colledge-Halliburton. She emigrated to Canada and sent a gold nugget to be sewn into a men's ba'. Alas the hailer had to part with it as times were hard and money was needed for his family. Ladies are among the keenest of supporters.

In 1982 Billy Gillies, a well known ba' player, wrote some verse about the game, a stanza of which gives a delightful insight into the atmosphere on the day:

> Hunners, they hae formed o' strow
> And often makes ye wonder how
> As mony folk get there tae play
> "A' Jetharts Here" on Handba' day
> And some hae come frae miles aroon
> And others, back tae their native toon
> Tae play the Ba'.

The game is held in high regard in Jedburgh, people returning annually to the town to watch and take part, and exiles remain keenly interested in the outcome of the contests.

Ancrum

Held on the Saturday after the Jedburgh game, at one time the sides were Ancrum (Uppies), and Jedburgh (Doonies) whose players travelled four miles. Present allegiance is determined by living above or below the village cross. The ba's are often presented by couples who marry during the previous year, and a ba' may be hung in the window of the bride's house for a few days before the event. In 2004 nineteen ba's were played, being donated to celebrate births, marriages, birthdays, and silver, ruby and golden weddings. Further support came from businesses and the Community Council.

The 'throw off' is at 1 p.m. from the village cross to contestants waiting in the square, and play continues until all the ba's have been hailed. There are no rules, and, particularly when numbers were greater, a ba' might be forced into Ale Water where the struggle continued. Nowadays a further game for those up to the age of sixteen is played, commencing at 11 a.m. As in other locations, from time to time old ba's are used, and these may have been handed down from generation to generation. At Fasternse'en 1967, one ba' was reputed to be 300 years old. The game ceased in 1974 and was restarted in 1997. During this pause Iain Heard maintained the old custom by carrying a ball on the appointed day from one end of the village to the other.

Part of a verse about the 1934 Ancrum Ba' is:

> Pit up the ba pit up the ba they're waitin in the square
> They're braw lads and bonnie lasses half O Ancrums there.
> Theres twa three Jethart lads aboot but no saw many ava,
> Sure they'll be landin here in droves come on pit up the ba.

Duns

The events on Fasternse'en 1724 are worth mentioning. Until that date 'all the idel people in that burgh were usually conveened by touck of drum to play at the football, which did always end and determine in the effusion of blood among the inhabitants.' In order to prevent these 'riots and tumults' John Gray, Bailie of the burgh and barony of Duns ordered that the drum be brought to his house. A crowd soon gathered outside and demanded its return. Unsuccessful in their efforts the mob departed to play at football, after which the winning side wished to signal its victory by exhibiting the ba' from the Tolbooth stair. This the losers would not permit unless the confiscated drum was brought forth, rioting broke out and continued that day and the next.[93]

Subsequently at an unknown date the Duns game, as in other parts of the Borders, became handball, and this was kept up till 1885 although for some years before that the custom had been declining. However, in the earlier part of the nineteenth century handball was quite an event in the town. A few days before Fasternse'en a number of young blades met in a local ale house and

[93] G. Watson, *Hawick Archaeological Society Transactions*, 1922, p. 5, where it is stated that the facts are contained in a document of complaint by Bailie Gray. This is preserved in Duns Castle and was reproduced in 1909 on pp. 43–45 of the fifth volume of the *Historical Manuscripts Commission*. See also F. P. Magoun, 'Scottish Popular Football', pp. 9, 10.

having made their plans, spent some evenings before the game parading the streets accompanied by a drummer and a fiddle, singing 'Never let the gree gang doon[94], for the gude o'oor toon'. They visited the neighbouring mansions, solicited subscriptions from the gentry, danced with the servants and partook of the refreshments that were liberally provided for them. Three ba's were required for the game; the first was gilt, the second silvered and the third coloured or spotted. A fourth was provided in case of mishap, and if not needed was presented to the subscriber whose entertainment had been most hospitable, the family at Duns Castle usually being the recipients.

On the forenoon of the great day the honour of throwing off the first ba' was auctioned in the Old Kirkyard, and there was keen competition among the trades for the privilege of starting the contest. Latterly the throw off was invariably performed by a member of the Duns Castle family.

At one o'clock the game began, the ba' being thrown-up in the Market Square. The married men attempted to 'kirk the ba' 'by putting it into the pulpit of the Parish Church, proclaiming their success by giving the church bell a most unecclesiastical jingle. The bachelors' goal was the hopper of any of the grinding mills of the district, the nearest of which was over a mile away As a token of victory the bachelor who succeeded in getting the ba' to a mill, had his cap and coat dusted with meal by the miller who then entertained him and those with him to pork and dumplings. The individual kirking or milling the first ba' got 1*s*. 6*d*., for the second ba' the reward was 1*s*., and for the third 6*d*. (Miss F. Marian McNeill, *The Silver Bough,* vol. 2, p. 137, believes that from this comes the saying: 'To mak' a kirk or a mill o't.') In the evening the 'ba' men' feasted themselves and their friends in one of the taverns of the town, using the balance of the subscribed money.

There was a great snow storm in February 1886 which prevented play that year. The game was revived as handball in July 1949 as part of the Duns Summer Festival, also known as Reivers Week. Commencing at the centre of the Market Square at 6 p.m., where play continues, between fifty and seventy men participate – much smaller numbers than in olden times although still with sufficient participants to ensure a noteworthy event. The sides are married and single men, and the goals are at the Post Office and the White Swan Hotel.

Three small, hand-stitched beribboned leather balls are used and play can often last for two hours or even longer, with the ball being kicked, thrown or held in a scrum. A member of the Hay family throws up the first ball painted gold; the silver ball is the preserve of the Riever's lass; and the third ball, resplendent in the

[94] Never let the importance diminish.

town colours of red and black, is turned up by the Wynsome Mayde o' Duns. A ball is hailed or goaled by depositing it in a barrel at each goal and at the conclusion of proceedings it is returned to the person who has started the contest, when it is redeemed for a token monetary prize: 15p, 10p and 5p respectively for the first, second and third ball. New balls are used each year.[95]

Denholm

The Ba' is played on the Monday after the Hobkirk game. In general the Doonies are men and youths living in the village, and the Uppies are the outsiders. At one time the game was between married and single men.

Hobkirk

Uppies play against Doonies on the Monday before the Jedburgh game. Originally the sides comprised those born above or below the church, but now allegiance is determined by location. Upwards of fifty players are involved. At one time it was the custom to throw the ba' over the church. In 1803 as a result of some very rough play the Heritors of Hobkirk met on 9 June and passed the following resolution: 'The Heritors taking into their consideration the pernicious effects of a vast number of people assembling from this and other parishes annually for the idle purpose of playing at Ball on the day preceding Fastern's E'en at and about the Parish Church, hereby order the Schoolmaster to lay an absolute prohibition upon his scholars from producing any Balls to be played on that day.' They also pledged themselves to prevent their own servants from coming to Hobkirk to play at ball, but their efforts to suppress the event were in vain.[96] The game is started or 'thrown out' from the wall of the church yard, but play is prohibited in the church yard itself.

Lilliesleaf

A boys ba' is played on the Wednesday after the Jedburgh game, the sides are 'Easties' and 'Westies', play starting in a field at Chirnot Cottage. The game may last for some two hours.

At the beginning of the century the Selkirk mill workers came to play at Lilliesleaf and the contest was so fierce that it was known locally as 'The Battle of Waterloo'!

[95] Information supplied in 2004 by Sheila Whitehead, Chairman, Duns Summer Festival, and from extensive notes supplied by Mr Wm. Renton, at one time Town Clerk of Duns.

[96] G. Watson, *Hawick Archaeological Society Transactions,* 1922, pp. 8, 9. G. Tancred, *Rulewater and its People*, p. 352.

Other Border Ba' Games

The St Boswells event took place on 12 March, the rivals being men from Ancrum, and the balls were donated by young people who had married during the year. The game lapsed during the Second World War, it was revived about 1946 but lasted only a few more years. Men no longer obtained a holiday for the occasion, and the loss of a day's wages was too much to afford.

Play in Lanton was celebrated after Fasternse'en, and at Campton the date was eight days before Fasternse'en, the sides being Uppies and Doonies.[97]

In Morebattle and Yetholm the contest was mass football rather than handball – married men against single men – and one of the few rules was that the oldest male inhabitant should throw up the first ba'.[98] In Melrose the tussle was indeed street football and caused so much inconvenience that it was abolished in 1900. In Morebattle the game, which came to an end just before the First World War, took place on New Year's Day.[99] The game was also played in Hawick.

Perhaps the most famous single occasion mass football match in Scotland occurred on Tuesday 5 December 1815 in a magnificent setting at Carterhaugh, before about 2000 spectators, including many of the titled and landed gentry. The sides consisted of men from the Vale of Yarrow and those from the parish of Selkirk, and a well-contested game ended in victory for the latter.[100] The Buccleuch banner was displayed and the Duke threw up the ba'. One side was backed by the Earl of Home and the other by Sir Walter Scott, a devotee of the game. Sir Walter wrote two songs for the event, one of which was entitled 'Lifting the Banner of the House of Buccleuch, At the great Foot-ball match, on Carterhaugh', and a stanza is as follows:

> Then strip lads, and to it, though sharp be the weather,
> And if, by mischance, you should happen to fall,
> There are worse things in life than a tumble on heather,
> And life is itself but a game at foot-ball![101]

[97] G. Watson, *Hawick Archaeological Society Transactions,* 1922, p. 8.

[98] G. Watson, *Hawick Archaeological Society Transactions,* 1922, p. 5.

[99] G. Watson, *Hawick Archaeological Society Transactions,* 1922, p. 5.

[100] In *Scotland, Social and Domestic, Memorials of Life and Manners in North Britain*, Rev. C. Rogers, 1869, pp. 189 and 190, it is stated that there was more than one game. Apparently the first struggle lasted an hour and a half and was won by the Selkirk men. The second game lasted three hours and was won by the men of Yarrow. As the light began to fail and great excitement prevailed it was decided that it would be wise to dispense with a third contest. See p. 187 of the book for description of annual Ba' playing in districts at the end of the eighteenth century.

[101] W. Hone, *The Every Day Book,* 1878, vol. 1, p. 777. G. Watson, *Hawick Archaeological Society Transactions,* 1922, p. 8. F. P. Magoun, 'Scottish Popular Football', p. 12.

Thus in Scotland there is a history of mass football stretching back to at least the beginning of the fifteenth century.

Where it has survived the game has become one of handball; familiar terms for the sides are Uppies and Doonies; in the true tradition of mass football there is a water goal in Kirkwall, and it seems likely that there was originally one in Jedburgh. At Kirkwall the Ba' is played on Christmas Day and New Year's Day, in the Borders the Fasternse'en Ba' still lives on in a few locations, and both these survivals provide a fascinating connection with a more rumbustious past.

FIG 103: Mens' Ba', Christmas Day 1994.

Bibliography

The publications listed below are those referring specifically to Orkney and Shetland. References to other books or manuscript sources consulted will be found in the footnotes in Part 4, 'Origin and History of Mass Football'.

Barclay, Robert S. *The Population of Orkney, 1755–1961.* W. R. Mackintosh, Kirkwall Press, 1965.

Dennison, Walter Traill. *Orkney Folklore and Traditions.* Herald Press, Kirkwall, 1961.

Fea, James. *Considerations on the Fisheries in the Scotch Islands; to which is prefixed a General Account elucidating the History, Soil, Productions, Curiosities etc. of the same, the manners of the Inhabitants, etc.* London, 1787.

Firth, John. *Reminiscences of an Orkney Parish.* W. R. Rendall, Stromness, 1920.

Gorrie, Daniel. *Summers and Winters in the Orkneys*, 2nd edn. William Peace, Kirkwall, n.d.

Hardy, E. W. *Life and Customs in the Shetland Isles.* Charles H. Kelly, London, n.d.

Horne, David. *Songs of Orkney.* Orkney Herald, Kirkwall, 1923.

Horne, David. *Under Orcadian Skies*. Orkney Herald, 1925.

Hossack, B. H. *Kirkwall in the Orkneys.* William Peace & Son, Kirkwall, 1900.

Johnston, A. W. *Orkney and Shetland Miscellany,* vol. 1. Viking Society for Northern Research, London, January, 1908.

Knudsen. *Træk Af Boldspillets Historie*. Gyldendalske Boghandel, Copenhagen, 1933.

Leask, J. T. Smith. *A Peculiar People and other Orkney Tales.* W. R. Mackintosh, Orcadian Office, Kirkwall, 1931.

MacGregor, G. A broadsheet entitled *History of the Game of the Kirkwall New Year's Day Ba.' (Stirring Events).* Kirkwall, January, 1914.

Mackintosh, W. R. *Curious Incidents from the Ancient Records of Kirkwall.* James Anderson, Orcadian Office, Kirkwall, 1892.

Marwick, Dr Hugh. *Orkney.* Robert Hale, London, 1951.

Marwick, Dr Hugh. *Orkney Farm Names.* W. R. Mackintosh, Kirkwall, 1952.

Mooney, John. *Songs of the Norse and other Poems,* Kirkwall, 1883.

Neill, Patrick. *A Tour Through some of the Islands of Orkney and Shetland.* A. Constable & Co., Edinburgh, 1806.

Rendall, Robert. *Orkney Variants and other Poems.* W. R. Mackintosh, Kirkwall Press, 1951.
Saxby, Jessie M. E. *Shetland Traditional Lore*. Grant & Murray Ltd, Edinburgh, 1932.
Stewart, George. *Shetland Fireside Tales.* T. & J. Manson, Lerwick, 1892.
Proceedings of the Orkney Antiquarian Society, vol. 1. Orcadian Office, Kirkwall, 1923.
Records of the Earldom of Orkney, 1299–1614, ed. J. Storer Clouston. Scottish History Society, 2nd series, vol. 7. Edinburgh, 1914.
The Karlamagnus Saga. Unger's edition, 1860.
The Orkneyinga Saga, trans. by A. B. Taylor. Oliver & Boyd, Edinburgh, 1938.
Scottish National Dictionary, vol. 4, part 6, 1956. Edinburgh, 1956.
The Story of Gisli the Outlaw, trans. from the Icelandic by G. W. Dasent. Edmonston & Douglas, Edinburgh, 1866.

Index